Tourism, Leisure and Recreation

Garrett Nagle

Contents

Chapter 1
Tourism, leisure and recreation

Tourism, leisure and recreation are among the world's largest, and most rapidly growing, industries. As standards of living have increased, and forms of transport have improved, the potential for travel has increased dramatically. In this chapter we look at the growth of tourism, the factors affecting growth, patterns of tourism, and the effect of tourism on the economy, society and the environment. Many of these effects are dealt with in detail in subsequent chapters. Models of tourism, as well as models relevant to the study of tourism are also examined in this chapter.

Chapters 2, 3 and 4 look at the impact of tourism in selected environments: coasts, mountains and wilderness areas. A variety of case studies, including those from developed and developing countries are examined, and at a variety of scales.

Subsequent chapters look at tourism in urban areas, including heritage tourism, theme parks andother day trip attractions, tourism in developing countries, the impact of safaris, and finally, sustainable ecotourism. Through the case studies, the changing nature of tourism, and its impact on societies and the environment are explored, and ways of managing tourism are assessed.

THE CHANGING NATURE OF TOURISM

Tourism is defined as all temporary visits to another region (domestic) or country (international) lasting more than 24 hours. This includes visits for holidays (Figure 1.1), sport, health, education (Figure 1.2), religion, business and visits to family and friends. **Recreation** is defined as all activities that are undertaken voluntarily for personal pleasure or enjoyment in a person's 'leisure time'. This definition includes home-based activities such as gardening, reading a book, or watching television, but also includes activities away from the home, involving a stay away from the home of less than one day. Hence a day trip to the seaside is a form of recreation, whereas an overnight trip is defined as a tourist visit. **Leisure** refers to all recreational and tourist activities whether they are home-based or not.

Figure 1.2 *Educational visit to Hiroshima, Japan*

The main reason for tourism is holidays. These account for 70% of all journeys undertaken.

There are many different types of holiday tourism. These include:
- mass tourism, such as coastal holidays in Mediterranean resorts
- charter holidays, such as to Florida and the Mediterranean
- short breaks, such as cultural and historical breaks in Bruges and York
- theme parks, such as Disneyland
- elite tourism, such as ecotourism
- offbeat tourism, such as tours to the Arctic Tundra
- unusual holidays, such as educational tours.

Figure 1.1 *One of the many forms of tourist attractions*

Visiting relatives is the second reason and business travel is third.

Mass travel dates from the nineteenth century. On July 5 1841, Thomas Cook, a printer and anti-alcohol campaigner took 500 people by train from Leicester to Loughborough for a temperance (anti-alcohol) rally. This was taken to be the world's first mass tourism movement and was the birth of modern tourism (Figure 1.3).

The growth of mass tourism is closely linked with:
● improvements in transport, notably railways and steamships
● the growth of conducted tours, such as those by Thomas Cook
● an increase in leisure time, disposable income and personal mobility.

Tourism has developed rapidly over the past decades and now is one of the world's largest industries. Together with telecommunications and information technology, it is one of the world's fastest growing industries. Since the Second World War there has been a huge increase in the number of tourists. In 1950 there were 25 million international tourists, but by 1997 international tourists numbered over 617 million. These were mostly from developed countries to other developed countries. However, there is an increasing demand for tourism to developing countries, although many tourists seeking to experience remote places still desire food, shelter and hygiene of the same standard as found in economically more developed countries (EMDCs). Tourism is largely the privilege of the urban and the rich (Figure 1.4). International tourism is currently growing at about 4% per annum.

There are few places in the world that have not been affected by tourism. Even remote and hostile environments such as Antarctica and the Himalayas are experiencing an increase in the number of tourists they receive, and the benefits and problems that they bring.

Figure 1.3
Early Thomas Cook posters

In the nineteenth century holidays were regarded as a luxury, even for the wealthy. Now however, among high-income earners, holidays are regarded as a necessary break from increasingly stressful and competitive work. By contrast, for people trapped in mundane, repetitive work, holidays relieve the tedium of their working day.

The growth of tourism is related to a number of factors that are examined in depth below. These include:
● the introduction of package holidays
● cheaper air travel
● an increased amount of paid holiday (Figure 1.5)
● an increase in free time
● a rise in disposable income.

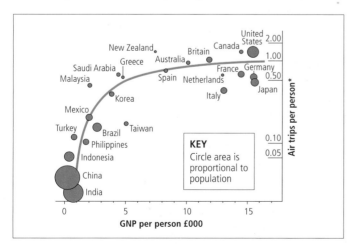

Figure 1.4 *The correlation between income and air travel, 1990*
Source: Booz, Allen & Hamilton, The Economist, January 10, 1998

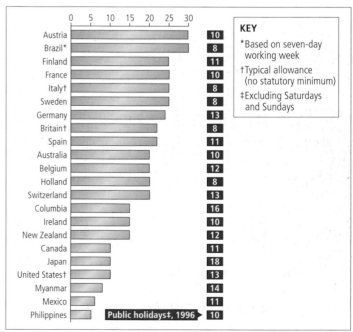

Figure 1.5 *Variations in paid holidays in the mid 1990s*
Source: The Economist, January 5, 1996

Cheaper air travel since the 1960s has led to a surge in travel and a change in holiday patterns: increasing volumes of tourists are travelling ever-increasing distances. The growth of long-haul travel is one of the industry's fastest growing sectors, particularly amongst younger European and American tourists who have the time to take advantage of lower air fares. Going abroad on holiday has become so common that even those holidays which were exclusive to the rich, such as skiing and cruising, have been packaged and made more affordable to a greater number of tourists.

Not all tourists have the same requirements. Some desire tranquility, whereas others want to be in locations where there are many activities on offer, and there are many other like-minded tourists. The main types of tourists are shown in Figure 1.6.

There are a variety of social, economic, environmental and psychological factors that affect the demand for tourism; the different types of traveller are reflected in the choice of different destinations and different activities.

Type of tourist	Type of tourist	Adaptation to local norms
Explorer	Very limited	Accepts fully
Elite	Rarely seen	Accepts fully
Off-beat	Uncommon but seen	Adapts well
Unusual	Occasional	Adapts somewhat
Incipient mass	Steady flow	Seeks Western amenities
Mass	Continuous influx	Expects Western amenities
Charter	Massive arrivals	Demands Western amenities

Terms

incipient mass	=	early stages of mass (large-scale tourism)
continuous influx	=	continuous arrivals/inflow
mass	=	volume
charter	=	package

Figure 1.6 Types of tourists and their adaptation to local norms
Source: Page, S., 1995, Urban tourism, Routledge

GLOBAL PATTERNS OF TOURISM

In 1997 worldwide over 617 million international tourists spent almost £300 billion. France was the top destination, attracting about 11% of the world tourist total (Figure 1.7), although the USA earns the most from tourism (Figure 1.8). In 1997 it earned some £50 billion, 16% of the world total. Domestic tourism is thought to be four times greater in terms of volume of people than international travel.

Between 1965 and 1993 there was a five-fold increase in the number of tourists worldwide from 110 million to over 510 million, with a slight dip in the 1980s due to the world-wide economic recession. Europe was the most popular destination, attracting over 60% of visitors, followed by North America, with over 15%. In the 1980s, tourism in developing countries accounted for only 13% of all tourism.

World's Top 40 Tourism Destinations
International tourist arrivals (excluding same-day visitors) (thousands of arrivals) – 1997

1985	Rank 1990	1997	Countries	Arrivals (000) 1997	% change 1997/96	% of total 1997
1	1	1	France	66 864	7.1	10.9
4	2	2	United States	48 409	4.1	7.9
2	3	3	Spain	43 378	7.0	7.1
3	4	4	Italy	34 087	3.8	5.6
6	7	5	United Kingdom	25 960	2.6	4.2
13	12	6	China	23 770	4.4	3.9
22	27	7	Poland	19 514	0.5	3.2
9	8	8	Mexico	19 351	-9.6	3.2
7	10	9	Canada	17 610	1.6	2.9
16(1)	16	10	Czech Republic	17 400	2.4	2.8
11	5	11	Hungary	17 248	-16.6	2.8
5	6	12	Austria	16 646	-2.6	2.7
8	9	13	Germany	15 837	4.2	2.6
18(2)	17(2)	14	Russian Federation	15 350	5.2	2.5
10	11	15	Switzerland	11 077	4.5	1.8
19	19	16	China, Hong Kong SAR	10 406	-11.1	1.7
14	13	17	Greece	10 246	11.0	1.7
15	14	18	Portugal	10 100	3.8	1.7
28	24	19	Turkey	9 040	13.5	1.5
25	21	20	Thailand	7 263	1.0	1.2
20	20	21	Netherlands	6 674	1.4	1.1
23	23	22	Singapore	6 542	-1.0	1.1
21	15	23	Malaysia	6 211	-13.0	1.0
17	22	24	Belgium	5 875	0.8	1.0
24	26	25	Ireland	5 540	4.9	0.9
56	55	26	South Africa	5 530	11.9	0.9
55	38	27	Indonesia	5 036	0.0	0.8
36	34	28	Macau	4 915	0.5	0.8
39	32	29	Argentina	4 540	5.9	0.7
49	36	30	Australia	4 286	2.9	0.7
33	29	31	Tunisia	4 263	9.7	0.7
26	28	32	Japan	4 223	10.1	0.7
41	31	33	Korea Rep.	3 908	6.1	0.6
–	18	34	Croatia	3 834	44.7	0.6
42	35	35	Egypt	3 657	3.7	0.6
32	37	36	Saudi Arabia	3 594	3.9	0.6
37	33	37	Puerto Rico	3 332	8.7	0.5
29	25	38	Morocco	3 115	15.7	0.5
35	53	39	Brazil	2 995	12.3	0.5
27	30	40	Romania	2 741	-3.3	0.4
			Total 1-40	**530 367**	**2.7**	**86.7**
			World Total	**611 964**	**2.8**	**100.0**

(1) Former Czechoslovakia. (2) Former USSR.

Figure 1.7 World's top forty tourism destinations
Source: World Tourism Organisation, 1998

World's Top 40 Tourism Earners
International tourist receipts (excluding transport) (US$ million) – 1997

1985	Rank 1990	1997	Country	Receipts (mn £) 1997	% change 1997/96	% of total 1997
1	1	1	United States	50 037	7.4	16.9
2	3	2	Italy	20 000	-0.1	6.8
4	2	3	France	18 877	-0.1	6.4
3	4	4	Spain	17 730	-3.9	6.0
5	5	5	United Kingdom	13 712	6.6	4.6
6	6	6	Germany	10 945	-6.5	3.7
7	7	7	Austria	8 262	-11.4	2.8
21	25	8	China	8 049	18.4	2.7
27	14	9	Australia	6 216	5.8	2.1
12	11	10	China, Hong Kong SAR	6 161	-14.7	2.1
9	9	11	Canada	5 952	0.7	2.0
23	13	12	Thailand	5 800	0.4	2.0
77	65	12	Poland	5 800	3.6	2.0
13	12	13	Singapore	5 328	0.4	1.8
8	8	14	Switzerland	5 306	-10.5	1.8
10	10	15	Mexico	5 062	9.5	1.7
18	21	16	Turkey	4 665	17.4	1.6
16(1)	23(1)	17	Russian Federation	4 446	-3.0	1.5
15	16	18	Netherlands	4 398	5.5	1.5
41	26	19	Indonesia	4 392	8.2	1.5
14	15	20	Belgium	3 998	1.8	1.4
34	18	21	Korea Rep.	3 466	-4.2	1.2
29	27	22	Argentina	3 379	10.9	1.1
24	17	23	Japan	2 881	6.0	1.0
24	19	24	Portugal	2 842	0.0	1.0
37	31	25	Malaysia	2 562	-1.9	0.9
47	44	26	Egypt	2 564	20.1	0.9
19	24	27	Greece	2 533	2.1	0.9
22	22	28	Sweden	2 523	3.6	0.9
33	29	29	Taiwan (Prov, of China)	2 470	1.9	0.8
55(2)	62	30	Czech Republic	2 466	-9.2	0.8
–	34	31	Macau	2 221	2.9	0.7
40	35	32	Ireland	2 166	8.2	0.7
20	20	33	Denmark	2 106	-7.8	0.7
32	33	34	India	2 101	6.4	0.7
30	40	35	Phillippines	1 887	4.9	0.6
26	37	36	Israel	1 866	-4.8	0.6
17	36	37	Brazil	1 734	5.4	0.6
56	50	38	Hungary	1 713	14.4	0.6
49	45	39	New Zealand	1 673	3.2	0.6
36	32	40	Norway	1 664	3.9	0.6
			Total 1-40	**261 962**	**1.8**	**88.6**
			World Total	**295 510**	**2.2**	**100.0**

(1) Former USSR. (2) Former Czechoslovakia.

Figure 1.8 *World's top forty tourism earners*
Source: World Tourism Organisation, 1998

In the 1990s, China and Eastern Europe became more popular, with a slight increase in visits to Africa, East Asia, the Pacific and the Middle East. This was due to a combination of favourable exchange rates, competition between airlines, and the growth of specialised tourism such as ecotourism. Nevertheless, Europe is still the main destination for the following reasons:

- most travellers are from Europe
- there are strong historic and linguistic ties between Europe and North America.

Over 80% of all tourists come from just twenty countries, mostly developed countries. The destination of tourists varies with their origin:

- most tourists to Africa are from Europe
- Australasia is increasingly important for East Asian and Pacific travellers, but still of minor importance for European and North American tourists
- the Middle East market consists mainly of European and East Asian travellers, but not Americans
- Europe remains internationally popular.

North America, Europe and Japan account for most of the global expenditure; Europe alone accounts for 48% of expenditure. The global contribution of tourism to tax, direct, indirect and personal is huge. Direct taxes include those paid at airports, for example entry airport tax, or VAT on hotel accommodation; indirect taxes include tax paid on souvenirs, at restaurants; personal taxes include taxes paid by those working in tourism. In 1994, £440 billion was spent and it is estimated this will rise to £1000 billion by 2005.

The popularity of tourist destinations has changed over time. For example, in the 1920s and 1930s Nice and Monte Carlo were fashionable. Spain was popular in the 1950s, whereas the Caribbean was renowned in the 1960s. Africa was favoured in the 1970s, the Pacific in the 1980s and increasingly, in the 1990s, Asia has attracted larger numbers of tourists – in 1991, Asia earned over £20 billion from tourism.

THE BRITISH ON HOLIDAY

In 1995, the British took 87 million holidays and breaks, spending £22.5 billion or about 5% of total consumer spending. Thirty-two million long holidays (five nights or more) were taken by the British within the UK, compared with 23 million long holidays abroad (Figure 1.9). However, expenditure was much greater on the foreign trips, amounting to 60% of spending. France and Spain accounted for 45% of holidays and the USA 7% (Figure 1.10). The most popular home destinations were the West Country and Wales, attracting 17% and 10% of tourists. However, there are a number of 'honeypot' destinations, including the Lake District, south Devon (the English Riviera), the north Devon coast, Blackpool, Great Yarmouth and the Scottish Highlands.

The most popular foreign destination for the British in 1998, was the Spanish Balearic Islands – best known for the resorts at Mallorca, Menorca and Ibiza – although the number of visitors fell 5%. The second most popular country was Greece, which achieved the fastest visitor growth rate of 33%. The World Cup boosted visitor levels to France, which were up 21%, while Italy suffered a decline of 13%. Trips to North America rose almost 25%, and travel to other long-haul destinations rose 14% in 1998 compared with 1997. Visits to Western Europe only increased by 9%.

Consumer spending on holidays can be divided between long holidays and short breaks abroad, worth £13.5 billion, domestic long holidays, worth £6 billion, and domestic short breaks, worth £3 billion. Average spending per person on a domestic holiday is between £100 and £160 whereas average spending on a holiday abroad is about £600.

	Millions		% total	
	UK	Abroad	UK	Abroad
Package holidays	3	15	9	65
Independent travellers	29	8	91	35
Main transport				
Car	24	3	75	13
Air	–	17	–	74
Other	8	3	24	13
Total	**32**	**23**	**100**	**100**

Figure 1.9 *The British on holiday, 1995*
Source: Adapted from New leisure markets, 1996. Special interest tourism, New Leisure Markets.

Domestic holidays	%	Holidays abroad	%
West Country	17	Spain/Canaries	25
Wales	10	France	20
Southern England	9	Greece	7
East Anglia	9	USA/Canada	7
Scotland	9	Portugal	4
South East England	7	Italy	4
North West England	7	Benelux	4
Other (England)	32	Turkey	3
Ireland	2		
Others	24		
Total	**100**	**Total**	**100**

Figure 1.10 *Principal holiday destinations for the British, 1995*
Source: Adapted from New leisure markets, 1996, Special interest tourism, New Leisure Markets

1   Natural landscape – mountains: the Alps; natural history: the Galapagos islands; coasts: the Great Barrier Reef; forests: Amazon Rain Forest; deserts; polar areas; wildlife; rivers; canyons

2   Climate – hot, sunny, dry areas are very attractive to most tourists; seasonality of climate leads to seasonality of tourism

3   Cultural – language, customs, clothing, food, architecture, and theme parks. Examples include recreation: Nice; religion: Lourdes; education: Oxford

4   Demographic factors – increasing affluence and leisure time, longer holidays, paid holidays, improved mobility and transport links, more working women

5   Economic factors – exchange rates (change in value of one currency relative to another), foreign exchange (foreign currency earned – in this case, through tourism), employment, multiplier effects,

6   Technological factors – improvements in air transport, communications and information technology

7   Political factors – political instability: the 1992 military coup in Thailand led to a 20-30% drop in the occupancy rate in luxury hotels; terrorism

8   Disease – outbreaks of malaria, Aids and cholera lead to a decrease in tourism; the 1995 Ebola virus in Zaire led to a drop in tourism

9   Sporting events – events such as the World Cup (USA, 1994), the Olympic Games (Atlanta, 1996), the Rugby World Cup (South Africa, 1995) led to a small boom in tourism.

Figure 1.11 *Factors affecting tourism*
Source: Nagle, G., 1998, Development and underdevelopment, Nelson

QUESTIONS

1   Distinguish between tourism and recreation.

2   Describe the geographic pattern of tourist destinations (as shown in figure 1.7 on page 6). How do you explain this pattern?

3   Study Figure 1.8. Which countries earn more money from tourism in relation to the percentage of tourists they attract?. How do you explain the differences between the percentage of tourists and the percentage of spending?

4   Study Figure 1.10 which shows the main destinations of British holiday makers within Britain and abroad. Choose an appropriate method, such as a choropleth, proportional circles or flowlines, to show variations in the popularity of the destinations. How do you explain the results you have shown?

FACTORS AFFECTING TOURISM

Tourism is a volatile business. Not only is it subject to climatic change, it is also influenced by political instability, currency fluctuations, changes in fashion and changes in the economy. Figure 1.11 lists some of the factors affecting the volume, type and impact of tourism (Figure 1.11).

Figure 1.13 Wide, sandy beach, Bettystown, Ireland

Physical factors include scenic locations (Figure 1.12), wide sandy beaches (Figure 1.13) and warm, sunny climates. These are examined in depth in Chapters 2 and 6. Other factors are discussed in this chapter, while the influence of culture (heritage) is discussed in Chapter 5.

Demographic factors

Life stage elements such as infants in the family or adolescents, recent empty-nest status (households in which the young people have just left home) or failing health can

Figure 1.12 Rugged scenery, Wicklow, Ireland

Stage in life cycle	Buying or behavioural patterns
1 Bachelor stage: young, single people not living at home	1 Few financial burdens; fashion opinion leaders; recreation oriented; buy basic kitchen equipment, basic furniture, cars, equipment for the 'mating game', holidays
2 Newly married couples: young, no children	2 Better off financially than they will be in near future; highest purchase rate and highest average purchase of durables; buy cars, refrigerators, cookers, sensible and durable furniture, holidays
3 Full nest I: youngest child under six (Figure 1.15)	3 Home purchasing at peak; liquid assets low; dissatisfied with financial position and amount of money saved; interested in new products; buy washers, dryers, television, baby food, chest-rubs and cough medicines, vitamins, dolls' prams, sleds, skates
4 Full nest II: youngest child six or over	4 Financial position better; more wives work; less influenced by advertising; buy larger-sized packages, multiple-unit deals; buy many foods, cleaning materials, bicycles, music lessons, pianos
5 Full nest III: older couples with dependent children	5 Financial position still better; many wives work; some children find jobs; hard to influence with advertising high average purchase of durables; buy new, more tasteful furniture, automatic cars, non-necessary appliances, boats, dental services, magazines
6 Empty nest I: older couples, no children living with them, head of the household in work force	6 Home ownership at peak; most satisfied with financial position and money saved; interested in travel, recreation, self-education; make gifts and contributions; not interested in new products; buy holidays, luxuries, home improvements
7 Empty nest II: older couples, no children living at home, head retired	7 Drastic cut in income; keep home; buy medical care products that improve health, sleep and digestion
8 Solitary survivor, in labour force	8 Income still good but likely to sell home
9 Solitary survivor, retired	9 Same medical and product needs as other retired group; drastic cut in income; special need for attention, affection and security

Figure 1.14 A traditional family life cycle in a developed country   Source: Page, S., 1995, Urban tourism, Routledge

Figure 1.15 *A young family coping with the crowded streets of Killarney, Ireland*

impose restrictions on the choice of holidays or guide the consumer towards a particular type of holiday (Figure 1.14). A source of friction can be the lack of adequate provision for different life stage groups at the chosen destination, for example, the provision of creche facilities or nightclubs. Some companies have exploited a niche market – the most notable ones being Club 18-30 for that age-group and Saga Holidays for the over 50s.

A higher level of education strongly influences the willingness of travellers to take calculated risks and seek adventure in return for satisfaction. The less well-educated tend to look for familiarity, security and predictability, and this may prevent some people from going abroad. The level of education in general influences levels of income, which has a strong influence on the type of holiday taken.

> **QUESTIONS**
>
> 1 For a tourist area in a developed country and in a developing country show how the factors listed in Figure 1.11 have influenced their development as tourist centres. List the main similarities between the two places, and list the main differences between them.
>
> 2 Study Figure 1.14 which shows the buying and behavioural patterns in a traditional family life cycle in a developed country. Describe and explain what types of holidays are likely to be taken at each of these stages.

Economic factors

Economic factors influence tourism in a number of ways. Exchange rates will influence tourists' choice of destination – a strong exchange rate, such as the German Deutsche Mark or the Japanese Yen, will deter visitors; abroad cheaper places, such as Turkey and Spain, will attract tourists as they get greater value for money.

In 1997, the growth in world tourism slowed down, due to the financial crisis in Asia. At the time Asia was the fastest growing region in terms of tourists and tourism, but its growth rates dipped to 4% in 1997, compared with 14% in the early-1990s. Pressures from the financial crisis were most felt in Thailand, but stretched across to the Philippines, Indonesia and Malaysia. Countries that usually receive many Asian tourists, such as Australia, were also badly affected. China, however, was unaffected by the crisis and its tourism receipts rose by 18% between 1996 and 1997 to £9 billion.

The Asian currency devaluation in the late 1990s made Asian countries more attractive to European and North American tourists: the devaluation of the Thai Baht and the North Korean Won made them more competitive and led to an increase in the amount of long-haul travel to the region. However, the increase in long-haul travel did not compensate for the huge decline in intra-regional tourism, i.e. the tourism within south-east Asia.

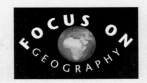

Case study: **Economic recession and visits by Asian Tourists to Australia**

Tourism is one of Australia's biggest industries. In 1997, it accounted for over £4.4 billion, 11% of total export earnings. The number of international visitors tripled between 1984 and 1995. There were about 1 million visitors in 1984-85, 2 million in 1990, and over 3 million in 1993-94. The growth rate was about 14% per annum. The number of tourists was expected to reach 6 million by 2000, with the Sydney Olympic Games providing a big boost.

Employment at Homebush Bay, site of the Olympics, increased from 405 000 in 1986 to 460 000 in 1993. It is estimated that by 2000, 600 000-700 000 people will be employed in tourism in Sydney.

Japan is the largest source of tourists to Australia and there were big growth rates in other Asian markets. In the mid-late 1990s, the emerging Asian middle classes, especially in the newly-industrialised countries (NICs) such as Taiwan, Hong Kong, Korea, Malaysia, and Singapore, are especially important. Australia is the nearest Western country to these Asian countries. In 1993, the New South Wales government carried out a £2.5 million advertising campaign to promote Sydney, largely directed at the Asian markets.

The Asian financial crisis in 1997 had a great impact on the whole of the Pacific Rim region. In Australia, nearly all sectors of the economy faced falling demand and prices, but the sector that felt the most immediate impact was tourism. Airlines and tourism operators had long prided themselves as Australia's biggest foreign exchange earner and generator of jobs, but feared that the collapse of Asian

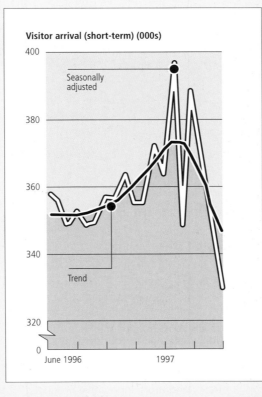

Figure 1.16 *Visitor arrivals in Australia (short-term), 1996-97*
Source: Australian Bureau of Statistics, 1998

business could reduce Australia's tourist revenue by 20-25%.

Official figures confirmed the industry's worst fears (Figure 1.16). The number of Asian tourists arriving in Australia fell 24% in 1998 contributing to an overall reduction in tourist numbers by 6%. The collapse in the South Korean market, Australia's second-largest source of tourists, was the most marked – in 1998, Korean arrivals fell 66% on 1997 figures. This collapse was most noticeable in Queensland, the most popular destination for Asian tourists, where the number of tourists was down by 90%.

The crisis intensified when Qantas Airways, Australia's largest carrier, halted some services to destinations including Indonesia, Malaysia and

Thailand, and cancelled all flights to South Korea. In an effort to attract passengers to and from other destinations, Qantas and Ansett, Australia's other international carrier, became locked in a bitter price war with Asian carriers on routes to Europe. Prices on the European routes were slashed, causing the Australian carriers to have to cut their profit margins drastically. Although Qantas dropped the price of a Sydney to London flight by nearly 25%, to the equivalent of £600, it was still unable to compete with some Asian airlines, which offered the same route for little more than £400.

The weakening of the Australian dollar has improved Australia's appeal in markets such as the US and Europe, but it faces difficulties making up for the losses from Asia.

Case study: **Tourism in Europe: the European Single Currency**

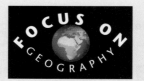

The implementation of European Economic and Monetary Union (Emu) between 1998 and 2002 (Figure 1.17) has considerable implications for travel and tourism in Europe. On the positive side, it should stimulate tourism in many non-Emu member countries such as Turkey and the North African states, as they will become more competitive if the European Single Currency (the Euro) settles at a strong rate.

One of the main effects of the price transparency (direct price comparisons in different countries) offered by the Euro will be to increase competition among destinations and tourism businesses. Faced with increased competition, tourism suppliers will be obliged to become more efficient. This means producing at a lower cost, rationalising tourism services for increased flexibility at the same price, whilst maintaining the quality of the services provided.

However, a strong Euro could have a negative impact on some places, notably Spain and Italy, which have traditionally attracted tourists from the wealthier countries of north-west Europe. To date their tourist industries, particularly in Spain have been based on cost-competitiveness. In the future, they may lose this competitive edge to the non-Emu countries and may have to improve their services and productivity, or even remodel their tourist industries.

May 2, 1998	Designation of countries which have formed the Euro zone: Austria, Belgium, Finland, France, Germany, Ireland, Italy Luxembourg, the Netherlands, Portugal, Spain.
Jan 1, 1999	Exchange rates set Euro can be used in non-cash financial transactions
Jan 1, 1999 to July 1, 2002	Euro bills and coins enter circulation and national currencies remain July in circulation
July 1, 2002	Euro only

Figure 1.17 *The Euro timeline*
Source: The World Travel and Tourism Council, 1998

The Euro is expected to become as widely accepted in tourism as the US dollar, and will stimulate Europe's tourism industry encouraging higher quality and more innovative products. The Euro will benefit tourists as it will stabilise prices; tourists will be able to carry one currency, compare prices in different countries and save on the costs and time involved in changing money.

Another benefit will be security, as tourists will not need to carry quantities of different currencies and should not be such an easy target for pickpockets. It is already easier to travel between most of the European Union countries and the liberalisation of air transport has brought down airfares.

According to the World Trade Organisation, the Euro zone is set to become the most important tourism zone in the world, outperforming the United States in all aspects: the number of incoming tourists, the number of outbound tourists, tourism receipts and tourism's importance in the economy. It is estimated that forty per cent of international tourism will take place in this Euro zone.

However, if the Euro is too strong as a currency, it will not attract tourists for a 'cheap' or bargain holiday. The introduction of the Euro and the transition period will create new costs as companies switch their accounting procedures, computer software and add dual pricing to travel brochures. These costs should be a short-term problem.

Political factors

There are a number of ways in which governments can encourage, discourage or control tourism and the number of tourists (Figure 1.18). Government involvement in tourism is important and is increasing in most places. This is because tourism is a major earner of foreign income and governments wish to increase the amount of revenue they receive.

Trade barriers and agreements play an increasingly important role in tourism. The World Trade Organisation (formerly **GATT** – the Global Agreement on Tariff and Trade) should increase tourism by allowing easier flow of goods across international borders. Fewer government restrictions on foreign ownership, multinational controlled hotels and travel agencies will also lead to increases in tourism.

Technological factors

Improvements in travel safety, decreased travel time and increase in communications information have also aided the spread of tourism. Technological changes in transport have led to mass air travel. The 707 jet aircraft was developed in 1954; this aircraft was capable of carrying 200 passengers, compared with earlier planes, such as the Comet that could carry only 70 passengers. By the 1960s, the world was in the jet age.

Increased volumes of tourism and more accessible travel are linked with:
● increased incomes
● decreased costs of air fares
● a greater variety of cheaper package tours.

Advances in computing and information technology have led to:
● increased safety, with better monitoring of aircraft and ships
● safer travel in bad weather, using satellite navigation
● easier, quicker and cheaper booking, reservations, and itineraries.

Medical advances are also important. Before the 1950s, international travel was associated with a risk of infectious disease. Now, however, with better immunisation, vaccination, improved water supply and sanitation, the risk of infectious diseases is greatly decreased. However, serious outbreaks of disease still occur, as is shown in the case of the Dominican Republic, discussed in Chapter 8.

Political factor	Explanation	Example
1 Development strategies	1 Land-use control, building control, pollution	1 Restrictions on number of tourists e.g. Namibia
2 Travel documents	2 Track the flows of tourists and immigrants	2 Passports, visas, permits etc. Lack of control into the EU
3 Quarantine regulations	3 Check spread of plant and animal diseases	3 Channel Tunnel between France and UK could aid the spread of rabies
4 Infrastructure	4 State funding for all kinds of infrastructure	4 Government sponsored/aided developments, such as sports events
5 Control of exchange	5 Limit the amount of money taken into a country	5 In Egypt and Bulgaria proof of money spent is needed
6 Legalised gambling	6 Casinos	6 Las Vegas; former 'homelands' in South Africa
7 Advertising, promotion	7 To increase the number and/or type of tourist	7 Northern Ireland and the Republic of Ireland's joint campaign from 1995
8 Deregulation	8 Decrease government control	8 US airline industry
9 Geo-political conflicts	9 War and political upheaval	9 Northern Ireland, former Yugoslavia
10 Sanctions by other countries	10 Boycotts	10 South Africa pre-1992
11 Government Dept. of Tourism	11 Coordination, planning regulation	11 Yellowstone National Park
12 Legislation	12 Creation of national parks, heritage areas etc.	12 National parks in the UK
13 Taxes	13 Direct and indirect	13 Departure tax in Japan, VAT in the UK.

Figure 1.18 *A summary of the impact of political factors on tourism Source: Nagle, G., 1998, Development and underdevelopment, Nelson*

QUESTIONS

1 With the use of examples, show how variaitions in currency/exchange rates influence the decision to take a holiday.

2 What are the advantages and disadvantages of a single currency in Europe for the tourist industry.

THE IMPACT OF TOURISM

Tourism is important for foreign exchange and balance of payments (Figure 1.19). Tourism is defined as an export earner because it brings new money from foreign countries into the economy. In Egypt and Jamaica over 60% of export income is derived from tourism. It is also very important in developed countries, such as France and Ireland. In Spain, it is the most important export earner.

The World Tourism Organisation believes that tourism will triple by 2020, with 1.6 billion tourists visiting countries abroad annually and spending more than £1300 billion annually (Figure 1.19).

Tourism creates much unskilled employment, such as porters, maids, and cleaners (Figure 1.20), as well as highly skilled employment, including accountants, managers, and entertainers. In developing countries, wages from tourism often exceed the national average. By contrast, in developed countries wages in tourism are usually below the national average (Figure 1.24 on page 17). Tourism is often very seasonal and this can lead to problems of seasonal unemployment and under employment.

Tourism also leads to developments in infrastructure, notably roads and utilities. These do not, however, always benefit the locals.

Tourism is important in terms of economic development. It generates employment in construction activity. Airports, hotels, roads, and other facilities need to be built and maintained. In addition, it has links with many important service industries. These include accommodation, entertainment, food and catering, guided tours, travel by air, road and rail, banking services, shop, laundry, cleaning, taxi, bus, car line, insurance, luggage suppliers, medical services, travel agencies, duty free shopping (Figure 1.21). These industries are very diverse and many are small-scale operations, such as restaurants and taxis. In addition, there are a small number of very large-scale operations, such as multinational hotel companies and air travel.

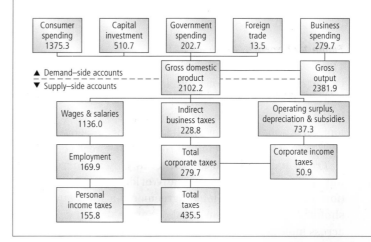

Figure 1.19 *The global impact of tourism, 1996 estimate*
Source: The Economist, January 1998

Figure 1.20 *Low paid employment at Miyajima Shrine, Japan*

The impact of tourism on the global economy is difficult to calculate. The World Travel and Tourism Council (WTTC) argues that calculations based on direct spending ignore the knock-on benefits of tourism to the economy, such as spending in restaurants or contributions to the retail trade. According to the WTTC, if these knock-on effects are included in the figures, tourism accounts for about £2400 billion or 11% of the world's gross domestic product. The industry accounts for about 230 million jobs directly, and is forecast to create another 100 million jobs by 2010 (Figure 1.22).

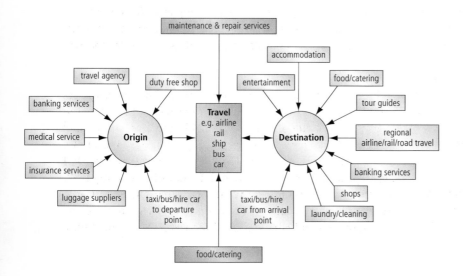

Figure 1.21 *Tourist links*
Source: Baker S. et al, 1996, Pathways in georgraphy, Nelson

Figure 1.22 *Prospects for travel and tourism*
Source: Baker S. et al, 1996, Pathways in geography, Nelson

World estimates	1996	2006	Real growth
Jobs	255m	385m	50.1%
Jobs (% of total)	10.7%	11.1%	–
Output	£2400bn	£4733bn	48.7%
GDP	10.7%	11.5%	49.6%
Investment	£511bn	£1067bn	57.3%
Exports	£507bn	£1000bn	51.2%
Total taxes	£435bn	£867bn	49.6%

National and local governments are keen to develop tourism for a variety of reasons:

- to improve the balance of payments
- to aid regional economic development
- to diversify the economy
- to increase income
- to increase tax revenue
- to create new jobs
- improve the structure and balance of economic activities
- to encourage entrepreneurial activity.

For national governments, job creation is one of the main attractions of developing a tourist industry. This is particularly so in countries with few natural resources and little capital. Increasingly, however, some countries in the developed world have looked to tourism as a means of creating employment in declining industrial areas. Examples in the UK include Liverpool, the Medway ports and Doncaster (Figure 1.22). The British government has targeted tourism as one of the most promising sectors for job-creation through its New Deal scheme to return unemployed young people to work.

Governments are taking an increased interest in the tourist industry because of its potential as a source of revenue from taxes. Some countries have chosen to increase entry fees and export taxes. For example, in 1998 the USA introduced an arrival tax at its airports and ports, while the UK's departure taxes were doubled in 1997. However, these increases have attracted criticism from some consumers' groups who claim that too many taxes are aimed indiscriminately at tourism because it is an easy target and because governments see tourism as a luxury. Tourism is also an export, the groups argue, bringing in foreign currency to the country, and governments should offer incentives to make travel and tourism easier and more affordable.

Tourism offers excellent potential for economic development because it creates an unparalleled number of jobs for the young and for women, and offers employment opportunities in areas of high unemployment such as some city centres, some rural areas and in developing countries.

However, because travel and tourism involves a large number of sectors and is a largely uncoordinated sector of the economy, governments often overlook it as a vehicle for large-scale economic development.

But there are major problems associated with tourism:

- it is fickle – destinations go in and out of fashion
- the demand for tourism varies with external factors, such as economic recession and political unrest
- it is price- and income-elastic (as income increases, the amount of money spent on tourism, recreation and leisure increases)
- it can lead to an increasing dependence on imported goods
- employment is often seasonal
- there can be leakages from the local economy
- there may be additional costs to the city authorities
- families can be separated if the bread-winner has to work away from home, i.e. by moving to a tourist centre
- the local culture may be destroyed
- there may be undesirable changes in land use
- an increased demand for buildings, which may spoil the environment
- farmers may leave the land thereby reducing agricultural production
- money is spent on tourist infrastructure to provide water, food, shelter, waste disposal, and entertainment.

Inset 1.1
Leakage

The **leakage** from tourism is the money that is generated by tourism but is transferred back to the other country. For example, in Kenya up to 17% of tourist expenditure leaks out, very often back to developed countries. Leakages can take place in five main ways:

1 foreign workers send the money home
2 travel costs to airlines and ships.
3 payment for goods and services imported for tourism
4 payment to foreign owners of hotels and other amenities
5 foreign debt in developing the infrastructure for tourism.

In Britain it is argued that the growth of the tourism sector is being held back by a skills shortage. In 1996, the Department of National Heritage published a report, *People working in tourism and hospitality* and stated that the tourism industry in Britain has a poor training record that led to poor staff motivation and difficulties in retaining staff. So great is the problem that the Department of National Heritage believe that unless action is taken to develop the workforce, the industry will lose out to overseas competitors.

The British tourism sector is threatened by a vicious circle of recruitment difficulties, shortages of skilled staff, relatively low pay (Figure 1.23), high staff turnover and a relatively unattractive image as an employer. Employers in the hotel and restaurant sectors have greater difficulty in filling jobs than the average across all industries (Figure 1.24). The low profile and poor image of the tourism industry deters many recruits. The report also criticised staff training. It found that over 45% of full-time tourism staff and 74% of part-time staff had received no job training since leaving full-time education. In fact, the report found that levels of training were below the all-industry average, and productivity levels were half those in the US and France. The fragmented nature of the industry – 81% of hotels and 94% of restaurants have less than 25 employees – means that many companies do not have the resources to train people.

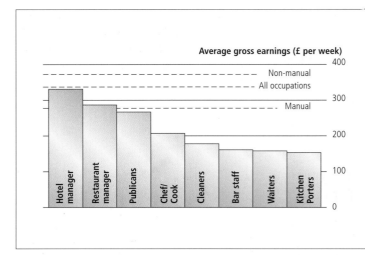

Figure 1.23 *Hotel employment: earnings compared with other sectors*
Source: HCTC, 1995, New earnings survey

Inset 1.2
The impacts of tourism

Positive impacts

1 **Employment** Tourism is labour intensive and has a **multiplier effect** (see Models of tourism on pages 20-22 for a discussion of the multiplier effect). This leads to more money in the local economy, demand for more buildings, more hotels, more entertainment , and guides etc.

2 **Environment** Tourism can have a positive impact on the environment. Tourism brings in revenue and this may lead to sustainable long term use and investment in the environment. In Mallorca, where much of the beauty of the south of the island has been destroyed by tourism, its tourist revenue is now being used to protect the landscape.

3 **Culture** Tourism may lead to the preservation of local customs and heritage. There may be increased local awareness of the importance of architectural and heritage sites, and there may be the development of craft and art industries to reinforce local cultural identity.

4 **Education** There may be an increase in the training and skills of local people, this may lead to the growth of information centres, visitor centres, and increased education in the visitor. The study tours run by the Japan Foundation are an excellent example.

5 **Infrastructure** Although these developments are mostly for tourists, there is a spin-off effect that may benefit local people. Roads and utilities, such as electricity, gas and water, may benefit the whole community.

Negative impacts

1 **Alienation** The contrasts between the tourist-haves and the indigenous-have nots are very great. Local resentment may develop against tourists; crime against tourists may occur; inflated prices for second homes and apartments may develop; local food production may decline; there may be terrorism against tourists. Examples of terrorism include Egypt in the early 1990s, the abductions in Cambodia in 1994 and in the Yemen and Uganda in 1999.

2 **Prostitution and paedophilia** In Thailand and the Philippines both are very common. They are linked very closely with poverty. One result has been a rise in the number of cases of Aids.

3 **Westernisation of culture** Multinational food chains such as Kentucky Fried Chicken, McDonalds and Coca-Cola are global and can destroy the unique quality of a place, as well as its agricultural base (see page 126). Global patterns in music, fashion and cinema also lead to a westernisation of cultures and society. This devalues the tourist experience. As well as damaging local systems, it devalues the tourist experience.

4 **Commercialisation of culture** For example religious dances are commercialised and packaged. Woodcarvings are trivialised and there is much production of cheap souvenirs.

5 **Environmental destruction** For example, habitat removal, loss of biodiversity, footpath erosion (Figure 1.25).

One of the biggest problems for the sector is a high rate of staff turnover. Almost half of those employed in hospitality (providing accommodation) had been with their employer for less than two years, compared with an all-industry average of less than 30%.

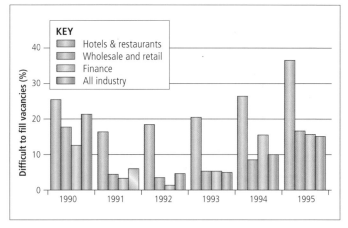

Figure 1.24 *Hotel employment: difficulty in filling vacancies compared with other industries*
Source: HCTC, 1995, New earnings survey

Despite the industry's favourable potential for employment and wealth creation, its rapid growth poses many problems. For example, it is questionable whether the infrastructure (airports, ports, roads, hotels and so on) will be able to cope with the anticipated increase in the number of tourists by 2020. The number of air passengers is expected to double within the next twenty years, and this may cause increased congestion in Europe and south-east Asia where much of the demand and supply of the tourism industry is forecast to grow.

Beautiful environments attract tourism. However, tourism may exceed the **carrying capacity** (see page 22) of an area and lead to environmental deterioration in terms of air-, water-, noise- and visual-pollution. Increasingly, there is growing concern for the long-term management of the environment. This is evident even among large tourist operators, such as British Airways, and they are putting pressure on some destinations to offer a higher quality environment. Paradoxically, the pressure for a better environment is not coming from public institutions but from market forces. Customers paying for a tourist experience are demanding higher standards, and this includes environmental quality.

Stressor activities	Stress	Primary environmental response
1 Permanent environmental restructuring (a) Major construction activity • urban expansion • transport network • tourist facilities • marinas, ski-lifts, sea walls (b) Change in land use • expansion of recreational lands	1 Restructuring of local environments expansion of built environments land taken out of primary production	1 Change in habitat Change in population of biological species Change in health and welfare of humans Change in visual quality
2 Generation of waste residuals • urbanization • transportation	2 Pollution loadings • emissions • effulent discharge • solid waster disposal • noise (traffic, aircraft)	2 Change in quality of environmental media • air • water • soil Health of biological organisms Health of humans
3 Tourist actiivities • skiing • walking • hunting • trail-bike riding • collecting	3 Trampling of vegetation and soils Destruction of species	3 Change in habitat Change in population of biological species
4 Effect on population dynamics • population growth	4 Population density (seasonal)	4 Congestion Demand for natural resourses • land and water • energy

QUESTIONS

1 Briefly outline the (a) positive effects and (b) negative effects of tourism.

2 Why is so much tourist employment
(a) seasonal,
(b) unskilled and
(c) low-paid?
What are the implications of this for economic development.

3 Describe and explain the environmental impact of tourism as shown in figure 1.25.

Figure 1.25 *Environmental impacts of tourism*
Source: Pearce, D., 1981, Tourist development, Longman

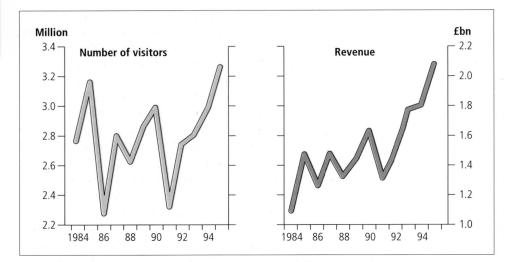

Figure 1.26 *Fluctuations in US visitors to the UK*
Source: ONS, Financial Times, 1996

THE FUTURE OF TOURISM

Changes in leisure time

Traditional thinking is that economic advances would improve the quality of life and lead to a new golden age of leisure. But far from leisure time continuing to increase throughout the world, the amount available for many people is likely to decline. Reductions in the working week have slowed considerably in the last decade as the world economy has become more competitive. As work pressures increase and where leisure time is constantly being squeezed, the quality of life may fall. For many employees, working hours have actually increased, because companies are facing ever more intense global competition. Competitive markets are forcing companies to downsize and to minimise employee costs – of which holidays and pensions are among the most expensive. At the same time technology is making employers less dependent on manpower. These factors encourage workers to attempt to safeguard their jobs by working longer hours.

Very few governments are considering bringing in legislation to reduce the length of the working week, increase paid holiday entitlements or introduce additional public holidays. France is an exception. Many countries are raising the age of retirement (or phasing out early retirement) and considering increases in contributions to pension funds to contain rising social security and pension costs. In these circumstances, trade unions are more concerned about stabilising employment and maintaining income than pressing for more leisure time.

The impact of these trends on the tourism industry worldwide could be significant. Although demand for holidays is unlikely to weaken, the current trend towards shorter holidays could continue at an even faster rate. Long holidays, which often need to be planned well in advance, may be more difficult to arrange, and holidays may become shorter and more frequent as people find more intensive breaks, often extended weekends, fit their schedules better. It will also favour the expansion of quickly accessible holiday destinations in the same time region or time zone. Thus it will benefit destinations where most of the tourists originate, i.e. those in western Europe and the USA.

New marketing opportunities are presented by the 'money-rich but time-poor' tourists. They will seek a range of widely different holidays in easily and quickly accessible destinations. Those who have time constraints rather than money constraints will also be looking for a higher quality product, with highly efficient ways of selecting and purchasing holidays.

Changes in air travel

The tourist industry depends very heavily on aircraft to carry its millions of customers around the world. Air traffic is expected to increase by over 5% annually until about 2007 and then at about 4.8% for the following decade. By 2017 airlines will be carrying nearly three times as much traffic as they are now.

There are a number of ways in which airlines will be able to cope with the increased number of passengers. One method is to pack more passengers into each aircraft, with less space per passenger, or a higher occupancy rate. For example, Airbus plans to develop a new generation of aircraft that will carry 600 people or more. In addition, medium-sized and large-sized planes will be modified. Airbus forecasts that the number of seats on each flight will increase from 179 in the late-1990s to 227 by 2017. In the Asia-Pacific region, airlines already have an average of 240 seats on their flights. This is forecast to grow to 320 by 2017.

Second, airlines are expected to buy more aircraft. Airlines will spend over £670 billion obtaining more than 1000 aircraft over the next two decades, both to replace their ageing stock and to expand their fleet.

Airlines are also looking at ways of moving passengers more efficiently and quickly. Ticketless travel, computerised check-in, and electronic tracking of passengers between flights have all been introduced to streamline the process. These developments have important implications for the electronics industry and there are major multiplier effects from changes in air travel, in all aspects of aircraft engineering and manufacturing.

A new generation of low-cost, no-frills airlines is competing with the major carriers. Companies such as the Dublin-based Ryanair can only compete with the large operators by offering very competitive prices. They have also speeded up the boarding process by not issuing seat numbers. People are offered seats on a first-come first-served basis at boarding time.

Improved technology and passenger management should help with the management of the increased volume of passengers that is forecast. The main obstacles to expansion are likely to be environmental issues such as pollution and the expansion of the transport infrastructure. For example, noise and fuel emissions are both potential problems. According to the British Airports Authority (BAA), the introduction of quieter aircraft means that levels of noise pollution are falling. Moreover, the zone exposed to high levels of noise (above 80 decibels) by a modern aircraft taking off is less than that of a high speed train. The 'noise footprint' made by the train stretches from the origin to the destination whereas that of a plane is only noticeable close to airports. The BAA argues that (per passenger transported) airports use land about five times more efficiently than rail, and six times more efficiently than road.

Travel and the Internet

'Surfing the Net' is a powerful way of matching specialised needs with specialised companies and independent suppliers. For example, the Internet allows consumers to check the cheapest air fares on offer, search for hotels in the area, see photographs of them, download a town map and decide which restaurants to visit and where to go shopping. It also allows visitors to check up on health warnings and to examine the risk of crime. However, it is not just as a provider of information that the Internet is valuable. It can be used to book and pay for holidays.

Nevertheless, travellers remain hesitant about booking and paying online. A survey by the International Air Transport Association (IATA) showed that while 55% of Americans, 38% of Europeans and 30% of Asians accessed flight information from the Internet, only 8% of all of them used it to book flights. Of those who did not book through the Internet, 42% stated that they preferred going to a travel agent; only 4% said that the Internet was too complicated and 4% that it was too slow.

The potential for online reservations is immense. Software is available to allow travellers to make bookings and change them, from anywhere in the world. One of the first online packages was Air Canada's Cyber Ticket Office.

In the USA, the total value of Internet travel sales was £1.2 billion in 1997 and is forecast to reach £18.7 billion by 2002. By contrast, the market penetration of Internet travel sales in Europe is tiny. In 1996, online travel bookings amounted to £5.2 million, just 7% of transactions. However, that figure is expected to rise rapidly to £1.1 billion by 2002, 35% of the European market, as the use of the Internet spreads. At present, many of those booking through the Internet are people looking for cheap, last-minute flights, but this is expected to change as more people become familiar and confident with the Internet.

In theory, the rise of the Internet could threaten High Street travel agents. Certainly, they will have to adapt to the changes that online information provides rather than ignore them. The role of the travel agent may well become that of 'master' of the Internet – the best informed person of its uses for travel. Travel agents can continue to provide a service for the many people who do not have access to the Internet or the time to surf and browse. Many consumers will always want human contact with an experienced travel agent who can offer sound, impartial advice.

CHANGING PATTERNS OF TOURISM IN THE UK

In the early 1990s, Britain's share of the world tourism market fell to a low of 4.4%. However, this rose to 5% in 1995 when 23.7 million visitors visited Britain. High-spending American tourists dropped off sharply during the Gulf War, 1990 to 1991, although by 1995 numbers had risen back to 3.3 million US visitors, spending over £2 billion, about a sixth of all tourism receipts (Figure 1.25). Increasingly, tourist authorities are trying to entice the over-50s, as this is the most affluent group.

Changes in tourism are notoriously short-term and unpredictable and affected by a number of factors. For example, during 1998, more UK tourists went abroad on holiday, driven away by poor weather, enticed by the enhanced buying power of the strong pound, the falling cost of foreign trips and the billions of pounds of windfalls from building societies. Almost 11 million people took foreign package holidays in the first nine months of 1998 – a rise of 13% on the same period in 1997. However, fears of a recession combined with the 1998 stock market turmoil, meant fewer people travelled abroad in 1999.

Tourism in the UK is examined in detail in Chapter 5, 'Urban and heritage tourism'.

TOURISM AND ETHICS

The tourist expects paradise, but at a knockdown price! However, holiday destinations are not paradise: they are where other people live and work. Attempting to balance the demands of the tourist (the consumer with money), the needs of the environment and the social and economic needs and rights of the local people constitutes a difficult task for any authority or organisation. Consequently, the WTO is preparing an international code of ethics for tourism to set out the responsibilities of all participants in the industry.

However, although the code will be monitored, it will not be binding. The code of ethics is being drawn up by a committee that includes Iran, Algeria, Egypt, Brazil, Portugal and Malaysia, some of whom have notorious human rights records. Indeed, only three of these countries are major tourist-receiving countries and none are major sources of tourists. So there is potential for conflict between those countries that draw up the code and those that are important sources of, and destinations for, tourists.

In their report, *Tourism and Human Rights*, Tourism Concern, a British organisation concerned with the impact of tourism on communities and environments, described a number of tourist activities that flout the Universal Declaration of Human Rights, by denying the local community access to their natural resources. For example, at a holiday destination in Goa, India, water is piped to the hotels but villagers are forced to depend on well water. There are increasing calls for the profits of tourism to make their way into local communities and local economies. At present less than 30% of the money spent by foreign visitors in Goa makes its way to local economies.

Environmental issues have frequently been ignored until the situation becomes critical. For instance, Mallorca, one of Europe's top package tour destinations was forced to rethink its water policy after its supplies diminished to a trickle in 1994. The local supply had become salty and islanders and visitors had to rely on water transported from Barcelona. A desalinisation plant which was opened in 1998 should overcome most of the problem although other strategies have also been implemented: the island has introduced the Law of Golf which allows only waste water to be used on golf courses.

In Calvia, Italy, a district of 30 000 people which attracts 1.2 million tourists annually, high-rise hotels which were built hastily during the rapid expansion of the 1960s and 1970s, are being upgraded or demolished. The renovated hotels have a number of sustainable features, such as water and energy conservation, and recycling facilities.

MODELS OF TOURISM

There have been a number of approaches to the study of tourism including:

- the supply of tourism facilities, such as the distribution of hotels, restaurants, entertainment facilities
- the demand for tourism, such as who visits tourist areas, why they go, where they come from, their behaviour, their demands for activities.

Butler's model of evolution of tourist areas

According to Butler (1980) there is a cycle in the development of tourist resorts. Initially visitors come in small numbers. Numbers are restricted by lack of access, facilities and knowledge, but as awareness increases, visitor numbers increase. With marketing and improved facilities, the popularity of the resort increases and more tourists visit. However, as the numbers increase, the carrying capacity is reached and the attractiveness of the area declines. Butler's model can be divided into six stages (Figure 1.27):

1 Exploration
   A small number of tourists, new location, exotic adventurous travel, minimal impact.

2 Involvement
   If tourists are accepted and if tourism is acceptable, the destinations become better known. There are improvements in the tourist infrastructure. Some local involvement in tourism may begin.

3 Development
   Inward investment takes place. Tourism becomes a big business. Firms from developed countries control, manage and organise tourism. This leads to increased package tours, more holidays and less local involvement.

4 Consolidation
   Tourism becomes an important industry in an area or region. It is not just the provision of facilities but also includes marketing and advertising. Former agricultural land is used for hotels. Facilities, such as beaches and hotel swimming pools, may become reserved for tourists. Resentment begins and there is a decelerating growth rate.

5 Stagnation

There is increased local opposition to tourism and an awareness of the problems it creates. Fewer new tourists arrive.

6 Decline

The area decreases in popularity. International operators move out and local involvement may resume. Local operators may be underfunded, however. Hence there is a decline in tourism. It is possible for the industry to be rejuvenated, such as some UK coastal resorts in the 1990s.

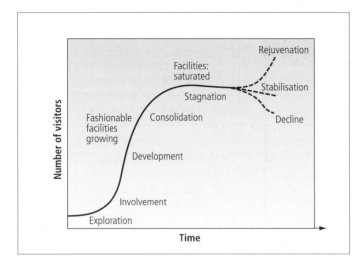

The core periphery enclave model

The economic core periphery model examines the social and economic influences on tourism and the effects of some types of tourism.

In this model, the flow of tourists is from the core, mainly developed countries, to the periphery, mostly developing countries (Figure 1.28). Tour operators, airlines, and hotel owners are generally located in the core. In addition, many tourists flows are dependent upon historic or colonial ties. These factors support the model and reinforce the inequalities in tourism – whereby a rich (western) population experiences and enjoys holidays, whilst the host population sees little of the benefits.

Tourist **resorts** and **enclaves** are specifically designed for tourists. These contain specialised facilities such as hotels, restaurants and recreational activities. Hence, there is very little contact between the resident population and the tourist population. Consequently, there is little experience of the reality of economic, social and cultural life. These self-sufficient enclaves have little multiplier effect in the local economy. Much of the profit generated by tourism goes to Western companies leaking out of the local economy.

Figure 1.27 *Butler's model of evolution of tourist areas*
Source: Chrispin, J. and Jegede, F., 1996, Population resources and development, Collins

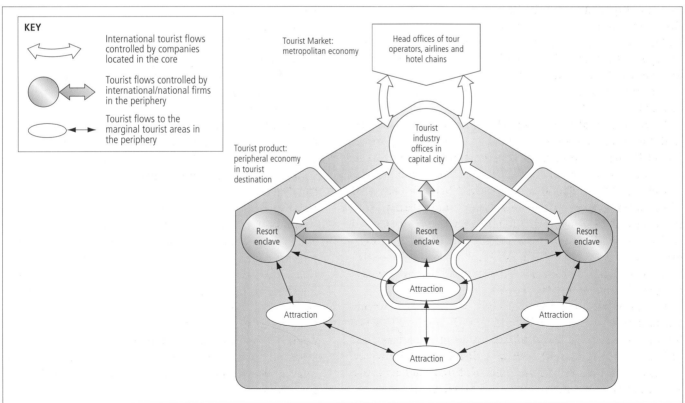

Figure 1.28 *The core periphery model of tourism*
Source: Chrispin, J. and Jegede, F., 1996, Population resources and development, Collins

Carrying capacity

The carrying capacity of a tourist resort is the number of visitors that can be catered for in a resort before the tourist experience declines and the resort becomes less attractive as a destination. It is also the ceiling or saturation level whereby the population is the largest which can be supported without causing irreversible damage to the environment.

Overpopulation occurs when there are too many people relative to the resource and the tourists ruin the attraction. This ties in with Doxey's irritation index of residents' attitudes to tourism (Figure 1.29).

Doxey's index of irritation (resident attitudes to tourism)

Doxey's index of irritation shows how residents' attitudes to tourists change over time. After an initial phase of acceptance and welcome, the atmosphere becomes hostile.

Multiplier effects

Multiplier effects are the processes that increase the amount of new investment and development in one area compared with others. It is the geographical equivalent of the rich getting richer, while the poor get poorer. The theory is based on the work of Gunnar Myrdal (1957). He believed that over time, multiplier effects cause economic forces to reinforce and increase regional inequalities rather than reduce them.

Initial **comparative advantages** such as location, natural resources or labour, provide the stimulus for development in a particular location. In turn, **cumulative**

Stages of development			
1	EUPHORIA	1	Initial phase of development, visitors and investors welcome, little planning or control mechanism.
2	APATHY	2	Visitors taken for granted, contacts between residents and outsiders more formal (commercial), planning concerned mostly with marketing.
3	ANNOYANCE	3	Saturation points approached, residents have misgivings about tourist industry, policy makers attempt solutions via increasing infrastructure rather than limiting growth.
4	ANTAGONISM	4	Irritations openly expressed, visitors seen as cause of all problems, planning now remedial but promotion increased to offset deteriorating reputation of destination.

Figure 1.29 *Doxey's index of irritation (resident attitudes to tourism)*
Source: Doxey, G., 1976, When enough's enough: the natives are restless in Old Niagara, Heritage Canada, 2 (2), 26-7

causation (the multiplier effect) occurs as **acquired advantages** are developed and reinforce the area's reputation, thereby attracting further investment (Figure 1.29). The acquired advantages include improvements in infrastructure, skilled workforce and increased tax revenues. Further investment makes the area increasingly attractive compared with other areas, thus attracting more investment.

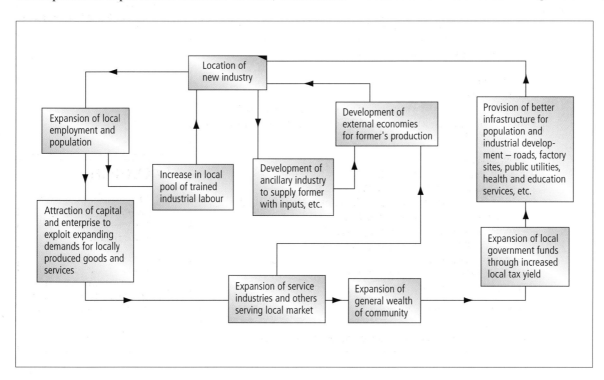

Figure 1.30
Multiplier effects (Myrdal's process of cumulative causation)
Source: Chorley, R. and Haggett, P., 1967, Models in geography, Methuen

Inset 1.3
Collecting and interpreting tourism statistics

In this section, and again in Chapter 5, 'Urban and heritage tourism', we look at some of the ways in which projects can be carried out. Here we look at ways of obtaining data on visitor numbers and the profile of the visitors. In Chapter 5 we look at the impact of tourism in an urban area.

There are major gaps in our understanding of the processes that contribute to tourism, i.e. its growth, development, operation and management. There are a number of areas in which we can gain statistics related to tourism:
- tourist arrivals in different regions
- the volume of tourist trips
- the types of tourism
- the number of nights spent in different regions
- tourist expenditure.

Gathering data is difficult because tourists are a transient and mobile population. However, there are three main types of survey – pre-travel studies of tourists' intended travel habits, studies of tourists in transit, and post-travel studies.

The most widely-used statistic for studying patterns of tourism is that of tourist accommodation. The number of beds and their occupancy rate are used to determine visitor numbers. Most hotels are situated in urban areas, so it can be relatively easy to collect the data. However, this does not take into account the number of tourists who stay with family or friends, or who go camping, caravaning, or who stay in bed and breakfast accommodation.

As well as counting numbers of tourists and facilities, it is possible to examine the **scale** of tourism in an area. This is influenced by a number of factors including:
- the nature of the area and the tourist product
- the volume and scale of tourist expenditure
- the state of economic development and economy in the area
- the size and nature of the local economy
- the extent to which tourist expenditure circulates around the local economy
- the degree to which the local economy has addressed the problem of seasonality and extends the appeal to all year round.

Getting reliable figures for these is difficult.

Techniques	Forms
Determining quantity of visitors Counters	• Counters for vehicles. Turnstiles, doorways and tracks for people. (compressed air tubes, pressure pads, spring-loaded switches and infrared beams) • Observations of numbers and/or group size
Administration	• Bookings • Visitor books • Receipts and income • Number of enquiries and amount of information (publications) distributed
Impact assessment	• Noting vehicle tracks, trampling, amount of waste and resource consumption (such as wood and water)
Determining profile of visitors Observation	• Visitor flow diagrams • Type and order of visitor experience • Timing length of experience (overnight/2 hours, etc) • Recording use of facilities (individual or photographic e.g. video and audio-time-lapse or motion-/sound-triggered)
Computers Surveys/interviews Focus groups Polling	• Recording behavioural characteristics (as above) • Programmes that record visitor choices made on interactive devices • Written, oral, and behavioural • Selected small groups in lengthy discussions • Phone, post and personal
Visitor numbers and profile Extrapolation from other sources	• Numbers at neighbouring sites • Past studies • General number of enquiries and complaints (written and verbal)

Figure 1.31 Techniques for determining visitor numbers and profiles
Source: Page, S., 1995, Urban tourism, Routledge

QUESTIONS

1 For a small area close to where you live carry out a survey of the attractions and facilities that are available to visitors.

2 To what extent do tourist facilities and attractions cluster in certain locations, such as near the city centre, or in areas of natural beauty?

SUMMARY

This chapter has shown how important and how complex tourism is. It is now one of the most important industries in the world and affects all parts of the globe. We have see that there are variety of types of tourirmtourism and tourists, and that the benefits and disadvantages that they bring to areas are wide ranging. Tourism is a very dynamic industry. It is affected by a variety of factors, and there are important short-term as well as long-term fluctuations in the industry.

QUESTIONS

1 How useful are models in our understanding of the tourism process?
2 Using examples, describe and explain how the factors that influence tourism change over time
3 Evaluate the positive and negative impacts of tourism.

BIBLIOGRAPHY AND RECOMMENDED READING

House of Commons, 1995, *The environmental impact of recreation*, HMSO

Jenner, P. and Smith, C., 1992, *The Tourism Industry and Environment,* The Economist Special Report 2453

Mathieson, A. and Wall, G., 1982, *Tourism economic, physical and social impacts,* Longman.

Pearce, D., 1981, *Tourist development,* Longman

World Trade Organisation (WTO), *Annual 1993 Year Book of Tourism Statistics 45th edition,* WTO

WEB SITES

British Tourist Association – http//www.visitbritain.com

The virtual tourist – http//www.tourist.com

Chapter 2
The impact of tourism in coastal areas

Figure 2.1 *Near-deserted sandy beach on the west coast of Ireland*

In this chapter we look at the impact of tourism in coastal areas. Coasts have long been a source of recreation and leisure, and in the second half of the twentieth century coastal tourism has changed certain places beyond all recognition. The impact has been experienced both in developed and developing countries. For some countries, such as those in the Caribbean, coastal tourism is seen as the way forward in the twenty-first century. For other countries, such as those bordering the Mediterranean, the costs of tourist development since the 1960s are very great. For yet others, such as the UK, there has been a decline in the popularity of the traditional seaside resort.

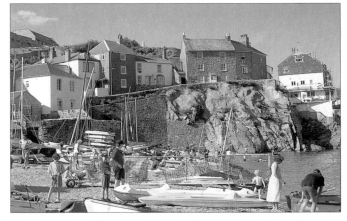

Figure 2.2 *A seaside resort on the south Devon coast that has kept its charm*

COASTAL TOURISM

Coastal tourism originated in the eighteenth and nineteenth centuries when it became fashionable to take the sea air, often on medical grounds. Important resorts included Blackpool, Brighton and Southport in the UK, whilst Venice was a favoured location in Europe.

The impact of tourism on coasts is not evenly distributed: coasts with sandy beaches in wave- and wind-dominated environments have experienced the greatest impact. By contrast, tidal coasts, such as estuaries, are far less popular. Moreover, some beaches do not have the climate to guarantee warm, sunny weather.

Figure 2.3 *Tourist pressure at Lulworth Cove, Dorset*

Ireland has a series of beautiful wide, sandy beaches but they are often deserted because tourists are not guaranteed good weather (Figure 2.1). The pressures in the more favoured resorts can be intense, since large numbers of people are confined to a relatively small area. Although some small resorts retain their charm (Figure 2.2), many developments degrade the coastal environment (Figure 2.3).

The management of coastal tourism involves a number of issues:
- providing access to the foreshore (beach) involving steps down cliffs or paths across sand dunes
- coping with pressures on coastal habitats, such as trampling and four-wheel drive
- maintaining a stable beach
- managing conflicts of interest, for example between naturists and walkers
- dealing with increased pollution, such as refuse, fires, sewage and air pollution, caused by the large influx of people
- developing new facilities to feed, accommodate and entertain tourists.

For example, sand dunes are very popular with tourists and with day trippers. But as well as their recreational function, they also have an important natural function – they are a temporary store of sediment and a natural defence from coastal flooding. When they are used for other purposes these functions are compromised. Sand dunes are fragile environments and are susceptible to visitor pressure; they are the most tourist-damaged coastal environment. Pressure often results in degradation. This takes many forms:
- a reduction of biomass
- changes in species structure
- sand erosion causing blow outs
- soil compaction and reduced oxygen availability to plants.

How the pressures of tourism have been managed in this type of environment (at Studland Beach, Dorset) are covered in depth in *Britain's changing environment* in this series.

The increasing popularity of golf is having a major impact on many coastal regions (see pages 98-9). On the one hand, golf courses restrict public access onto sand dunes giving potential for environmental management and conservation.

Figure 2.4 *Tourism life cycle for the Costa del Sol, Spain Source: Baker, S. et al, 1995, Pathways in senior geography, Nelson*

	stage 1	stage 2	stage 3	stage 4
	1960s	**1970s**	**1980s**	**1990s**
Tourists from UK to Spain	1960 = 0.4 million	1971 = 3.0 million	1984 = 6.2 million 1988 = 7.5 million	1990 = 7.0 million
State of, and changes in, tourism	Very few tourists	Rapid increase in tourism. Government encouragement.	Carrying capacity reached– tourists outstrip resources, eg. water supply and sewerage.	Decline – world recession, prices too high – cheaper up-market hotels elsewhere.
Local employment	Mainly in farming and fishing.	Construction work. Jobs in hotels, cafés, shops. Decline in farming and fishing.	Mainly in tourism – up to 70% in some areas.	Unemployment increase as tourism declines (20%). Farmers use irrigation.
Holiday accommodation	Limited accommodation, very few hotels and apartments, some holiday cottages	Large blocks built (using breeze block and concrete), more apartment blocks and villas.	More large hotels built, also apartments and time share, luxury villas.	Older hotels looking dirty and run down. Fall in house prices. Only high-class hotels allowed to be built.
Infrastructure (amenities and activities)	Limited access and few amenities. Poor roads. Limited streetlighting and electricity.	Some road improvements but congestion in towns. Bars, discos, restaurants and shops added.	E340 opened – 'the highway of death'. More congestion in towns. Marinas and gold courses built	Bars/cafés closing. Malaga bypass and new air terminal opened.
Landscape and environment	Clean, unspoilt beaches. Warm sea with relatively little pollution. Pleasant villages. Quiet. Little visual pollution.	Farmland built on. Wildlife frightened away. Beaches and seas less clean	Mountains hidden behind hotels. Litter on beaches. Polluted seas (sewerage). Crime (drugs, vandalism and mugging). Noise from traffic and tourism.	Attempts to clean up beaches and seas (EC Blue Flag beaches). New public parks and gardens opened. Nature reserves.

1	Overdevelopment	Unplanned growth of hotels and tourism facilities with little regard to visual impact or local architecture has led to visual degradation over vast areas. Land has been used for the recreational facilities such as golf courses and theme parks. Major roads and airports encroach on protected areas, such as Ria Formosa National Park in the Algarve, Portugal.
2	Visitor related development pressure	For example, agricultural development aimed at meeting tourists or catering needs around the National Park in Southern Spain at places such as Coto Donana, where wetlands are threatened by water abstraction and pesticide run off.
3	Loss of habitat and loss of biodiversity	Over 75% of the sand dune systems from Gibraltar to Sicily have been lost since 1960. This has led to the loss of breeding grounds for species such as the Loggerhead Turtle. Over five hundred Mediterranean plant species are threatened with extinction. In France alone, one hundred and forty-five species are on the verge of extinction or have already disappeared.
4	Species impact	Tourism pressure on nesting sites of the Loggerhead Turtle and Green Turtle led to a curtailing of the building of a hotel at Dalyan in Turkey in 1986. However, the very act of protecting the turtles has led to an increased influx of tourists, 5000 every summer, creating other environmental pressures such as waste dumps.
5	Lack of sewage and effluent treatment and disposal	Only 30% of municipal waste water from Mediterranean coastal towns receives any treatment before being discharged. As a result some Mediterranean beaches fail EU bathing water quality tests. For example, in 1992 7% of Spanish beaches and 13% of French beaches failed the test. The total cost of developing the necessary level of sewage treatment is over £6 billion. Spillages from pleasure boats were also a major source of pollution.
6	Unsustainable exploitation of natural resources	This includes excessive abstraction of drinking water and exploitation of fisheries resources. Over-abstraction of water for drinking, bathing, golf courses and water theme parks has led to increased forest fires.
7	Traffic congestion	On coastal roads traffic congestion, and the associated problems of noise and air pollution, are becoming an increasing problem.
8	Changes in traditional lifestyle	Where local populations are outnumbered by tourists, such as in the poorer regions of the Balearics, Turkey, Croatia and Cyprus, over-dependence on tourism threatens traditional lifestyles.

Figure 2.5 *The impact of tourism in the Mediterranean*   Source: Nagle, G., 1998, Development and underdevelopment, Nelson

On the other hand, indigenous plant species such as marram and sea couch are not wanted on golf courses because they are too long and coarse, so alien species in the form of fine, closely-cropped grasses are introduced into the environment.

In the case of salt marshes, walkers trample and destroy the vegetation on the upper parts of salt marshes; the lower parts are much less affected, partly because they are too dangerous to walk on and partly because they are repaired by frequent tidal inundation.

TOURISM AND THE MEDITERRANEAN

The adverse impact of tourism in coastal areas is highlighted in the Mediterranean region. The Mediterranean coast is the world's most important tourist location, accounting for 35% of international tourists. The nature of tourism and its impact on the local and national economy have changed dramatically since 1960 (Figures 2.4 to 2.7). The problems caused by tourism in this area are so intense because of the sheer **concentration** of tourists, accommodation, infrastructural development, traffic and waste generation. The number of tourists in the area rose from 54 million in 1970 to 157 million in 1990. Current predictions show that the numbers are set to rise to 380 million by 2025, 760 million if the world economy is strong. As an added pressure, population growth in Mediterranean areas is forecast to rise from 350 million in 1985 to 570 million by 2025.

Over half of the tourists to the Mediterranean are concentrated in coastal regions, causing increased pressure on fishing, industry, urban development and energy development as well as tourism and recreation. Figure 2.5 describes some of the adverse effects resulting from these pressures.

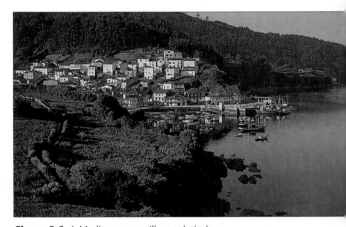

Figure 2.6 *A Mediterranean village relatively unscathed by development*

Figure 2.7 *A Mediterranean village after development*

The growth of tourism has been especially noticeable in Greece and Turkey where the numbers have increased six-fold and fourfold respectively between 1983 and 1991. The concentration of tourists has reached alarming levels in certain places. For example, the Tarragona, Costa Brava, Spain contains up to 4250 tourists per square kilometre in high summer. For the whole of the Mediterranean area, the tourist infrastructure was spread over 4400 square kilometres in 1984, of which over 90% was in Spain, France and Italy; it is estimated that this will double by the year 2025. Nearly 3 million tonnes of solid waste was generated in 1984 and it is forecast to rise to between 8.7 and 12.1 million tonnes by 2025. Similarly, waste water is predicted to rise from 0.3 billion tonnes to between 0.9 and 1.5 billion tonnes during the same period.

Global warming and tourism in the Mediterranean

According to the environmental pressure group Greenpeace, shrinking beaches, water and food shortages could all become the norm around the Mediterranean Sea as a result of global warming (Figure 2.8). More than 100 million people visit the sea's extensive, sunny coastline each year, and this number has been projected to rise to as much as 340 million by 2025. As the possible impacts of climatic change become more fully understood, it is clear that the coast is under threat.

The Greenpeace report is based on estimates for sea level and temperature rises in the next century made by the United Nation's Intergovernmental Panel on Climate Change.

Inset 2.1
The Mediterranean Blue Plan

By 1970, the Mediterranean Sea was a dumping ground for untreated sewage, industrial and chemical waste, agricultural chemicals and oil. This led to the growth of red algae, toxic to humans and marine life. 'Red tides' of algae blooms made the beaches unsafe and threatened tourism. In 1976, eighteen countries bordering the Mediterranean signed the Mediterranean Blue Plan. Their aim was threefold:

- to build more sewage treatment works
- to control industrial waste
- to reduce the use of pesticides.

However, the project is extremely expensive, costing over £1 billion to treat the sewage. The poorer countries in the south and east cannot afford the cost. There is a marked difference in attitude between the richer countries, France, Spain and Italy, which are basically the causes of most of the pollution, and the poorer countries. The rich want to clear up the beaches, whereas the poor want to create new industries and develop economically. Its continued operation is very much in doubt.

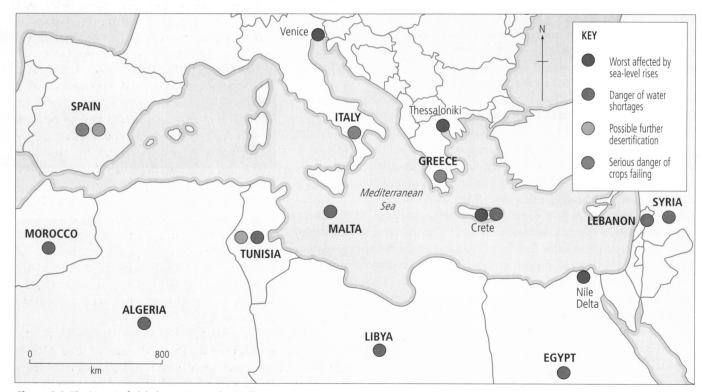

Figure 2.8 *The impact of global warming on the Mediterranean* Source: *The Independent, October 98*

Greenpeace has chosen to emphasise the worst-case scenarios for 2100. In this case, temperatures are expected to rise by up to 4°C over many inland areas. Annual rainfall is projected to fall by 10-40 per cent over much of Africa and south-eastern Spain, with smaller but potentially significant changes elsewhere. As oceans expand and glaciers melt in a warmer world, sea levels could rise by almost one metre by the end of the next century. Venice, the Nile Delta and Thessalonika in Greece could witness sea level rises effectively 50 per cent higher than that, as a result of continued subsidence. In Egypt, it is estimated that a sea level rise of only 0.5 metres would displace 16 per cent of the population, if the coastline and riverbanks of the Nile Delta were not defended against the rising sea. Beach resorts could lose much of their appeal, as the sand would be covered by the higher water level. Warmer conditions are likely to increase cases of malaria, schistosomiasis, yellow fever and dengue fever. The implications for tourism are serious, *if* the worst case scenario occurs.

Redirecting tourism in the Canary Islands

The Canary Islands lie in the Atlantic Ocean off the west coast of Africa; they are part of Spain (Figure 2.9). Over the past two decades, the Canary Islands have become a very popular destination for package holidays. The majority of the nine million people who visit the islands each year go there to enjoy the warm temperatures during the European winter. So much tourism is concentrated in these winter months

Figure 2.10 *Intense visitor pressure, Gran Canaria*

that local planners and business people are worried that the Canaries have become something of a tourism monoculture, with tourists staying very close to the beach and spending little time inland visiting the attractions and facilities outside the coastal hotels.

Investment in tourism is concentrated on the coastlines of the busiest islands – Gran Canaria, Tenerife and Lanzarote. The growth of the tourist infrastructure in Gran Canaria has been chaotic, destroying vast amounts of natural resources and rural landscapes. Motorways, hotels and apartments (Figure 2.10) scar the southern coastline of Gran Canaria, home of the spectacular and protected dunes of Maspalomas. To date there has been too much concentration on satisfying the demands for bed space. There is a need for more organised growth, as well as more quality growth. Local planners are therefore attempting to control new developments and to restrict development to one hotel room per 60 square metres, producing a lower density of development. By contrast, developments away from the existing coastal-tourist developments are less restricted.

However, by increasing the amount of land available for tourist development, and decreasing the density of development, there will be a reduction in the amount of land available to the 1.5 million local people. As the number of tourists is growing at 5% annually (less rapid than in the 1970s and 1980s) compared with a 1% growth among the local population, the pressure is on developers to provide land for the tourist industry.

The Canaries have certainly benefited from tourism: the service sector accounts for over 80% of GDP and 77% of employment. However, employment in agriculture fell from 18% in 1983 to 7% in the late 1990s, and its contribution to GDP fell from 11% to 9%.

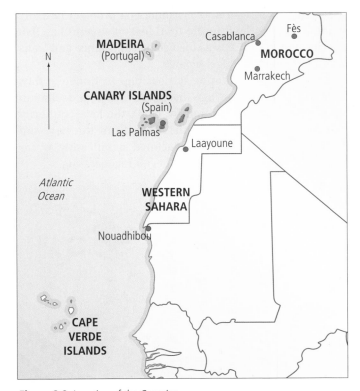

Figure 2.9 *Location of the Canaries*

QUESTIONS

1 Why is the Mediterranean so polluted?

2 To what extent are the attempts to improve the quality of the Mediterranean Sea influenced by (i) economic motives and (ii) environmental concerns? Give reasons for your answer.

3 With the use of examples, describe and explain the impact of tourism on coastal areas.

4 How will pressures on coastal areas change in the future? What impact will they have? Give reasons to support your answer.

5 Why are the implications of global warming 'serious' for tourism in Mediterranean countries?

6 How far do you agree that by using the 'worst-case scenario' Greenpeace are over-exaggerating the effects of global warming and will therefore be ignored? What would be the environmental impact of the 'best-case scenario'?

CORAL REEFS

After sand dunes, coral reefs are the most tourist-damaged coastal environment. Nearly two-thirds of the world's coral reefs are now at risk from human activity (Figure 2.11). Reefs are very attractive because of their diverse range of flora and fauna, and their warm, shallow, clear waters. Destruction takes many forms – collection of specimens, trampling, berthing of boats, oil spills, mining for building and the cement industry, and indirect causes such as sedimentation and discharge from agricultural wastes. Coastal development, destructive fishing practices that include cyanide poisoning and dynamiting, and pollution from both land and marine sources are all threatening reefs across the world.

Coral reefs are often thought of as 'the rainforests of the sea' because of the huge number of species they contain and their vulnerability to degradation. Occupying less than 0.25% of the marine environment, they nevertheless shelter more than 25 per cent of all known fish species.

Until 1998, there was little information about the state of coral reefs worldwide. It was believed that about 10% of the world's reefs were dead and 30% were likely to die by 2015. However, a 1998 survey by the World Conservation Monitoring Centre suggested that nearly 60% of the world's reefs are at risk of dying due to human impact. South-east Asia is the worst affected region, with more than 80% of the reefs in the Philippines and Indonesia at risk, followed by the Caribbean, where 65% are in danger. In the Indian Ocean, the Red Sea and the Arabian Gulf, more than half are threat-

ened. Only the Pacific is in relatively good shape – more than 60% of its reefs are thought to be 'low risk'.

In Sri Lanka, for example, rapid unplanned tourist development in the 1980s and 1990s had a severe impact on the reefs, largely though increased sewage, and increased sediment loads as a result of land clearances. In addition, about 40% of the raw material for the Sri Lankan cement industry comes from coral, while in Madagascar, coral is used for building.

The growth of coastal cities and towns generates a series of threats. These include outright destruction caused by the building of airports and harbours, dredging to keep shipping channels open and mining for construction materials. Most damaging are the indirect effects of development – sewage and agricultural pollution produce algal 'blooms' which block out the sunlight that corals need to survive. Unregulated tourism produces trampling, destruction of coral for souvenirs, sewage discharge and the overfishing associated with resorts. Overfishing is a problem in many places, and can lead to the total loss of several key fish species that in turn upsets the ecological balance and leads again to destructive algal blooms.

However, rehabilitation is possible. In Kaneohe Bay, Hawaii, increased sewage discharges led to a decline in reefs during the 1970s, but by 1980, the local authority redirected all sewage outfalls away from the bay, and by 1983 nutrient levels had declined significantly, water clarity increased, and the coral began regenerating.

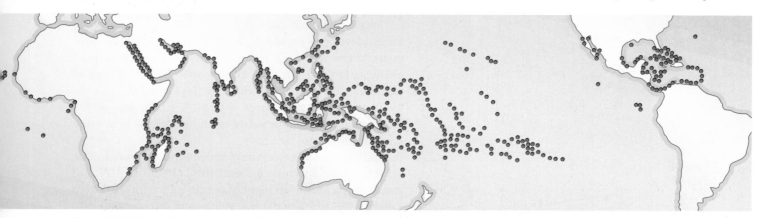

Figure 2.11 *The world's endangered coral reefs Source: World Conservation Monitoring Centre, 1998, Reefs at risk, World Conservation Monitoring Centre*

Protecting reefs makes sound economic as well as environmental sense. Good management produces booming and sustainable fish-yields and huge revenues from tourism, while leaving an economically crucial heritage for future generations. Global revenues arising from coral reefs are as high as £245 billion and over 100 countries stand to benefit from tourism-related income derived from their reefs.

Despite continued destruction in some areas, there are a number of success stories, such as the Great Barrier Reef in Australia, which has been kept healthy by careful management.

The Great Barrier Reef, Australia

The Great Barrier Reef, off Queensland, Australia, is a world-renowned tourist attraction. This coral reef extends for over 2000 kilometres and covers an area of 343 800 square kilometres (Figure 2.12). It consists of over 2900 reefs and is the world's largest living structure. It is also the most-used marine park in the world.

The Great Barrier Reef contains 1500 species of fish, 400 species of coral, and 4000 species of molluscs (Figure 2.13). It is a major feeding ground for many endangered species and is a nesting ground for many species of turtle. It was placed on the list of World Heritage Sites in 1981. World Heritage Sites are sites considered worthy of UN recognition on account of their culture, history, beauty, etc., and which need to be preserved.

Today the Reef is carefully managed (Figure 2.14). Before it was managed, the reef suffered badly from the effects of tourism, agriculture and recreational and commercial fishing. Each year 77 000 tonnes of nitrogen, 11 000 tonnes of phosphorus, and 15 million tonnes of sediment are washed into the coastal waters from Queensland. This, and waste from boat engines, and suspended sediment from farming reduces the clarity of the water, thereby killing the coral.

The Great Barrier Reef Marine Park Authority is responsible for the management and development of the reef.

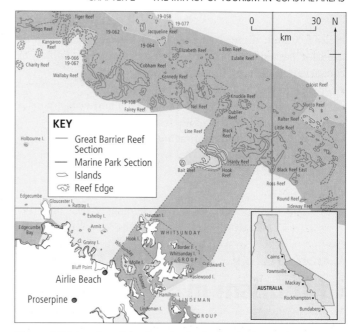

Figure 2.12 *Location of the Great Barrier Reef and visitor zoning*
Source: Baker S. et al, 1995, Pathways in geography, Nelson

It follows the Agenda 21 philosophy, namely that resources must be used and managed in such a way that they are not destroyed or devalued but are conserved for future generations. The main type of management is that of land use

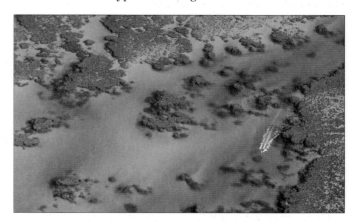

Figure 2.13 *The Great Barrier Reef is a World Heritage site due to its natural beauty*

	Bait netting and gathering	Camping	Collecting (recreational – not coral)	Collecting – (commercial)	Commercial netting (see also bait netting)	Crabbing and oyster gathering	Diving, boating, photography	Line fishing (bottom fishing, trolling etc)	Research (non-manipulative)	Research (manipulative)	Spear fishing	Tourist and education facilities and programs	Traditional hunting fishing and gathering	Trawling
General Use 'A'	Yes	Permit	Limited	Permit	Yes	Yes	Yes	Yes	Yes	Permit	Yes	Permit	Permit	Yes
General Use 'B'	Yes	Permit	Limited	Permit	Yes	Yes	Yes	Yes	Yes	Permit	Yes	Permit	Permit	No
Marine National Park 'A'	Yes	Permit	No	No	No	Limited	Yes	Limited	Permit	Permit	Yes	Permit	Permit	Yes
Marine National Park 'B'	No	Permit	No	No	No	No	Yes	No	Permit	Permit	No	Permit	No	No
Scientific Research	No	No	No	No	No	No	No	No	Permit	Permit	No	No	No	No
Preservation Zone	No	No	No	No	No	No	No	No	Permit	Permit	No	No	No	No

Figure 2.14 *Permissible activities in the different zones of the Great Barrier Reef*
Source: Baker S. et al, 1995, Pathways in geography, Nelson

zoning, which divides the reef into separate areas to be used for particular purposes, such as recreation, fishing or conservation. The main aims of zoning are to:

- ensure permanent conservation of the area
- provide protection for selected species and ecosystems
- separate conflicting activities
- preserve some areas untouched
- allow human use of the reef at the same time as protecting it.

QUESTIONS

1 Using an atlas and Figure 2.11 describe the conditions that are necessary for the growth of coral.

2 Using examples, describe the variety of pressures that affect coral reefs.

3 Why is the Great Barrier Reef a World Heritage Site?

4 Study Figure 2.14 that shows the land use zoning for part of the Great Barrier Reef. What is meant by the term 'land use zoning'?

5 How do the types of activities that are allowed in the Preservation Zone compare with the activities that are allowed in General Use 'A'?

Case study: **The environmental impact of tourism in St Lucia**

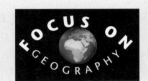

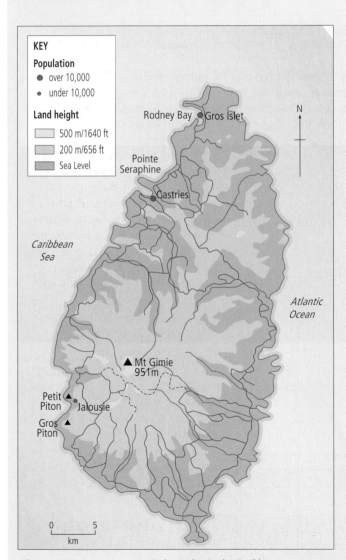

Figure 2.15 *St Lucia – a tropical paradise in the Caribbean*
Source: adapted from World Reference Atlas, 1994, Dorling Kindersley

St Lucia is a sub-tropical volcanic island in the eastern Caribbean (Figure 2.15). The natural environment is the key element in the promotion of the island as a tropical paradise which is 'Simply Beautiful'. White sandy beaches, natural harbours, coral reefs, sulphur springs, rainforest and the Piton mountain peaks are important resources for the tourism industry. Tourism is the most important earner of foreign exchange. Its role will increase with additional foreign investment, construction of large-scale hotels and increasing cruise ship activity. Visitor arrivals to St. Lucia in 1996 totalled 425 382, of which 56% were stayover tourists and the rest were cruise passengers. Most of the tourist development is low density, and is located around the coastal areas. However, St Lucia's transition to mass tourism is placing strains on the environment,

A model that has been used to describe growth and change in industry is the product life cycle (Figure 2.4). The product life cycle shows how an industry (in this case tourism) changes over time, and how its impact changes over time. Initially, there is little impact on the local economy and local environment, but as tourism takes off, the effects on both economy and environment increase dramatically. At a later stage, tourist developments may have ruined the area so much, that tourism begins to decline. In this study of St Lucia, the holiday 'product life cycle' includes the development of the transport infrastructure, infrastructure operations, transport, use and consumption patterns and the disposal of waste.

The construction of the built environment has had the greatest impact on the environment (Figure 2.16). Most hotels have been built on the beach front, and clearing the land has led to slope instability and erosion and the subsequent sedimentation of the shallow offshore environment.

Figure 2.16
A well-designed and managed forest trail in St Lucia

Figure 2.17 The Rodney Heights Development, Rodney Bay, Gros Islet

These developments have had a negative impact on the nesting grounds of endangered turtles. Over-exploitation of sand for building and construction, and in some places for artificial beaches elsewhere, has led to significant increases in beach erosion and environmental degradation. Although many hotels are artificially replenishing the beaches, the introduced sand is rapidly eroded and causing problems for offshore coral reefs that require clear water.

At Gros Islet, wetland habitats were destroyed in 1969 when the land was reclaimed to be used for building and to create an artificial lagoon to expand the Rodney Bay resort (Figure 2.16). The wetlands had been a breeding ground for sand flies, which had become a nuisance in the resort area and reclaiming the land was expected to solve the problem. The results of the reclamation were unforeseen. The ebb and flood tide patterns were modified, creating stronger currents, which increased erosion on nearby beaches. In addition, local fisheries declined as the offshore waters became murkier, and the problem of the sand flies remained, because there were still sufficient wetlands for the flies to breed. The construction of the transport infrastructure has caused destruction

of land, disruption of ecosystems and water pollution, although not all the transport infrastructure is provided solely for tourists. The construction of two runways has used a large amount of the flat land in St. Lucia, while the construction of roads has caused serious runoff problems that have increased sediment deposition on near-shore coral reefs. The building of the Pointe Seraphine cruise facility altered wave and swell patterns significantly in the harbour.

In terms of transport operations, the most significant impacts are emissions from combustion and increased congestion in the Castries area, in part due to tourism.

Tourists are great consumers of water and energy. Over-abstraction of water can lead to a decline in the amount of water available as well as a decline in its quality. As freshwater supplies become reduced, saline water intrudes into the aquifers thereby contaminating supplies. The use of detergents by hotels has led to water pollution, especially where there is little treatment of waste water.

Tourists use and consume goods and services while resident in St Lucia. The provision of food and beverages,

excursions and activities has an impact on the environment, although most of this impact does not occur on the island, since most of these goods are imported. However, a rising demand for fish is increasing pressure on fish stocks around St Lucia. The environmental impact of excursions depends on the nature and organisation of the activity. For example, well managed nature excursions in the rainforest (Figure 2.17) do not appear to disturb wildlife, but there is concern about unregulated tour operators on private lands. Scuba diving is increasing and efforts have been made to minimise the impact of divers on coral reefs. The development of marine leisure craft facilities has led to the loss of mangrove swamps. Boating activities also damage the marine environment: dropping anchors on the coral is a problem; there are no facilities at marinas for the collection of liquid and solid waste from recreational craft; the lack of holding tanks leads to the discharge of sewage by yachts straight into the sea, which contributes to near-shore marine pollution.

Solid and liquid waste disposal are amongst the greatest environmental challenges facing St Lucia; the tourism industry generates more solid waste per capita than any other sector. Cruise ships generate the highest amount of waste both in total and per capita, but in general this is not disposed of in St. Lucia as port facilities are very limited. The amount of solid waste generated per stayover tourist is estimated to be double that of per capita residential waste, and the total amount of waste increases with the expansion of hotel accommodation.

Solid waste management by the public sector has been inadequate and sanitary landfilling has not been widely practised. The discharge of poorly treated waste water into coastal waters poses environmental and health risks; nutrient loading has led to the loss of coral productivity (Figure 2.18). There are no facilities for special wastes and no recycling infrastructure. This reduces the attractiveness of the tourist experience and raises issues of health standards, the freshwater and marine environment, and the aesthetics of the island.

However, this issue of waste disposal is now being addressed by the government through a national environmental levy on both stayover and cruise passengers, designed to recover the costs of a comprehensive national solid waste plan. This will allow the government to establish much higher standards for solid waste management.

Figure 2.19 shows the environmental impact of tourism in St Lucia. The greatest environmental impacts arise from:
- land consumption and habitat loss and disturbance to ecosystems for site and infrastructure development
- destruction of coral reef through increased sedimentation from land clearing for construction of hotels and roads and artificial beach maintenance

Figure 2.18 Sedimentation causes a decline in the quality of coral

Figure 2.19 Comparison and ranking of environmental impacts of tourism Source: UK CEED, 1998, An assessment of the environmental impact of tourism in St Lucia

Source of impact	Water pollution	Air pollution	Noise impacts	Aesthetic impacts	Habitat loss (land)	Natural resource exploitation	Disruption of natural cycles
Tourist infrastructure	high (sedimentation)	low	low	moderate	high	moderate (sand)	high (coastal processes)
Infrastructure operations	moderate	moderate (detergents)	low (energy production)	–	low	moderate (water)	moderate (water abstraction)
Transport	high (sedimentation)	moderate	moderate	moderate	moderate (airports)	low (imports)	moderate (runoff, wave patterns)
Use and consumption	moderate (boating activities)	–	low (activities, excursions)	low	moderate (golf, marinas)	low (souvenirs)	–
Waste	high (sewage, leaching)	moderate (incineration)	– (dumping of solid waste)	moderate (landfill)	moderate	–	low

Specific to an all-inclusive product
All guest services in pre-paid package price
Non-individual pricing of tourism activity
Most guest services on site
Strict regulation to control entry
Advanced inventory control
'Stand alone' potential i.e. all guest services are provided within a self-contained site

Figure 2.20 *Characteristics of all-inclusive resorts*
Source: UK CEED, 1998, An assessment of the environmental impact of tourism in St Lucia, Table 2

- water pollution as a consequence of hotel waste water plants not working or operating below optimal capacity, with evidence that certain areas of the coastline are periodically contaminated by sewage
- inadequate solid waste management and disposal systems, which have led to the leaching of pollutants from landfill sites
- water pollution and anchor damage to reefs from boating activities.

The impact of the all-inclusive resorts

The all-inclusive resort, prevalent in St Lucia, is becoming increasingly popular with holiday-makers. Figure 2.20 lists the main characteristics of this type of resort.

The marketing of all-inclusive holiday products emphasises the range of high quality facilities, security at the resort and absence of limits to consumption, as once a package is purchased, many guest services are complimentary. However, the all-inclusive resort package is a controversial issue, having environmental, economic and social impacts.

The environmental impacts of the all-inclusive resorts

All-inclusive resorts are generally associated with significant negative environmental impacts, for example, the habitat loss following the construction of the 'Jalousie' resort between the Piton peaks. 'All-inclusives' tend to have greater environmental impacts than most conventional hotels because they tend to be large-scale resorts, which occupy land on the beach front.

In terms of infrastructure development, all-inclusive resorts have a distinctive impact because of their 'stand-alone' capacity. This allows them to be located in remote areas, which are often of high ecological value. The development of all-inclusives may restrict the development of other forms of tourism, such as nature heritage tourism, since all-inclusive visitors are not generally consumers of these activities. Moreover, the marketing of all-inclusives promotes a holiday product that has limited reference to the island's natural and socio-cultural environment.

All-inclusive resorts are efficient in that they achieve economies of scale and operate effective management systems. This enables several all-inclusives in St Lucia to implement energy and water conservation measures, innovative waste water treatment systems, recycling programmes and to offer guest education initiatives. Another distinctive impact of all-inclusive resorts is the reduced demand for transport by guests. The provision of food and beverages, activities and excursions as part of the holiday package is also a particular feature of all-inclusives.

Overall, the environmental impacts of the all-inclusive holiday are similar to, but of a higher magnitude than, package holidays. In most instances this is because all-inclusives tend to be larger beach resorts belonging to international chains.

Economic impact of the all-inclusive resorts

Evidence suggests that there is limited involvement of the ancillary sector (e.g. restaurant owners, taxi drivers and street vendors) in all-inclusive operations and less visitor expenditure outside the hotel complex. All-inclusives exhibit superior economic performance to conventional hotels due to higher year-round occupancy and profitability, but most of the profit goes to the international chain and there is limited tourist spending in the local economy.

Socio-cultural impacts

For many local residents, the negative effects of all-inclusive developments far outweigh the positive (such as employment and supplying food). In particular, local people are often denied physical access to resorts because they are part of an all-inclusive resort.

Reconciling tourism with local needs

For tourism in St Lucia to be sustainable, action is needed to reduce its negative impacts. For example, tour operators need to:

- monitor the capacity of the destination's infrastructure, such as waste management systems, to accommodate additional tourists and should deal with any adverse consequences of expansion
- develop 'benchmark' targets for hotel consumption of water and power and production of waste per guest-night
- emphasise the importance of comprehensive environmental management programmes for hotels
- work co-operatively with the public and private sector to raise standards in the tourism product
- seek to increase the diversity of St Lucia's tourism assets, for example, focus on cultural events, natural attractions and other forms of alternative tourism
- include environmental criteria on the list of specifications when product managers visit and select hotels for the holiday product.

Similarly, the St Lucia government should:

- develop comprehensive physical planning and development control legislation which provides for Environmental Impact Assessments of all major hotel projects (programmes which determine the environmental effects of new developments, e.g. beach erosion, loss of habitat, destruction of coral reefs, building of new access roads, etc.)
- adopt zoning plans

- implement the Coastal Zone Management Plan (a plan to manage the coastline and new coastal developments)
- enforce the sand moratorium (to prevent sand from being removed from beaches)
- introduce the Systems Plan for Parks and Protected Areas (a plan to protect the rain forest and other natural ecosystems), developed under the auspices of the St Lucia National Trust
- promote alternative types of

tourism, such as nature heritage tourism which contribute to conservation and the social and economic advancement of local communities
- develop national policies with regard to waste water management, solid waste management, water conservation, and energy conservation
- review large-scale tourism development projects because of their potential to alter the country's low-density tourism style and put

Figure 2.21 *Environmental Destination Factsheet – St Lucia Source: Adapted from UK CEED, 1998, An assessment of the environmental impact of tourism in St Lucia*

Geography
St Lucia is a tropical mountainous island located in the Windward islands of the Eastern Caribbean, with an area of 610 sq. km. The capital is Castries.

History
St Lucia was discovered by Europeans in the 16th century when it was occupied by Caribs who resisted attempts to colonise the island. The settlers developed plantations using slave labour. For two centuries, the island was fought over by the French and English until it became a British colony in 1814. St Lucia gained independence in 1979.

Population and culture
The population of St Lucia is about 145 000, of whom 90% are of African descent and Roman Catholic. There is a strong and distinctive Anglo-French Creole culture. English is the official language but Creole ('Kweyol') is the national language. Whilst on holiday try to learn a few words of Creole and take time to listen to the local people. Respect the privacy and dignity of others and inquire before photographing residents.

Nature
Just under one tenth of the island is covered with rainforest. There are several native species of birds and reptiles. The rare, brightly-coloured St Lucia parrot is the national bird and can be seen in Forest Reserves. Endangered turtles nest on the island, including the Leatherback, which is the largest turtle in the world.

Marine environment
St Lucia is surrounded by coral reefs, which are rich in marine life, particularly on the west coast. This can be enjoyed by snorkelling and scuba diving. Be careful not to stand on the coral as it is a fragile living organism. Also do not remove any living or non living organisms or material from the beach or the sea.

Land environment
Remember to take appropriate footwear to explore the rainforest trails and other nature reserves. Whilst enjoying these areas, help to minimise wildlife disturbance by keeping to paths and not making undue noise. Take litter home – leave only footprints and take only photographs.

Souvenirs
The buying and selling of coral is illegal in St Lucia. The purchase of conch shells is limited to one per tourist. Try to buy local crafts and other produce to support the local economy.

Water
Hotels are large consumers of water in St Lucia. On average, a tourist consumes about 75 litres of water per day. Try to conserve water. If the hotel provides the option, consider not having your towel laundered each day. This will reduce the use of detergents as well as water.

Energy
Hotels are also large consumers of energy in St Lucia. Typically a tourist consumes 26 kW of electricity per day. The island depends on imported petroleum to provide electricity. Combustion of fossil fuels produces gaseous emissions, which cause air pollution and climate change. Try to conserve energy by remembering to switch off lights, fans and especially air conditioning when you leave your room.

Transport
Try to see the island on organised tours and use local public transport (minibuses) to visit the capital. This will reduce the use of energy and other environmental impacts.

Waste
A tourist in a hotel generates double the amount of waste of a resident in St Lucia and the small island has very limited space suitable for the disposal of rubbish. Before you visit St Lucia, where possible remove all wrapping from packaged goods. There are no recycling facilities in St Lucia but some bottles are returnable so try to use these. Do not throw anything away that you can take home to re-use or recycle.

Awareness
While in St Lucia, if you see or become aware of actions or activities which damage the environment, notify your tour operator. Tell the local people how much you appreciate their environment and wildlife.

Hotels
Ask your hotel manager and staff questions about the environmental policy of your hotel to demonstrate that you take an interest in the protection of the environment. This will encourage them to take appropriate action. Comply with any environmental policies operated by the establishment.

Excursions
Ask your rep about excursions organised by conservation bodies such as the National Trust, the Naturalist Society and the Forestry Department. By participating in these nature heritage activities you will learn more about St Lucia and support organisations working to preserve the environment.

		J	F	M	A	M	J	J	A	S	O	N	D	Total
Plymouth	(°C)	7	8	9	10	13	15	17	15	14	12	10	8	
	(mm)	110	75	70	53	60	55	70	72	75	96	105	110	951
St. Lucia	(°C)	21	22	24	26	31	32	31	26	26	25	24	22	
	(mm)	128	98	82	105	158	216	237	261	246	231	228	200	2290

Figure 2.22 Climatic data for Plymouth (UK) and St Lucia

excessive demands on the available infrastructure. These reviews will study the potential impact of new developments and produce new guidelines for further developments.

There are many examples of environmental codes of conduct for tourists. A 'Destination Factsheet' (Figure 2.21) can inform tourists about environmental and socio-economic issues relevant to their holiday location.

Like many other emerging destinations, St Lucia's transition towards mass market tourism has been associated with increasing environmental stress. Issues that require attention include conservation of coastal habitats, especially beaches and reefs, improvements to sea water quality and the management of waste. The trend towards greater environmental stress brings into question the long-term viability and sustainability of this vital economic sector, based as it is on the quality of the natural environment and the amiability of the local people. UK CEED's research also suggests that there is an opportunity for the all-inclusive sector to be the driving force for the introduction of environmental manage ment in the local tourism industry. As they are the fastest-growing sector of St Lucia's tourism, they could cause the greatest damage in the decades ahead.

Therefore, it is imperative that the government's guidelines on environmental management are adhered to, enforced and inspected.

QUESTIONS

1 Figure 2.22 provides climatic data for Plymouth, in the UK, and for St. Lucia. Use the data to plot climatic graphs for each of the two locations. What are the advantages and attractions of St Lucia's climate compared with that of Plymouth?

2 What are the other attractions of St. Lucia as a holiday destination?

3 Describe and explain the environmental impact of tourism in St. Lucia.

4 With reference to specific examples, explain how tourism in St. Lucia can become more sustainable.

CRUISING HOLIDAYS

Cruising is one of the most rapidly expanding sectors of the tourism industry. Cruising developed as a luxury product and some companies, such as Cunard, still specialise in that sector. However, most companies now offer cruise holidays aimed at the mass market as an alternative to traditional land-based holidays. The typical passenger begins the cruise by flying to a destination such as the Caribbean or the Far East and then joining a cruise ship for between one and two weeks (Figure 2.23).

Cruising is no longer just the preserve of the elderly rich, although they still make up a the majority of those who take a cruising holiday. Cruising is in a transitional stage, with many companies now targeting the younger, more energetic population. A look at the age structure of the passengers on some of the newer cruise ships reveals interesting results: on Carnival Cruise Lines the average age of passengers is 40 years, and families with young children account for 20% of the market. This change in image has

Figure 2.23 Cruise ship at dock in Castries harbour, St Lucia

led to a rapid increase in the number of cruise passengers and to a building boom for cruise ships in the late 1990s. In 1997, 4.86 million Americans took a cruise holiday, an increase of almost 9% on the previous year. North American passengers account for about three-quarters of cruise passengers.

Despite the widening of the cruise market, it still attracts most of its customers from among the wealthy; cruise passengers are typically people with savings rather than people paying off a mortgage. This means that cruise operators are better able to weather a recession in the tourist industry than other sectors of the industry, such as package holiday operators.

Europe is the second largest source of cruise passengers, with about one million people taking a cruise each year. Growth is rapid in Britain – the British cruise market increased by 50% between 1996 and 1998 to over 600 000. By comparison, long-haul holiday sales amount to between 80 000 and 100 000 people each year, thus cruises are a very important part of the luxury holiday market. Average spending per person in 1995 was £1255, giving a total of over £440 million

The operators for UK-based cruises are led by P&O and Cunard. However, most British people take their cruises in the Caribbean or the Mediterranean with fly-cruises.

Investments made by cruise companies in new and refurbished ships and in new itineraries will mean continued growth for many years to come. The growing popularity of cruising has attracted 'new' companies such as Disney, Atriums, Thomson Holidays and Saga Holidays. These companies have helped to popularise the image of cruising by providing a more relaxed, informal, family-orientated and more affordable type of cruising. By contrast, the established companies have expanded the size of their fleets with ever-larger vessels. The Grand Princess, owned by Princess Cruises and launched in 1998, was at the time the largest cruise ship, weighing 109 000 tonnes.

At the end of 1998, despite the slow-down in global tourism, P&O and its American subsidiary, Princess Cruises, had placed orders for six new cruise ships, an investment of over £1 billion. This will increase the company's capacity by 12% per annum between 1999 and 2003. The fears that large ships would swamp the market have largely been unfounded. The present concern for most companies is that they are not building enough large ships to meet demand. Studies of the North American cruise sector suggest the potential size of the market is between 35 million and 50 million passengers annually.

The larger vessels now being built are impressive in size. The Princess Grand has 1296 rooms accommodating 3300 passengers and a crew of 1100. The trend towards ever-larger ships is driven by the economies of scale (Inset 2.2) which make large ships increasingly cost-effective in cater-

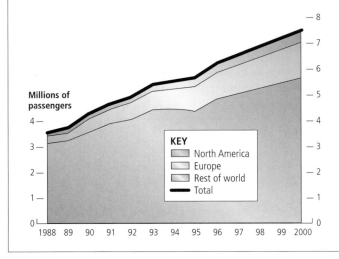

Figure 2.24 *Trends in the cruise sector, by origin of visitor*
Source: G.P. Wild (International) Projections

ing for the demands of a rapidly growing industry. The launch in 1999 of the 250 000 tonne World City cruise ship, owned by Seattle-based Westin Hotels, brought the scale of cruising to new heights. Over twice the size of its nearest rival, it can carry over 8600 passengers and crew. Three-quarters of the passengers rooms are in eight storey hotel towers. The cruise liner seems to resemble a floating hotel or floating new town. In order to achieve a high occupancy, the owners' have targeted the conference market as well as incentive travel (discount travel to loyal customers), the resort market, cruising between such resorts as Venice and Istanbul, or between Caribbean resorts, and the traditional cruise market.

However, there are limits to the size of ships that can be built. For example, the largest cruise liners cannot pass through the Panama Canal, and the number of destinations which can provide shore facilities to the very largest ships is relatively limited. Nevertheless, there are signs that a new type of cruise ship could be developed. The Cruise Bowl would comprise a 'mother' ship of 240 000 tonnes with two detachable satellites of 130 000 tonnes each. The mother ship would comprise a 12 000 seat arena to stage concerts and sporting events, while the satellites would provide cabins, shops and poolside areas.

Inset 2.2
Economies of scale

Economies of scale occur in large-scale organisations and developments, making average costs lower than in small-scale organisations, thereby making large-scale operations more efficient. There are internal and external economies of scale. Internal ones include specialisation, lower equipment costs, bulk buying and more competitive loans. External economies include positive multiplier effects.

It is likely that the cruise market will suffer casualties over the next decade. As we have seen with the product life cycle model, a period of rapid growth is often followed by stagnation or even decline (as shown in Chapter 1, and Figure 2.4). At that point, some producers diversify and reinvent their product. Change, flexibility and adaptability are the key to success. As cruising becomes more popular there will be increased competition and heavy discounting, forcing cruise companies to ensure effective marketing, cost control, improved efficiency, and maximisation of marginal revenues

The impact of cruising in the eastern Caribbean

Tourism has been referred to as the 'last resort' for the small island economies in the eastern Caribbean, such as Trinidad and Tobago, Barbados, Grenada, Antigua and Dominica. Many of the islands face a familiar dilemma: how to conserve the quality of their fragile island environments, which is the basis of the tourism product, whilst maximising the income from tourism. Cruise ship tourism is an increasingly significant part of the Caribbean tourism industry. For example, between 1986 and 1996, the volume of passengers visiting the Caribbean increased from 5 million to 10.6 million, with the eastern Caribbean attracting 41% of these visits.

The growing volume of cruise ships in the Caribbean presents serious environmental problems for the islands, especially with regard to the disposal of waste. Ineffective liquid and solid waste management and coastal marine resource degradation are a major concern. These issues threaten public health, the environmental quality of the islands and therefore the future of the islands' principal economic activity, tourism. Although there are clearly negative socio-economic and environmental impacts of cruise ship tourism (such as economic dependency on tourism and solid waste management), the governments of these tourism-dependent islands have been investing heavily in cruise ship port facilities. The governments are keen to encourage the tourists, who spend money on souvenirs and meals – but the amount of money these activities bring in is limited.

To tackle the problems of ship-generated and shore-based waste, the World Bank produced a Solid Waste Management Plan for the Organisation of Eastern Caribbean States (OECS). In order for the island governments to obtain loans to implement comprehensive national waste plans, an environmental levy was introduced on tourists to recover the costs of the management plans. The levy of 90p is charged on each disembarking cruise passenger and on all land-based tourists – with the support of hoteliers. Cruise companies strongly resisted the imposition of the levy; Carnival Cruise Lines threatened to boycott Grenada if the tax was introduced. In response to this, the eastern Caribbean governments united and all agreed to uniformly impose the environmental tax.

THE DECLINE OF SEASIDE RESORTS IN BRITAIN

The traditional seaside resorts of Britain, such as Scarborough, Skegness and Blackpool (Figure 2.25) have either declined in recent decades or undergone a transformation. They developed in the nineteenth century when the railways opened up the coastal areas and it became fashionable to take trips to the seaside. Moreover, falling rail prices and an increase in the amount of paid holiday leave (see page 96, Figure 6.13) allowed large numbers of working class people to visit the seaside. These were partly for relaxation but also for the supposed health benefit that sea air brought.

However, since the 1950s, traditional seaside resorts have been in decline. There are a number of reasons:
● the growth of mass tourism in the Mediterranean at places such as the Costa del Sol and their attractions –

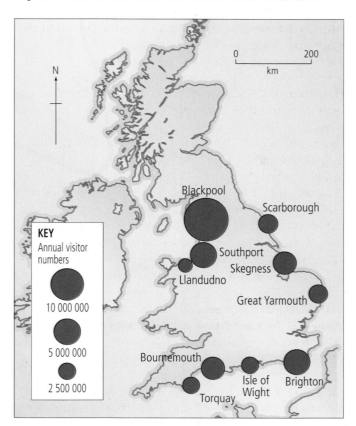

Figure 2.25 *Major seaside resorts in the UK*
Source: Carr, M., 1997, New patterns, Nelson

QUESTIONS

1 Account for the increasing popularity of cruise holidays.

2 What are the main impacts of cruising on the environment? Use specific examples to support your answer.

3 Why are cruise tourists more able to weather recession than most other tourists?

such as a more reliable climate, a more exotic location and new facilities
- rising standards of living and increased aspirations
- the decline of the 'works holidays' (the closure of factories for a couple of weeks in the summer and the mass movement of the workers to the resorts on their holidays)
- the lack of tourist revenue to reinvest in modern services and facilities
- the growth of other forms of tourism such as country parks and theme parks (see Chapter 7).

Attempts have been made to revive seaside resorts and some of these have been very successful. Bournemouth, for example, is a thriving conference centre, a regional shopping centre, and a number of firms have relocated there from London. Brighton, too, has been a notable success, again concentrating on conferences and the up-market end of the tourist trade. However, those outside the south-east, such as Porthcawl in South Wales, and further away from centres of population growth, such as Margate in the South East, have found it difficult to adapt. In addition, in areas of high unemployment, such as parts of north Kent and parts of south Wales, degeneration of the town may repel visitors. Buildings become degraded, and unemployed young people gather around amusement arcades. A period of tourist decline may set in.

EXAMINATION WORK

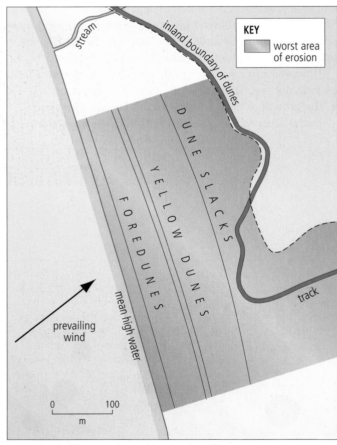

KEY

[ ] worst area of erosion

Figure 2.26 *The Hillend Burrows sand dunes, Gower Peninsula, South Wales*
Source: AQA, Summer 1990

In this section we look at a typical synoptic Geography paper. It includes an Ordnance Survey map, visual material, opposing viewpoints, and requires a decision to be made – and justified. This is a small-scale exercise similar to the large-scale exercises that governments, developers and planners must make before they decide whether to allow a development to take place.

QUESTIONS

1 Using all the resources provided, select the combination (not more than five) of management solutions that would best protect the natural environment of the sand dunes and still allow some access to the area.

2 Make a copy of Figure 2.26 and show clearly where you would locate each of your chosen solutions.

3 Justify your choice of methods to protect the sand dunes.

Marram grass

Figure 2.27 *Details of the main users of the sand dunes at Hillend Burrows, Gower Peninsula, South Wales*
Source: AQA, Summer 1990

Picnickers and sunbathers	Windsurfers and surfers	Anglers
I usually park as close to the beach as I can and take my family straight down to the beach for a picnic. The route we follow is carving a line through the dunes and seems to be wearing away the vegetation. Last winter the wind blew away the sand along the usual path leaving a big gap in the dunes. After our picnic, we usually look for a quiet place in the dunes where we can sunbathe and the children can roll down through the dunes and play games. When they roll down they thoroughly enjoy themselves and sometimes get buried in all the sand and vegetation they loosen. Last time a National Trust Warden told them off for all the damage they caused.	We come down here on a day when the wind comes from the south-west. We cut straight through the dunes from the car park towing the surf boards on trolleys. This is now easier as we used to have to climb up over the dune and drop down to the sea. Now the winter storms have formed a blow out where a lot of the sand has been blown away leaving a more level route. Stupidly some fence posts and signs are sometimes used to make a fire after finishing surfing. The sport of surfing is now so popular that a local club has been formed in Llangennith and we hold club meets here at weekends when as many as twenty members may turn out.	A big surf is a good time for fishing. When the surf is strong we get large bass. Often people will travel from Swansea, as well as the Gower Peninsula, to fish here. Rarely are there more than 35 anglers here at any one time. A few years ago you could not see the sea from the car park. Walking over the crest of the yellow dune you would feel the full force of the sand on reaching the crest. It scratched your face and bit like sandpaper. Since the blowout was formed this winter you are blasted by the sand before you even leave the car park.

Brushwood fencing

Information boards

Duckboard walkway

Figure 2.28 *The views of involved parties about the management of Hillend Burrows*
Source: AQA, Summer 1990

Farmer / Camper / Residents	Surfer / Angler / Tourist	Naturalist
Farmer If the dunes are not managed and rebuilt, the sea will break through and flood my low-lying farmland. Already the crops suffer from the wind. **Camper** I don't want any restrictions placed on my access to the dunes. I like finding a quite place to sunbathe, and I don't want to have to climb fences to find privacy. It is difficult getting to the beach as I keep sinking into the sand. A walkway made out of wooden slats would help. **Residents** For many years the dunes have been a peaceful place for a walk. In recent years I have seen more people visiting the area, particularly since the camping and caravanning site was opened. Now the dunes are heavily eroded and once the vegetation is worn down, the wind can blow the sand away.	**Surfer** The only way I use the dunes is when my friends hold a party in the dunes, some weekends. All I want to do is get straight from the car park to the beach. If they fence off the area I will not be able to get to the sea. **Angler** I want to get straight down to the sea. A better path will make it easier to carry my fishing tackle. If they fence off the area they should leave access to the beach. **Tourist** I visit the dunes with my family once a year on holiday. We can have a sheltered picnic in the dunes and the children can have fun playing in the dunes. I haven't noticed the dunes getting eroded, apart from the flat route to the beach. Somebody told me the winter storms had blown the sand away. I thought that the council had improved access to the beach.	**Naturalist** It used to be possible to see the rare orchids and other plants all over the dunes. Now it is only possible to see these in parts well away from the car park. I have seen the marram grass being worn down along the access routes, and then the sand blowing onto the farmland. The eroded area is getting bigger all the time. I think that some areas that are not too badly eroded should be fenced off to allow natural regeneration. Some of the least affected areas should be fenced off to make them nature reserves. The worst affected areas should be managed by encouraging the sand to be trapped. When this has happened, marram grass could be planted and the area re-opened when the environment is once again stable; fenced paths could then be created from the car park to the beach.

Fencing off

Raised walkways

QUESTIONS

1 Figure 2.27 shows the views expressed by the main parties affected by any management of the sand dunes at Hillend. Study Figure 2.27 and make two lists, one showing those parties who favour **some** action to protect the sand dunes and one listing those parties who wish to see **no** change.

Identify one party from each list that you think has strong views about dune management. For each party describe their view and explain why this is likely to be held. For each type of user, describe and explain the harmful impact they may have on the sand dune environment.

2 Figure 2.28 shows management solutions that could be adopted to protect the sand dunes. Using a table, state one advantage and one disadvantage of each of the possible solutions.

SUMMARY

As we have seen, tourism has great potential in developing countries. This is examined in more depth in Developing countries (Chapter 8). However, unplanned, unchecked tourism has the potential to do great damage including allowing beach erosion, sewage pollution and destruction of natural habitats. This conflict, between economic returns and environmental management and conservation, is likely to increase in the near future. For the Caribbean countries that are trying to diversify their agricultural base, the need to conserve their resources is vital.

QUESTIONS

1 How and why has coastal tourism changed since the 1950s?
2 To what extent does the tourism life cycle (Figure 2.4) account for changes in seaside resorts in (i) Britain and (ii) the Mediterranean?
3 What are the economic implications for British coastal resorts of the changing nature of tourism?

WEB SITES

UK CEED -
   http//www.ukceed.org
WORLD TOURISM ORGANISATION -
   http://www.world-tourism.org

BIBLIOGRAPHY AND RECOMMENDED READING

Dixey, L., 1998, *Environmental tax on cruise tourists in the Eastern Caribbean,* UK CEED Bulletin, 54
French, P., 1997, *Coastal and estuarine management,* Routledge
UK CEED, 1998, *An assessment of the environmental impact of tourism in St Lucia,* UK CEED
Pearce, D., 1981, *Tourist development,* Longman
World Conservation Monitoring Centre, 1998, *Reefs at Risk: A Map-Based Indicator of Potential Threats to the World's Coral Reefs,* World Resources Institute and the International Center for Living Marine Aquatic Resources

Chapter 3
Mountains, high ground and rugged relief

Figure 3.1 The English Lake District

Figure 3.2 Visitors to Hound Tor, Dartmoor

Mountains (over 1000 m) and highlands (over 300 m) account for 30% of the earth's land area but are difficult environments to exploit. A combination of steep slopes, thin soils, harsh climates, unstable environments and low agricultural potential have traditionally kept population densities low. However, in certain places, such as the Alps, mountains and highlands are being evaluated as environments with considerable potential for tourism. The same is true for gorges and areas of rugged beauty such as the Lake District (Figure 3.1), Cheddar Gorge (Figure 3.26 on page 55) and Dartmoor (Figure 3.2). In this chapter we examine the potential for expanding mountain tourism, and at the same time look at some of the problems that tourism has brought and which continue to be contentious issues.

Here we concentrate on examples largely from Britain and Europe. Other chapters, such as Chapter 8, 'Developing countries', look at the Himalayas, whilst Chapter 6, 'Sport', examines the impact of the Winter Olympics in Nagano, Japan. This chapter examines mountains that are accessible to large numbers of people and consequently are placed under severe environmental stress. By contrast, mountains in remote parts of Russia and China are under less stress from tourism.

MOUNTAIN ENVIRONMENTS

One of the main problems in trying to develop mountain environments is the steep slopes that make them inaccessible and relatively isolated. In addition, gravity influences mass movements, so mountain areas are subject to a number of natural hazards such as avalanches, rock falls, landslides and slumping. These hazards are increasing. As we saw in *Hazards* in this series, human exploitation of mountainous areas, in particular the removal of its forest cover, has resulted in an increase in the amount of overland runoff, flooding and landslides.

Mountain environments are complex and consist of a number of micro-environments such as high altitude glacial and periglacial environments, free faces and debris slopes, degraded middle slopes and ancient valley floors, active valley slopes, and valley floors (Figure 3.3). Each of these zones differs in terms of climate, natural hazard, agriculture and tourist potential.

In addition, tourist developments in some mountainous areas are discouraging potential investors in other industries. For example, heavy tourist traffic is one of the reasons given by senior executives in some companies for being reluctant to invest in the Lake District in Cumbria. Other negative aspects include its remoteness from markets and suppliers, and poor road and rail communications. In addition, the siting of the Sellafield nuclear waste reprocessing complex in West Cumbria is a disadvantage.

Tourism in the Alps

In many parts of the Alps there are few alternatives to tourism as a source of employment. In the Swiss Alps, for example, 40% of employment (out of a total of just 500 000 inhabitants) is provided by tourism; this is likely to increase as the only other alternative, agriculture, declines due to rising costs and falling prices for produce. Over 75% of accommodation is outside the hotel sector. This includes bed and breakfast accommodation, holiday apartments, holiday houses and campsites.

Tourism in the Alps grew rapidly during the 1960s and 1970s as the demand for winter sports increased (Figure 3.4). Development of the transport infrastructure made the area more accessible and less remote. This growth has had both positive and negative consequences. Positive effects include population growth, a youthful age-structure and increased employment and earnings. Many of the new jobs created are not in tourism but in linked industries, such as construction. The 60s and 70s were a boom time for builders with hotels and holiday homes being built to satisfy tourist demand. On the other hand there have been negative effects (see also Inset 3.1). The demand for land has pushed up land prices and many local people have been priced out of the housing market or have sold land to speculative developers

KEY

1. **High altitude glacial and periglacial**
   glacial/periglacial conditions, glacial erosion, mechanical weathering and solifluction. Landforms include cirques, angular ridges, peaks, U shaped valleys.

2. **Free rock face and associated debris slopes**
   steep rock slopes and cliffs with intense weathering and active mass movement. Avalanches and rocks slides may be frequent. Scree slopes weather to provide talluvium.

3. **Degraded middle slopes and ancient valley floors**
   gentler slopes, deeper soils, river terrace sediments and fan deposits. Extensive soil creep and soil wash.

4. **Active valley slopes**
   high rates of chemical and mechanical weathering and mass movement. Debris slides, rock slides and mud slides.

5. **Valley floors**
   valley flows of alluvium deposited by main rivers or tributaries.

Figure 3.3 *Composite diagram of a mountain ecosystem to show micro-environments*
Source: Geo Factsheet, April 1997

(Figure 3.6). Environmentalists claim that the multimillion-pound ski industry is destroying the Alps.

Other problems are more regional in scale. In some areas, there appears to be an excess concentration of facilities and the proposed government decentralisation of facilities and services threatens to relocate these developments in areas as yet untouched by tourism. In addition, there is a clear conflict between winter and summer users of the Alps. The former visit the area mostly for skiing and are relatively unaware of the environmental damage they cause. By contrast, summer visitors tend to be walkers and naturalists, only too aware that the natural beauty of the Alps is being destroyed by inappropriate development (Figure 3.5).

However, not all of the damage is caused by tourism. Entire rivers have disappeared due to the proliferation of hydroelectricity schemes over the past sixty years. The biggest threat is from new roads. Eighteen major cross-border roads through the Alps are planned, all of which would damage the environment and increase pollution. For example, the German and Italian governments fiercely

	Pays d'Enhait	Aletsch	Grindelwald
Type of tourism 	Agro-tourist periphery. Rural villages based on extensive farming. Small number of hotels, usually owned by non-residents.	Development of cable-cars in the 1950s led to huge expansion of tourist beds. Agricultural employment in decline.	High, steep sided mountains, broad valleys. Large tourist resort. Rapid development during the 1960s and 1970s of parahotellerie – a group term for condominiums, second homes and their infrastructure
Population dependent upon tourism	30%	80%	90%
Population trend	Declining	Increasing	Increasing
Seasonality of tourism	Winter > summer	Winter >> summer	Summer > winter
Problems	Increasing pressure to develop tourist facilities and for agriculture to rationalise	Ecological and landscape damage from winter sports. Loss of native young people. Pressure on farmers to sell land for further hotel developments.	Seasonal unemployment. Conflict between expectations of summer and winter tourists. Serious traffic congestion at peak periods.
more important >	much more important >>		

Figure 3.4 *Regional variations in tourism in the Swiss Alps Source: adapted from Geo Factsheet, April 1997, 'Social and economic geography of mountains'*

oppose attempts by Austria and Switzerland to cut pollution by restricting traffic through the Alps. Likewise, in the western Pyrenees, controversy surrounds the construction of a four-lane highway through the Aspe valley, the last home of the Pyrenean brown bear. Environmentalists who argue that the road will ruin the landscape have repeatedly delayed building work. Regional governments around the Pyrenees are therefore trying to coordinate environmental protection by organising a joint forum between developers, environmentalists, planners and local people.

The impact in Eastern Europe

The problems are not limited to the Alps. The unplanned, uncontrolled development of ski centres in many central and eastern European countries, such as the High Tatra mountains in Poland, is threatening the environment there, and conflicts between those concerned about mountain environments and developers are common. New fashions, such as snowmobiles and skiing from helicopters, are particularly damaging to wildlife.

The worst environmental disasters have occurred in the mountain ranges of eastern Europe. For example, whole

Figure 3.5 *Inappropriate developments in the Alps causing environmental damage*

forests in the Giant Mountains between Poland and the Czech Republic have been destroyed by pollution from coal-burning power stations. Grazing sheep, goats and cattle is steadily degrading mountain habitats in Albania, Bulgaria, Romania and Ukraine. In the Tatra Mountains, the privatisation of land over the last thirty or forty years has spawned a new generation of village landowners who want to exploit the land rather than preserve it.

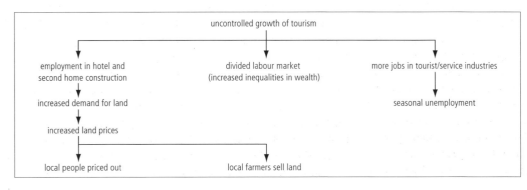

Figure 3.6 *Some negative consequences of the uncontrolled growth of tourism in the Swiss Alps Source: adapted from Geo Factsheet, April 1997, Social and economic geography of mountains*

Inset 3.1
The impact of skiing on mountain areas in Europe

Europe is one of the most densely populated areas in the world; its mountains are one of the few remaining areas there that are relatively uninhabited and relatively untouched by human activity. However, mountain areas are becoming increasingly popular destinations for tourists. Most of the tourism in mountainous areas of Europe is concentrated in the Alps, which receives about 100 million tourists each year. Alpine regions are fragile environments, and recently-introduced human activities, especially skiing, have led to environmental hazards and have threatened delicate ecosystems; there has been an increase in levels of pollution, deforestation, and soil erosion.

In 1990 some 50 million people took an alpine ski holiday. Over 40 000 ski runs and 14 000 ski lifts were needed by the late 1980s to cope with the demand (Figure 3.7). The trend of development is well illustrated by the case of Switzerland. There, the number of ski lifts increased from about 250 in 1954 to nearly 2000 by 1990.

Figure 3.7 *Chair lift carrying skiers to the summit*

The environmental impacts of skiing are far-reaching. They include the construction of the ski piste, related facilities such as access roads, parking, cafeterias and toilet facilities. These are very major impacts on the environment. Skiing removes habitats, when for example forests are cut down to allow building of ski lifts. Deforestation removes the natural protection against avalanches and degrades the natural landscape. Exhaust fumes from private cars and coaches

have led to further forest damage leading to the loss of wildlife; in Switzerland, 70% of domestic and foreign tourists arrive at their destination by car.

Forest clearance has led to an increased incidence of avalanches. Over 100 square kilometres of forest have been removed throughout the Alps, which has led to higher rates of avalanches with greater impact. In Austria, the creation of just 0.7 square kilometres of ski runs in 1980, for the Winter Olympics, led to a major mud slide. New resort construction involves bulldozing, blasting, and reshaping of slopes. This increases slope instability and leads to a higher incidence of avalanches. Natural forest barriers are often replaced with concrete, plastic and wooden barriers associated with developments. These reduce the environmental visual amenity and lead to visual pollution.

Another increasing hazard is water pollution and sewage disposal. In the French Pyrenees, sewage from summer tourist resorts discharges directly into streams. In the Alps, chemicals used in preparing thirty-six glaciers for skiing have caused increases in nitrogen and phosphorus levels in drinking water.

The unsustainable use of water is also increasing the potential for hazards. By 1992, 4000 snow cannons were producing artificial snow to lengthen the ski season in the Alps. These used 28 million litres of water per kilometre of piste. In Les Meunieres, France, 185 snow cannons installed for the 1992 Olympics were supplied by drinking water sources.

The artificial snow melts more slowly than natural snow, reducing the already short period of time for the alpine vegetation to regenerate. Furthermore, skiing in sparse snow conditions contributes to erosion and damages sensitive vegetation. The result is a severe reduction in water absorption and holding capacity for the mountain slopes. There is also an increased risk of runoff and avalanches.

When resorts experience low snow fall:
• skiers move higher up the slopes, onto glaciers
• lifts higher up the slopes are used more regularly.

These trends may increase the environmental problems because they bring skiing to more sensitive areas.

Elsewhere in Europe, such as at Jotunheimen, Norway, skiing and other activities have had a negative impact on animal species. Brown bears, wolverines, lynx, Arctic foxes, otters and even wild reindeer have all become less common. Road construction, power lines, visitor impact and long-range air pollution have all added to a decline in the wilderness value of the area and in the productivity of the ecosystem. The use of ski lifts, off-piste skiing, use of all-terrain vehicles and compaction of snow on-piste all disturb rare species. In the French Alps, rare species such as the Black grouse have been decapitated by overhead wires, displaced from their breeding grounds and can face competition for space with cable car installations.

The European avalanches of 1999

The avalanches that killed up to eighteen people in the Alps in February 1999 were the worst in the area for nearly one hundred years. Moreover, they occurred in an area that was thought to be fairly safe. In addition, precautionary measures had been taken, such as an enormous avalanche wall to defend the village of Taconnaz, and a second wall to stop the Taconnaz glacier advancing on to the motorway that runs into the mouth of the Mount Blanc tunnel. However, the villages of Montroc and Le Tour, located at the head of the Chamonix valley had no such defences.

The avalanche that swept through the Chamonix valley killed 11 people and destroyed 18 chalets (Figure 3.10). The low temperatures (-7°C) which caused the snow to compact, and made digging almost impossible, hampered rescue work. The avalanche was about 150 metres wide, 6 metres high and

December	10%
January	22%
February	32%
March	23%
April	13%

Figure 3.8 *Occurrence of avalanches in the French Alps*
Source: adapted from Symons, L., and Morth, H.,1992, 'Avalances', Geography Review, 5, 4, 2–6

Altitude	No. of avalanches	Per cent of total
> 3000 m	326	3
2500 – 2999 m	2210	24
2000 – 2499	3806	41
1500 – 1999 m	2632	28
Below 1500 m	394	4

Figure 3.9 *Avalanches and altitude in the French Alps*
Source: adapted from Symons, L., and Morth, H.,1992, 'Avalances', Geography Review, 5, 4, 2–6

travelled at a speed of up to 90 kilometres per hour. It crossed a stream and even travelled uphill for some 40 metres (Figure 3.11). Residents were shocked, since they had never before experienced an avalanche so powerful, so low in the mountains, and certainly not one capable of moving uphill.

Figure 3.10 *The Montroc-Le Tour avalanche*

Nothing could have been done to prevent the avalanche, and avalanche warnings had been given the day before, as the region had experienced up to two metres of snow in just three days. However, buildings in Montroc were not considered to be at risk. In fact, they were classified as being in the 'white zone' almost completely free of danger. By contrast, in the avalanche danger zones no new buildings have been developed for many decades. Avalanche monitoring is so well established and elaborate that it had caused villagers and tourists in the 'safe' zone to think that they were completely safe. In Montroc the probability of the avalanche occurring was the equivalent of an extinct volcano – the last time the snow above Montroc had caused an avalanche was in 1908.

Meteorologists have suggested that disruption of weather patterns resulting from global warming will lead to increased snowfall in the Alps, both heavier and later in the season. This would mean that the conventional wisdom regarding avalanche safe zones would need to be re-evaluated.

Figure 3.11 *The causes and consequences of the Montroc-Le Tour avalanche Source: adapted from The Independent and The Daily Telegraph, 11 February 1999*

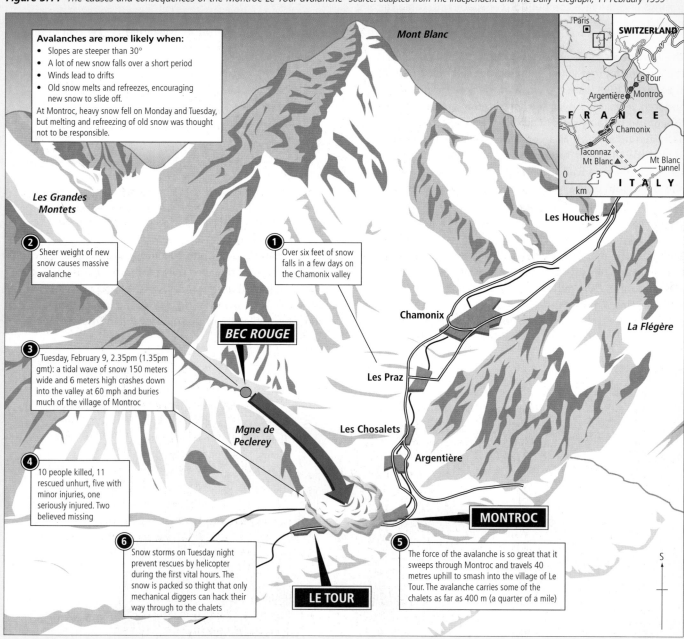

Avalanches are more likely when:
- Slopes are steeper than 30°
- A lot of new snow falls over a short period
- Winds lead to drifts
- Old snow melts and refreezes, encouraging new snow to slide off.

At Montroc, heavy snow fell on Monday and Tuesday, but melting and refreezing of old snow was thought not to be responsible.

2 Sheer weight of new snow causes massive avalanche

1 Over six feet of snow falls in a few days on the Chamonix valley

3 Tuesday, February 9, 2.35pm (1.35pm gmt): a tidal wave of snow 150 meters wide and 6 meters high crashes down into the valley at 60 mph and buries much of the village of Montroc

4 10 people killed, 11 rescued unhurt, five with minor injuries, one seriously injured. Two believed missing

6 Snow storms on Tuesday night prevent rescues by helicopter during the first vital hours. The snow is packed so thight that only mechanical diggers can hack their way through to the chalets

5 The force of the avalanche is so great that it sweeps through Montroc and travels 40 metres uphill to smash into the village of Le Tour. The avalanche carries some of the chalets as far as 400 m (a quarter of a mile)

Mont Blanc

Les Grandes Montets

BEC ROUGE

Mgne de Peclerey

Chamonix

La Flégère

Les Praz

Les Chosalets

Argentière

Les Houches

MONTROC

LE TOUR

SWITZERLAND
Paris
F R A N C E
Le Tour
Argentière • Montroc
Chamonix
Taconnaz
Mt Blanc ▲
Mt Blanc tunnel
I T A L Y
0   3
km

The implications of the avalanches for tourism are important. As many of the avalanches took place in areas where the risk was thought to be low, it suggests that other 'safe' areas could be at risk, or that the risk of avalanches is changing. Much of the tourist related accommodation is located in safe areas, and many of these areas will need to be re-assessed. Moreover, people skiing off-piste caused some of the avalanches. Off-piste skiers may in future be held responsible for avalanches, and in the event of death or destruction, legal cases may be brought.

In addition, much of the infrastructure and accommodation that was destroyed needs to be rebuilt. This will have to be paid for by the government and/or the local community, which may need to raise local charges to cover the cost.

If avalanches become more common, and more people are killed each year, there may be a decline in skiing as a holiday activity – especially for school groups, where parents have little control over where their children go.

Figure 3.12 *Map of the area affected by the avalanche of February 1999 Source: Didier Richard, Les tracts grand air 8, Pays du Mont Blanc, 1:50 000*

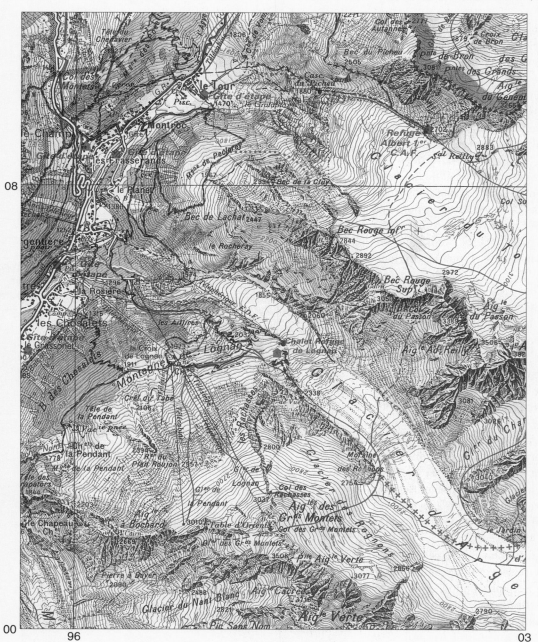

QUESTIONS

1 What is an avalanche?

2 What factors increase the risk of an avalanche?

3 Choose an appropriate method to display the data shown in Figure 3.8. Why are avalanches clustered in the months between January and March? Give at least two reasons.

4 Figure 3.9 shows the distribution of avalanches with altitude in Switzerland. The tree-line is at about 1500 metres and the snow line is at 3000 metres. Choose a suitable technique to show the distribution of avalanches with altitude. How do you explain this pattern?

5 What conditions in Europe in February 1999 led to widespread avalanches?

6 How and why may the threat of avalanches change in the next decades?

7 Figure 3.12 shows the areas affected by the avalanches. Describe the site of Montroc and Le Tours.

8 What are the attractions for tourists as shown on Figure 3.12? Use the grid provided to give grid references.

9 What map evidence is there to suggest that the area is at risk of hazardous events?

TOURISM IN THE BRECON BEACONS

The Brecon Beacons National Park is located in the south of Wales and is one of the national parks closest to large centres of population such as South Wales, Birmingham and Bristol. This makes the Park attractive to day-trippers and overnight tourists, and increases the pressures put on it. In addition, like all national parks in Britain, much of the land is privately owned, and there are conflicts between local people and tourists.

As a result of the increasing pressures on the Park a comprehensive survey was carried out in 1994 to:

- estimate the number of visitors using the Park
- identify where visitors had travelled from and how they arrived
- establish why they had visited the Park and to determine which parts of the Park were visited
- discover which features the visitors enjoyed and which they did not.

The National Parks of Britain were established under the 1949 National Parks and Access to the Countryside Act. They had two main functions, namely, to preserve and enhance the natural beauty of the area, and to promote their enjoyment by the public.

The National Parks in Britain are not owned by the state. Rather they are owned by a mixture of private individuals and organisations, and conflicts between these owners and visitors are common. The conflict centres on reconciling the recreational demands of visitors against the landscape conservation wishes of the National Park residents and local users such as farmers.

The Brecon Beacons cover an area of over 1350 square kilometres and contain over 110 main roads and hundreds of minor roads (Figure 3.13). Over 32 000 people live and work within the area covered by the Brecon Beacons National Park.

A survey of visitor and visitor habits was carried out between March and November 1994. It consisted of a survey of vehicles and their occupants, visitors at key sites, and a self-completion questionnaire.

The survey showed that the number of people visiting the Brecon Beacons during the period March to November was about 3.3 million. Of these, just over half were day trips and just under a half were overnight stays. The Brecon Beacons have a wide sphere of influence: although the majority of day trip visitors are from adjacent counties, almost 40% came from further away (Figure 3.14)

Most visitors staying in the Brecon Beacons used self-catering facilities and of those in serviced accommodation, most used bed and breakfast accommodation. This partly reflects the length of stay in the Brecon Beacons (Figure 3.15). About 80% of visitors come to the region for its landscape and scenery (Figure 3.16) and for peace and quiet

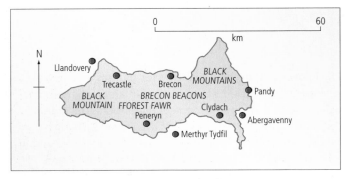

Figure 3.13 *The Brecon Beacons National Park*
Source: adapted from Geo Factsheet, April 1997

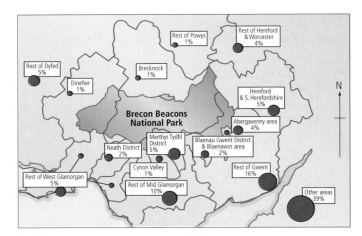

Figure 3.14 *Origin of day trip visitors to the Brecon Beacons National Park*
Source: Geo Factsheet, April 1997

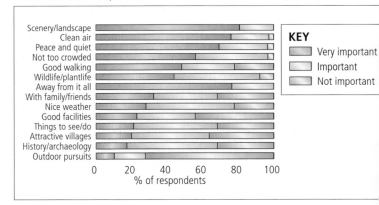

Figure 3.15 *The attractions of the Brecon Beacons National Park*
Source: Geo Factsheet, April 1997

Figure 3.16 *Scenery and landscape of the Brecon Beacons*

Figure 3.17 *Tranquil scene from the Brecon Beacons National Park*

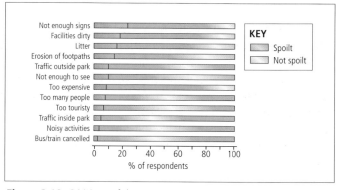

Figure 3.18 *Criticisms of the Brecon Beacons National Park*
Source: Geo Factsheet, April 1997

(Figure 3.17). Overcrowding by people or cars did not appear to be a major concern for most visitors. Insufficient signposting was the most commonly mentioned criticism (Figure 3.18).

The Llanthony Valley

The Llanthony Valley has seen an increase in tension and conflict between the different user groups (Figure 3.19). For over 200 years Llanthony has been a microcosm of the problems and opportunities of rural recreation. The Llanthony Valley covers just 55 square kilometres and the Afon Honddu runs through it for about 12 kilometres south from its source at Hay Bluff. The valley has 240 inhabitants, of whom 40% of the heads of households are farmers, 20% work within the valley, 20% are commuters and 20% are retired. The population of the valley declined from 645 people in 1845 to 248 in 1979 and has since stabilised. Only four families in the valley benefit from tourism, from bed and breakfasts and pony-trekking.

The valley's scenic beauty, with its rich history, has attracted increasing numbers of tourists. There are several historic sites, including Llanthony Priory, a twelfth century Augustine Priory and a late Victorian monastery at Capel-y-ffin. The valley has links with the poet Wordsworth, the

sculptor Eric Gill and the writers Raymond Williams and Bruce Chatwin. However, there had been relatively little attempt to interpret the valley's history and geography on-site, by erecting information boards, until very recently. Other attractions in the valley include hillwalking, hang-gliding and mountain-biking.

Most visitors to the valley drive straight through. In one survey, on August Bank Holiday 1992, almost two-thirds of visitors did not stop. Thus the visitors bring minimal benefit to the valley. Of those that stopped at the Hay Common car park, two-thirds barely left their car (walked less than 10 m) and most of these did so to buy ice-cream; the other third walked less than 100 m.

A survey of the resident community found that farmers in particular had problems with the numbers of tourists using the Llanthony Valley road. They found it difficult at times to move animals and large machinery, found their gates blocked by cars, and were disrupted by slow-moving pony trekkers and sightseers.

Thus the Llanthony Valley is an example of all that is negative about tourists: they bring little or no benefit or revenue to an area but cause disruption, irritation and problems for local people (Figure 3.20). For the tourist, the trip is merely a pleasurable drive and they gain little or no understanding of the community or the landscape and the heritage that they have passed through.

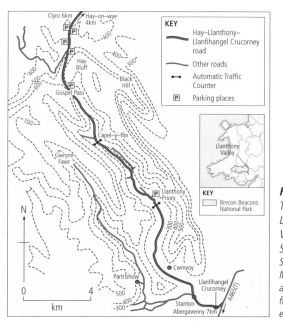

Figure 3.19
The Llanthony Valley, South Wales
Source: Price, M. (ed), People and tourism in fragile environments

Figure 3.20 *Car-based visitors often find themselves in conflict with local people*

Inset 3.2
Involving local communities

Not all tourism has a negative impact and it is possible to involve local communities in tourism. One such attempt is the South Pembrokeshire Partnership for Action with Rural Communities (SPARC). The SPARC area is much larger than the Llanthony Valley and consists of about 400 square kilometres, some of it within the Pembrokeshire Coast National Park. The area has an average income of just 75% of the European Union average and unemployment is above average, 16%. One SPARC action plan improved infrastructure, footpaths and routes that linked tourist sites, creating over 350 kilometres of linked and marked footpaths. Small-scale tourism information points were established in 24 village shops and post offices across the area. This type of tourism provides immediate benefits to the community, as it allows local residents to become involved in tourism developments and it allows them to provide services to tourists. This is done in many ways:

- local produce is used wherever possible
- the majority of visitors stay in locally-owned and managed accommodation
- the service sector is locally owned
- local manufacturers are encouraged to tap the tourist market by producing gifts, souvenirs and crafts.

QUESTIONS

1 How does the location of the Brecon Beacons National Park affect the visitor pressure exerted on the Park?

2 What conflicts result from visitor pressure in the Brecon Beacons, and in the Llanthony Valley in particular?

3 Briefly outline ways in which tourism could be made more beneficial to the residents of the Llanthony Valley.

CONFLICT IN THE CAIRNGORMS, SCOTLAND

In April 1996 in Coylumbridge near Aviemore in Scotland, ministers and senior scientists from more than twenty countries attempted to agree a strategy to preserve the fragile and threatened environment of Europe's mountains. The conference was one of a series of intergovernmental meetings aimed at fulfilling the international commitment to 'sustainable mountain development' made at the 1992 Earth Summit in Rio. But with mountains everywhere under increasing threat from pollution, roads and ski developments, the prospects for sustainable development are bleak. Throughout mountainous areas wildlife is killed by acid rain, landscapes wrecked by roads, and slopes shredded by downhill skiing. The skiing denudes the slopes of vegetation, compacts the thin soils, which thus lose their infiltration capacity, resulting in increased overland runoff and erosion.

Ironically, at the same time as the Coylumbridge Conference and only a few miles away, there was a classic example of the clash between environmental issues and economic gain. Since 1987, the Cairngorm Chairlift Company had been trying to win approval for a scheme to develop a funicular railway to just below the summit of Cairn Gorm which would scar the landscape forever – although it would encourage more visitors to the area (Figure 3.21).

The central Cairngorms mountain range includes four of the five highest mountains in Britain: Ben Macdui (1309 metres), Braeriach (1296 metres), Cairn Toul (1291 metres) and Cairn Gorm (1245 metres). The arctic conditions there provide a home for unique high-altitude plant life, including rare mosses, lichens and dwarf shrubs. The mountain tops are an irreplaceable refuge for rare birds such as golden eagles, ptarmigan, snow buntings and dotterels, while the slopes support some of the most important remnants of the ancient Caledonian pine forest that used to cover most of Scotland.

Figure 3.21 Location of the proposed funicular railway and associated buildings on Cairn Gorm
Source: New Scientist, 20 April 1996

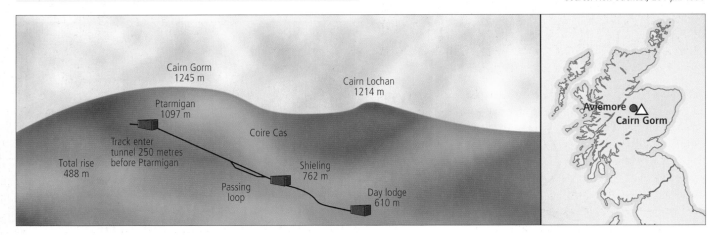

The area holds a large number of conservation designations, illustrating its importance. There are three large Sites of Special Scientific Interest (SSSIs), and proposed special protection areas to protect birds and important natural habitats. However, the area does not have National Park status. Nevertheless, in 1996, the Scottish Office proposed the Cairngorms as a World Heritage Site, a designation bestowed by the United Nations on places such as Uluru (Ayers Rock), the Great Barrier Reef in Australia and the Galapagos Islands in the Pacific. Despite these acknowledgements of its importance, the area is not protected and it has never been managed by a single authority. In the absence of any overall policy framework, developments such as the proposed funicular railway make a mockery of conferences about sustainability. At present it is difficult to establish government responsibilities for mountain issues.

The Cairngorms are a classic example of the pressures that are placed on beautiful yet fragile environments. The worst scenario is that the tourist-related developments and tourists will destroy the very attractions that they come to see, including the views (Figure 3.22). The Cairngorm Chairlift Company, which has run skiing facilities on the northern flanks of Cairn Gorm since 1961, has tried twice since 1980 to expand west into Lurcher's Gully. On both occasions the Scottish Office rejected the company's plans after heated opposition by environmental groups. In 1997, the company was granted permission to build a £17 million, two-kilometre funicular railway to within 150 metres of the summit of Cairn Gorm. This will be the highest funicular in Britain.

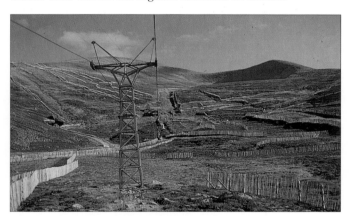

Figure 3.22 *A chairlift and fencing in the Cairngorns*

The development also includes a new chairlift, three new ski tows, four new ski runs and provision for 150 extra car parking spaces, a 250-seat restaurant and an 'interpretive centre'. The latter two developments will be built at the top of the funicular, tripling the capacity of the existing 'Ptarmigan' snack bar. The aim of the development is to attract more visitors in the summer and improve facilities for skiers in the winter; the plan is to quadruple the number of summer visitors, from 60 000 to 225 000.

The threat of increased trampling on the vulnerable summit during the short growing season alarms conservationists. They fear that plants will be crushed, birds disturbed, soil compacted and eroded, and the landscape irreversibly damaged. The World Wide Fund for Nature (WWF) and the Royal Society for the Protection of Birds maintain that the railway and the visitors it brings pose a significant risk to the protected snow bunting, dotterel and ptarmigan. At the planning inquiry the judge rejected arguments that the funicular company should guarantee no adverse environmental impact.

To control the effects of the increased visitor numbers, the chairlift company developed a 'visitor management plan' aimed at controlling the movement of walkers. Access to the summit plateau may be limited by charging people, or else people may be confined to the restaurant and visitor centre: people will not be free to walk wherever they want to.

Doubts over the feasibility of the plan led to the government's conservation agency, Scottish Natural Heritage (SNH), initially opposing the development.

Despite the environmental opposition, many organisations are in favour of the development. Local businesses and skiing groups, Highlands and Islands Enterprise and the local authority, Highland Regional Council, all the major political parties and the European Union back the development. Scotland's mountain ranges have less statutory protection than almost any of the world's uplands. Nevertheless, the natural habitats of the Cairngorms are in better condition than those in England and Wales. In

Figure 3.23 *OS Map of the Cairngorms*
Source: Ordnance Survey, Landranger 36, Grantown, Aviemore and Cairngorm, 1:50 000

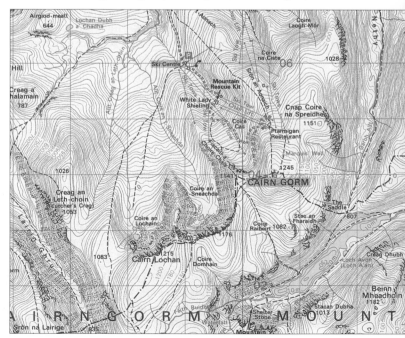

Snowdonia and the Lake District overgrazing and acid rain have degraded large areas. Consequently, upland mosses and dwarf shrubs have been replaced by grass, which supports a much less diverse range of wildlife.

Highlands and Islands Enterprise will build the railway and put £3 million towards the cost of the building and then rent it to the chairlift company. The EU is also contributing another £3 million. Work on the railway began in 1998 and is due to be completed in 2001. Backers claim that the development will be a big attraction and ensure sustainable tourism. The Cairngorm Chairlift Company believes that it will create 60 jobs and take 200 000 people a year close to the summit of Cairn Gorm, although summer visitors will not be allowed to walk indiscriminately. More skiers will be brought to the summit in winter, but, the lack of winter snow in the 1990s and the possible future impact of global warming on the region, may make skiing a less than viable sector to invest in.

QUESTIONS

1 What are the economic arguments in favour of the funicular railway and the associated developments?

2 What are the environmental arguments against the development?

3 Describe the environment associated with high mountains, such as the Cairngorms. The map extract (Figure 3.23) may be helpful. What are the implications of the Cairngorm's climate for environmental rehabilitation following disruption? Justify your answer. (N.B. The climatic data for the Cairngorms are based on observations at Cairn Gorm and at Craibstone, located 75 kilometres north-east of the Cairngorms at an altitude of 91 metres.)

Figure 3.24 *Climatic data for Craibstone and Cairn Gorm*

		J	F	M	A	M	J	J	A	S	O	N	D		
Craibstone	(°C)	3	3	5	7	9	12	14	13	12	9	6	4	8	(Av)
	(mm)	78	55	53	51	63	54	95	75	67	92	93	80	856	(Total)
Cairn Gorm	(°C)	0.2	-0.8	3.9	3.1	6.9	7.3	13.6	12.7	9.8	5.6	2.5	3.3	5.7	(Av)
	(mm)	n/a	n/a	n/a	n/a	n/a	n/a	n/a	n/a	n/a	n/a	n/a	n/a	n/a	(Total)

TOURISM ISSUES AT CHEDDAR GORGE

Cheddar Gorge in the Mendip Hills of Somerset is a tourist 'honeypot' (Figure 3.25). It is an excellent example of an area of rugged relief about which there is conflict of interest. Tourist-related businesses want to bring more visitors into the area, whereas mining companies want to continue to quarry the limestone rock. However, many residents and environmentalists want to preserve the character and tranquility of the region. They wish to preserve the unique landscape of gorges, caves, potholes, cliffs and other spectacular limestone scenery, as well as unusual plants and birds.

Nearly one million people a year visit the caves at Cheddar Gorge and Wookey Hole, while Bath – whose hot springs draw their water from the Mendip Hills – is the second most popular tourist centre in Britain. Visitors to the attractions created by Mendip limestone bring about £23 million a year into the area.

The Gorge is a stunning feature (Figure 3.26). It is one of the most dramatic landforms in the south-west of England. Due to its close proximity to the M4 and the M5, it is in an accessible location, which increases tourist pressure on the Gorge and the Mendip Hills.

Tourism has been important in the town of Cheddar for over 200 years, beginning in the 1790s when it was fashionable amongst the middle classes to take an interest in rocks, caves and their formations. In 1800, the first road was put through Cheddar Gorge and it became easier to visit this now-famous beauty spot. Over the years, the type of visitor changed. In 1867 a rail link reached Cheddar, bringing cheap day excursions within the reach of most of the population of south west and central England, and South Wales.

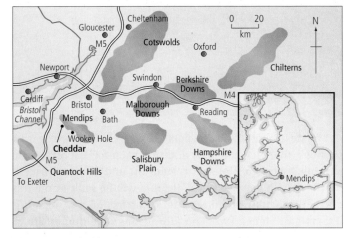

Figure 3.25 *Cheddar Gorge*
Source: Nagle, G., Autumn 1998, Managing Cheddar Gorge and the Mendips, GeoActive, 194, Stanley Thornes Publishers

Figure 3.26 *Cheddar Gorge – a spectacular landscape in the south-west of England*

Cheddar became one of the beauty spots which workers from large cities such as Bristol, Cardiff and Exeter visited.

Many of the tourist-related activities and attractions at Cheddar Gorge are owned and run by the Cheddar Showcaves company. The caves include a variety of impressive caves, tunnels and limestone deposits such as stalactites, stalagmites and pillars. The scale of Cheddar Showcaves' operations has a significant impact on the local economy. The area owned and managed by Cheddar Showcaves includes 300 acres at Cheddar, covering the whole south side of the Gorge (Britain's highest inland limestone cliffs), about 50 caves, woodland and grassland.

The strategic objectives of the company are to 'To make the Limestone Gorge and its Caves accessible to visitors in a way which increases visitor awareness of their value, while responding to the social needs of our visitors and protecting the natural environment for future generations; to earn from the Gorge and Caves a surplus of income over expenditure sufficient to maintain our operations, in ways which are compatible with this aim'. The company also states that 'While our activities must be self-financing, the main objective is to protect the fragile environment rather than to make money'.

More than 500 000 visitors a year spend time in Cheddar Gorge and of these up to 80% visit the Showcaves. However, with more people taking their holidays abroad and an increasing number of rival British attractions, visitor numbers have not risen significantly since the mid-1970s. In addition, most visitors to Cheddar Gorge are from social classes with the least disposable income (groups C2, D, and E) and couples aged 25 to 44 years, with or without children. Although school groups, European students and coach parties of pensioners are the most visible types of visitor, they only account for ten per cent of the total. Part of the Cheddar Showcaves management plan is to encourage wealthier visitors, winter visitors, repeat visitors, older and younger visitors, and local residents.

Tourism is the most important industry bringing money into the local economy. Up to 1000 residents in the village of Cheddar derive an income indirectly from tourism, and without these earnings Cheddar would be unable to support many of its facilities and amenities, such as its swimming pool, sports centre, shops, pubs and cafes.

Tourism and conflicts in Cheddar

The development of tourism as Cheddar's main industry has brought problems, pressures and conflicts. The conflicts at Cheddar Gorge are easy to see: one of the greatest natural features of southern Britain has been scarred by a large number of tea rooms and souvenir shops (Figure 3.27). It has many amusement arcades which are unattractive, and there is an air of over-exploitation: the stunning scenery has been spoiled by the growth of tacky souvenir stores keen to make as much money as possible from the tourists. But many local people make their living from providing these facilities; and it seems to be what many visitors want.

Other problems are not so immediately obvious, but can be more serious for those affected: ramblers straying from paths, gates left open allowing flocks of sheep to escape, litter thrown in residents' gardens and alleged shoplifting by young tourists. On a busy summer day, Cheddar's residents may have to share their village with 5000 strangers who arrive in 2000 cars. This influx detracts from the residents' enjoyment of living in the Cheddar area, and the perceived hostility of some of the residents detracts from the enjoyment of the tourists.

The Gorge and Showcaves are delicate and vulnerable habitats and it is impossible for hundreds of thousands of people to visit them every year without some damage. Many Mendip caves now have strictly restricted access to prevent cavers damaging the caves and reducing their scientific importance. There are often conflicts between visitors with different interests. For example, motor-cyclists frighten horses, horses make paths too muddy for walkers, walkers are at risk from mountain-bikers and may leave farmers' gates open or pick rare flowers. Cheddar Gorge is one of the most popular areas in the country for rock climbing and cav-

Figure 3.27 *Honeypot congestion and developments at Cheddar Gorge*

ing. The best climbs are above the Gorge car parks where there is a risk that climbers will damage the cliff faces and bring loose rocks down onto other visitors. And this is in addition to the conflicts between mining and tourism!

Mining began in 1756, close to Cheddar, but large-scale quarrying of the Mendip limestone started in 1870 with the arrival of the railways. Between 1756 and 1966, 60 million tonnes of limestone were blasted out of the Mendips. By 1988, only 22 years later, 190 million tonnes more had been removed. At one time about 40 large quarries were open – of these, 16 are still working or temporarily inactive. In total, about 6 per cent of the limestone outcrop has been quarried.

Limestone is used as a building stone, as crushed rock, for desulphurisation (it de-acidifies waste products), in cement making, in the smelting of iron ore, as a neutralising agent (for liming acid soils, as well as in smelting), and the calcium is also used widely (for example for toothpaste). It is also cheaper to quarry limestone than other rocks, because the outcrops are larger and it is fairly pure.

The value of the 250 million tonnes of limestone that has so far been quarried is about £900 million at current prices. Sales of limestone aggregate (crushed rock used for road ballast and foundations) from Mendip quarries are worth about £43 million a year.

In the Mendips, annual production of hard limestone 'aggregate' rose from three million tonnes in 1965 to 10 million tonnes in 1980. In Britain it rose from 60 to 86 million tonnes over the same period. Since the mid-1980s, the Mendip quarries have produced more than 12 million tonnes of limestone annually, and production from East Mendip will rise to 15.3 million tonnes in 2005.

The impact on the Mendip scenery has been dramatic. A small limestone hill at Vobster has disappeared and larger hills at Sandford, Milton and Dulcote have shrunk by between one-quarter and two-thirds of their volume. Quarrying has shrunk or polluted five of the Mendip springs, once large and clear. About 600 000 people in Somerset and Avon get their water supply from springs in the Mendips, which, thanks to their high rainfall of between 1000 and 1200 millimetres a year, produce at least 40 per cent more water per unit of area than any other aquifer in southern England. Some researchers argue that deep quarries, when abandoned, will fill with water to become vast reservoirs but waste disposal companies in Somerset and Avon are keen to use old quarries more profitably as rubbish tips.

Already, the road infrastructure cannot support the scale of quarrying. More stone could go by rail, but only two quarries have railheads so millions of tonnes of limestone are carried by lorry through narrow country roads. The increase in lorry traffic means that on some days there are over 3000 outward journeys from East Mendip quarries.

	Hard limestone	Granite	Basalt	Gritstone
Aquifer	Good 4	No 0	Poor 1	Occasional 2
Landscape	Very good 5	Very good 5	Good 4	Very good 5
Attractions (examples in British Isles)	Cheddar Gorge Malham Cove Burren pavements	Dartmoor tors Exmoor tors Fingal's Cave	Giant's Causeway,	Pen-Y-Fan, Croagh Patrick, Co. Mayo
Caving	Yes 5	No 0	No 0	No 0
Walking, climbing	Very good 5	Very good 5	Good 4	Very good 5
Open space	Yes 5	Yes 5	Yes 4	Yes 5
Paleolithic remains	Yes 5	No 0	No 0	No 0
Mines, minerals	Many 5	Many 5	Few 1	Few 1
Agricultural soil (where present)	Good 4	Poor 2	Very good 5	Poor 2
Fauna and flora	Very diverse 5	Limited 2	Good 4	Limited 2
In situ score	48	28	27	26

(The scale 0 (worst) to 5 (best) is a subjective scale)

QUESTIONS

1 What are the attractions of limestone areas for tourists?

2 Using an atlas and Figure 3.25, explain why Cheddar Gorge receives so many visitors each year.

3 What are the advantages of tourism for the Cheddar region?

4 Study Figure 3.28. Explain the values of limestone when it is not quarried.

5 What are the disadvantages of mining for tourism?

Figure 3.28 *Why the best place for limestone is in situ*
Source: adapted from *New Scientist, May 1989*

SUMMARY

In this chapter we have examined the impact of tourism in mountains, highland and areas of rugged relief. There are considerable differences between the Alps, the Brecon Beacons, the Cairngorms and Cheddar Gorge in terms of size, population density, impact of tourism and so on. However, all areas have limited land use due to the nature of the slopes and the soils. Mountainous areas are often remote and inaccessible, and the resulting increased cost of purchasing goods, fewer alternatives in terms of employment, shopping, etc., and fewer social contacts create extra pressures on people living there. Tourism is a mixed blessing. Although it increases the number of jobs and raises incomes, it can inflate land prices, lead to deforestation, increased natural hazards and resentment between tourists and visitors. The studies in this chapter have shown that tourism brings conflict with its impact on the economic, social, political and natural environment.

QUESTIONS

1 Describe and explain the effects of tourism on mountain areas, areas of high ground or rugged scenery. Use examples to support your answer.
2 How are pressures on mountain areas, areas of high ground or rugged scenery likely to change over the next few decades? Justify your answer
3 What are the social and environmental problems associated with tourism in mountainous areas, areas of high ground or rugged scenery? Use examples to support your answer.
4 What disadvantages can tourism bring to a mountainous area?
5 What factors make mountainous areas, areas of high ground or rugged scenery vulnerable to tourist developments?

BIBLIOGRAPHY AND RECOMMENDED READING

Brecon Beacons National Park, 1994, *Visitor Survey Brecon Beacons National Park*

Fitton, M., 1996, 'Does our community want tourism? Examples from South Wales' in **Price, M.,** (ed) *People and tourism in fragile environments,* Wiley

North York Moors National Park, 1990, *Visitors and the national park landscape*

North York Moors National Park, 1993, *North York Moors National Park Visitor Survey*

WEB SITES

British Geological Society – http//192.171.148.40/bgs/home.html

Chapter 4
Wilderness and protected areas

In this chapter we look at some of the pressures from tourism in a number of the most fragile environments in the world. These environments include Antarctica, described as the last great frontier, Banff National Park in the Canadian Rocky Mountains, the Galapagos Islands in the Pacific and Hwange National Park in Zimbabwe. In addition, we look at problems that affect wilderness areas and national parks in general. The problems differ in each of the examples chosen, and the solutions are equally varied. In many cases there are no complete solutions, only options and choices to be made, based on the information available and the political will and economic incentives to see them through.

THE IMPACTS OF TOURISM

Tourism and recreation in wilderness areas and protected areas have a number of impacts. For example, in the protected areas of Europe, problems include overcrowding, changes in the habitats of native animals, introduction of exotic species, footpath erosion and conflicts between competing users.

Nature and national parks are under extreme pressure from the demand for outdoor activities and the development of tourism facilities, such as large hotels on the Mazurian Lakes in Poland. Overcrowding occurs at peak periods. For example, in Hohe Tauern, Austria, visitors are concentrated into six summer months, while in Ojcow, Poland, 60% of tourists visit during the three summer months. Most visitors to both places are day trippers arriving by car (over 90% to the Hohe Tauern region), leading to traffic congestion, congestion of car parking spaces and litter problems. In Triglav National Park, Slovenia, two

million tourists outnumber residents during the summer months by almost one thousand to one.

Changes in habitats of native animals occur as a result of tourist developments. Wildlife attracts visitors, who disturb breeding patterns, leading to a fall in animal numbers. The species become rarer and more people come to 'see it while you still can'. By contrast, in Tenerife (Canary Islands) more than a dozen plant species have invaded the Teide National Park, having been carried from other countries as seeds on vehicles, clothes or tents of visitors.

Conflicts occur between tourism and nature conservation. For example, the Coto Donana National Park in south west Spain is an important breeding ground for many of Europe's birds, and is home to endangered species such as the Imperial Eagle and the Spanish Lynx, but it is now threatened by water extraction for tourism and local agriculture.

ANTARCTICA – THE LAST RESORT

Antarctica is one of the world's last wonders for scientists and visitors alike. Two-thirds of the world's fresh water is locked up here as ice. Some layers of its snow date back a million years. Its glaciers are populated by seals and penguins. Underneath this are thought to lie potential riches in the form of iron ore, coal, uranium and oil that could be the flashpoint for environmental battles in years to come.

It boasts spectacular scenery, sunny, albeit cold, weather and unusual wildlife (Figure 4.1). Tourism to Antarctica is increasing: in 1997, nearly 5000 people visited Port Lockroy in British Antarctica, an increase of 16% on 1996, as the search for more exotic holidays continues. Port Lockroy, with its large penguin population, was restored in the mid-1990s as an Antarctic base and declared a historic site.

Antarctica is remote and people perceive it as the last wilderness, although for some, travelling to it may be a luxurious experience. Orient Lines, the biggest cruise line operating to the area, market the area as a 'wonderful destination and surprisingly sunny. The temperatures are around 45°F (8°C) so it's rather like going on a skiing holiday'. Cruises for 1998 were fully booked, leading to more cruises being introduced in 1999.

Australia is leading the field in its attempts to develop tourism in Antarctica. It is one of seven countries with territorial claims to Antarctica, along with Argentina, Britain, Chile, France, New Zealand and Norway (Figure 4.2). The

Figure 4.1 *Antarctica's spectacular scenery!*

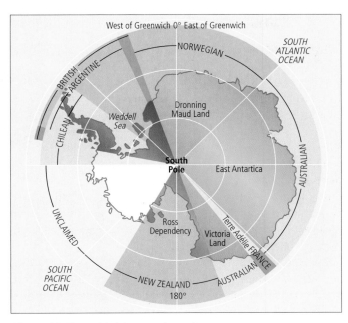

Figure 4.2 *Territorial claims over Antarctica*

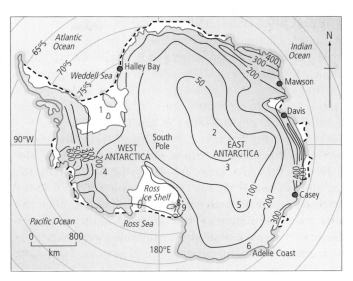

Figure 4.3 a) *Antarctica's climate with isohyets of annual precipitation in terms of the water equivalent, i.e. millimetres per annum. The numbers on the map refer to the following places: 1 Filchner ice shelf, 2 highest point on the plateau (3570 m), 3 Vostok, 4 Byrd, 5 Dome C, 6 Dumont D'Urville, 7 Mt. Erebus, 8 Lake Vanda, 9 McMurdo Sound*

Figure 4.3 b) *Antarctica's climate with isotherms of annual mean temperature (° C) and the directions of katabatic winds*

Source: Linacre, E. and Geerts, B., 1997, Climates and weather explained, Routledge

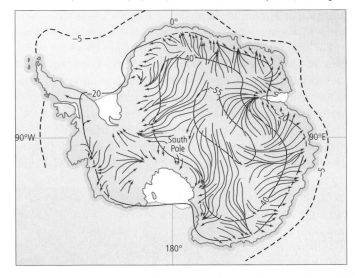

Australian claim covers about 43 per cent of the continent, almost as large an area as Australia itself.

Australia has proposed closing two of its three research bases in Antarctica and turning them into summer bases for adventure tourists. Australia wants to relocate research at its Casey and Mawson bases to its third base, Davis. Australia's three bases are about 1000 kilometres apart, each with its own transport system and infrastructure. Duplication of infrastructure and resources, and transport between the three bases uses up about two-thirds of Australia's £26 million Antarctic budget each year, leaving only one-third for research. It has proposed leasing the other two bases to other countries or allowing tourists to go there on strictly controlled expeditions. The Australian government report, Australia's Antarctic Programme Beyond 2000, argues that Australia should be sharing facilities, research equipment, personnel and supply lines with France, New Zealand and Norway – neighbouring countries with Antarctic claims. This would leave more money for research.

Britain, New Zealand and Russia already allow tourists to visit Antarctica, but only by ship. There are occasional tourist flights over the continent from Australia and New Zealand, but no tourists have been allowed to camp there because of fears for the security of the penguin rookeries and Antarctica's delicate ecosystem. Given the very low temperatures (Figure 4.3 a and b), decomposition of garbage, including oil, and biodegradable products, is very slow.

QUESTIONS

1 What are the main attractions of Antarctica as a tourist destination?

2 To what extent should Australia be allowed to develop Antarctica as a tourist destination?

3 Study Figure 4.3 a and b which shows temperature and rainfall for Antarctica. What are the implications of Antarctica's climate for the provision of tourist facilities and the disposal of tourist waste?

THE GALAPAGOS ISLANDS

At another latitudinal extreme are the Galapagos Islands, a series of equatorial volcanic islands located in the Pacific Ocean, 850 kilometres off the coast of Ecuador (Figure 4.4). At first glance, the Galapagos Islands are not luxuriant. According to Darwin, they were 'a broken field of black basaltic lava, thrown into the most rugged waves and crossed by great fissures ... everywhere covered by stunted, sunburnt brushwood, which shows little sign of life.' However, they are famed for their rich biodiversity and unique species of iguana, sharks, blue and red-footed boobies, penguins, giant tortoises (Figure 4.5), and the palo alto tree. The native species of the islands are unique because they have evolved over three million years in the absence of competing species and predators. Washed by the cold Humboldt ocean current flowing from Antarctica, the Galapagos islands have their own unique climate as well as their unique biodiversity. The climate is temperate except for a few months when the Humboldt current reverses and the climate becomes sub-tropical.

In 1959, a century after the publication of Darwin's *Origin of the species*, Ecuador declared all of the Galapagos a national park, except for land that was already colonised by Ecuadorean fishermen – today 97% of the archipelago is a managed national park, with access restricted to 50 000 tourists per annum and only 3% is freely open to tourists.

The Galapagos have enjoyed a tourist boom since about 1970. The number of visitors has risen from about 10 000 a year in 1970 to over 50 000 a year in 1998, and the local tourist industry now earns over £30 million annually. As a result, the islands have attracted an increasing number of mainland Ecuadorians keen to profit from the tourist trade. There were barely 1350 residents on the islands in 1950, now there are more than 12 000 and the population is growing at 8% per annum, the fastest population growth rate

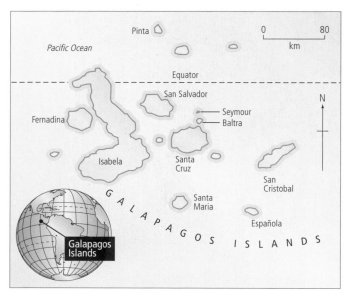

Figure 4.4 *The Galapagos Islands*
Source: adapted from World Reference Atlas, 1994, Dorling Kindersley

in South America. The main centre of population is Puerto Ayora on Santa Cruz island. It includes most of the tourist facilities and services: bars, restaurants, disco, and souvenir stores.

Until the mid-1980s, regulations on tourism in the Galapagos worked well, but with increasing numbers of tourist developments, these regulations have proved ineffective (Figure 4.6). The tourists come to see, among other wildlife, the giant tortoises, and the wide sandy beaches become pressure spots. The Galapagos problem is not just ecological, it is social as well. Tensions have increased as older residents seek autonomy from the mainland and special legislation to stem the flow of immigrants from mainland Ecuador. Fishermen have threatened to disrupt the tourist industry and conservation programmes if they continue to

Figure 4.5 *Giant tortoise – unique to the Galapagos Islands*

Figure 4.6 Tourists approaching a sea-lion on the Galapagos Islands

be blamed for the decline of marine life and are prevented from fishing lucrative species. Tensions also arise because some fishermen feel they are valued less than the Galapagos's rare species. For example, a giant tortoise with an injured leg was flown to Florida for special treatment. Would a fisherman who had broken his leg get the same treatment?

At the headquarters of the Galapagos National Park and the Charles Darwin Foundation, giant tortoises are also bred in captivity, free from the dangers of recently introduced species, such as dogs, goats, and pigs. These new species may prey on the indigenous species, or compete for the same food supplies.

Geographical isolation is not without its problems. Many of the animals and birds on the islands are unafraid of humans because they have had limited contact with them; yet humans are the biggest threat to the islands because they demand hotels, roads, food and water, and create waste materials – all of which degrade the environment. Human impact on the islands and their biodiversity has a long history, although it was initially limited because of their isolated position. In the late seventeenth and eighteenth centuries, the Galapagos Islands were a refuge for pirates and buccaneers, while in the eighteenth and nineteenth centuries they were used by British and American whaling ships. The ships stopped in the Galapagos for fresh water and meat. The giant tortoise was highly prized because it could be kept alive, unfed for months, on a ship. By 1929, giant tortoises were extinct on one of the islands, Floreana. Since then, another of the island's thirteen different species of giant tortoises has disappeared.

Currently, the illegal fishing of sea cucumbers is a great problem, despite a ban imposed in 1992. Sea cucumbers act as filters, purifying sea water, and their larvae are food for many fish, so their disappearance could create serious problems in the islands' food chains. Sea cucumbers are

considered a great delicacy in Asia and a fisherman can earn up to £2000 a month from fishing for them. This is a great deal of money and very easy to earn, but, in time, it will decimate the local population of sea cucumbers. In 1992, following the extinction of sea cucumbers in other parts of the Pacific, Asians turned to the Galapagos Islands. Illegal fishing for shark fins and lobster had been an ongoing problem for years, but the increased threat from sea cucumber fishing led the government to impose their ban.

It is the wilder, more beautiful parts of the Galapagos Islands that are the most threatened: they are more fragile and less resilient and roads need to be built for tourists to reach these areas, the alternative is four-wheel drive vehicles which may destroy the landscape. In the areas where tourists are based, the government controls new developments such as hotels, roads and ports; developments in the national parks, are controlled by the national parks authority. Without controls, a rapid development of tourist infrastructure without any long-term management plans or assessment of possible impacts would be likely to ensue.

Profits made by tourism companies based on the Ecuador mainland go back to the mainland and the companies do not invest in the islands. Without investment in local education and social facilities, the problem of inequality will become worse as local people will be unable to benefit from tourism, and will turn to illegal fishing. Some of the tourist developments – hotels, airstrips and roads – are having an adverse impact on the islands' biodiversity, for example, at Puerto Villamil an airport is being built close to a nesting ground of flamingos.

The Ecuador government is working to control emigration to the islands, impose a quarantine on plants and animals imported into the island, set up more efficient policing of fishing boats with a new radar network and patrol boats for the archipelago, and maintain tighter rules on tourist development. But the Galapagos Islands are just a poor part of a poor country. As we have seen, tourism can be a great economic boost for developing countries, generating jobs, income and hard currency. But there are deep social tensions between the government, conservation groups, tourist organisations and local inhabitants: conservationists want to preserve the Galapagos Islands in all their biodiversity; tourist organisations wish to get more tourists to the islands and thus increase their profits, and local organisations want to increase their gains from tourism.

QUESTIONS

1 Suggest, and explain, at least two reasons why the Galapagos Islands have unique flora and fauna.

2 Why are the Galapagos Islands vulnerable to tourism?

THE INCREASING PRESSURES ON BANFF, CANADA

Having looked at the pressure of tourism on an area in an undeveloped country, Antarctica, and islands in a developing country, the Galapagos Islands in Ecuador, we look at some of the pressures facing one of the world's most beautiful national parks, Banff, in the Canadian Rocky Mountains. It shows us that the pressures on wilderness areas in developed countries – even those protected by law – are just as great as in developing economies.

The Rocky Mountains, and in particular Banff National Park, are becoming increasingly popular among tourists. Banff National Park, which straddles the Canadian Pacific track, attracts over 4 million people each year to view its stunning scenery, including mountains and the world famous Lake Louise (Figure 4.7), as well as its wolves, bears and other wildlife.

This popularity is due mainly to the increased accessibility of the park, which has occurred because of new links; such as the opening in 1886, by the Canadian Pacific railway company, of its transcontinental link through the Rocky Mountains. Tourism was being encouraged, and part of the reason for opening the railway was to encourage tourists to the Rockies: 'If we can't export the scenery, we will import the tourists' went the slogan. Banff National Park now straddles the Canadian Pacific track. The busy Trans-Canada highway has since been built through the middle of the park, and at the town of Banff several routes converge.

Banff (Figure 4.8) lies just inside the park's eastern boundary (Figure 4.9). In recent years it has grown rapidly, and now it resembles a suburban business district. As with other favoured tourist destinations, the cost of land has risen dramatically and house prices in Banff are comparable to those in Vancouver or Toronto, and many local people are unable to afford housing. Numerous houses offer bed and breakfast, and over 40 hotels have sprung up; the shops include Polo Ralph Lauren, the Body Shop and Allders duty-free. The 830-room Banff Springs Hotel, originally built in

Figure 4.8 *Banff village*

Figure 4.7 *Lake Louise, Banff National Park*

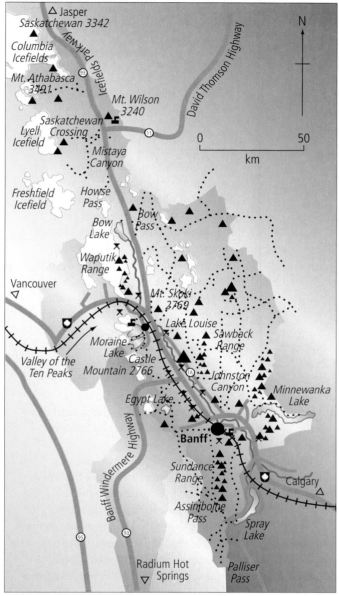

***Figure 4.9** Banff National Park*
Source: Cahill, M. and Yenne, W., 1991, The pictoral atlas of North America's National Parks, Brompton

Concern about the state of the national park is increasing amongst environmentalists, conservationists and local people, with the key issues being:

● can a wildlife sanctuary withstand so much pressure?
● should the numbers of visitors be limited, and if so, to what number?
● what can be done to protect the animals, fish and plants?

Problems are not restricted entirely to Banff. The three ski resorts in the national park pose a threat to local ecosystems, and some of the mountain lakes, such as Lake Louise, 50 km from Banff, also have their problems. At Lake Louise there are so many visitors that lichen and wild flowers are being destroyed, and the park authorities have had to build paved pathways. Fish introduced into the lake, possibly to improve fishing for the tourists, have eaten and eliminated some species of crustacean, and the park's only indigenous fish, the Banff long-nosed dace, has disappeared.

The problems which are developing have been at least partly recognised, and measures have been introduced to protect the animals and ensure their natural habitats and feeding patterns survive. Areas to have benefited are those such as along the Trans-Canada highway, which has since its construction been found to cross many prime animal migratory and feeding corridors. To allow continued migration and feeding several 50m wide animal overpasses have been constructed. In spite of the problems, as a result of good management, there are now more large animals, and more people, in the park than ever before.

There have also been attempts to address the inequalities in visiting tourist numbers throughout the year, so in an effort to balance the summer rush with winter visitors, the Banff and Lake Louise Tourist Association devotes over 80% of its promotional efforts to the ski season, extending from early November to early May. And Parks Canada, the organisation that manages Canadian national parks, is trying to lure people away from the most crowded parts of the Park as part of a 'demand management' strategy.

Although developed areas still cover less than 2% of the park, limitations on future developments have been imposed, and Banff's town boundaries are set by law: no new hotels or ski resorts are being allowed inside the park. Limiting facilities within the park has, however, raised other issues. With development in Banff at a near standstill, a building boom has developed outside the park boundaries, which could push up the number of day-trippers as well as causing serious environmental problems of its own.

the 1890s to provide meals to train passengers, to save hauling dining cars over steep mountain passes, now has a new conference centre and golf course.

The resident population of Banff is only about 6500, but its sewerage system is designed to cope with a transient population of about 45 000.

QUESTIONS

1 Explain why Banff is a popular National Park.

2 Describe and explain the problems caused by development within Banff National Park.

3 Explain why tourism is vital to the economy of Banff.

Case study: **Managing wildlife and tourism in Hwange National Park, Zimbabwe**

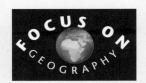

Figure 4.10 Hwange National Park – an important wildlife refuge

In the study of Hwange National Park, we examine in some detail the problem of managing a wilderness area and, more importantly, integrating the local population into its development. As shown later in Chapter 7, 'Theme parks and day trip attractions in the UK', rural communities in developed countries are often marginalised by tourist developments. The same was once true of the whole of Zimbabwe, although that has now changed in certain areas.

Hwange National Park is one of the most important wildlife sanctuaries in the world. It consists of almost 15 000 km² of semi-arid savanna and is the largest national park in Zimbabwe. It is Africa's third largest national park after Serengeti, Kenya and Kruger, South Africa. It is home for over 100 species of mammal, 400 species of bird and 70 species of reptile and amphibians (Figure 4.10). Many species are protected: the cheetah, white and black rhinos, aardwolf and African python.

Hwange is Zimbabwe's most accessible and most visited national park, being located on the tourist route to Victoria Falls (Figure 4.11). The park forms the north-eastern edge of the Kalahari Desert and consists largely of flat, gently undulating country. About two-thirds of the park is covered by deep wind-blown Kalahari sands and no natural watercourses exist here. The northern part of the park consists of more broken terrain, containing moist savanna woodland. The animal life is therefore limited to species that can tolerate semi-desert and savanna landscapes, i.e. those able to tolerate seasonal drought. There is a particularly large elephant population. Wildlife is now controlled by a boundary game fence surrounding much of the north and east of the park (Figure 4.12). This was erected to prevent the spread of foot and mouth disease by buffalo.

Traditionally, the area was used by hunter-gatherers (the San or bushmen people) and for grazing in the dry season by pastoralists in the south. During the British colonial period in the nineteenth and early twentieth centuries, a number of commercial farms were established in the north and east of the present park for wheat and cattle ranching.

Figure 4.11 Hwange National Park showing its position relative to Gwaai River and Victoria Falls Source: Rough Guides: Zimbabwe and Botswana

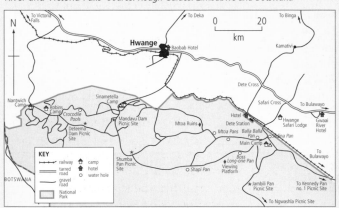

Figure 4.12 The boundary fence of Hwange National Park

Because much of the soil was unsuitable for agriculture, and rainfall was low and variable, the area was established as a Game Reserve in 1930 and became a National Park in 1949. In the 1950s there were unsuccessful attempts to acquire more land for the park in order to create a game corridor between the park and the Gwaai River, the only water source to the south of the park. Without a permanent source of water, very few of the game could survive the seven-month dry season and would migrate out of the park to find water sources on the Gwaai River. In order to overcome the shortage of water, park wardens used artificial methods of water provision during the dry season. After a number of unsuccessful attempts to produce watering pans (water holes) made of natural materials, concrete pans (Figure 4.13) were built. These pans were built into the natural pans and were designed to withstand trampling and allow clean water to spill over into the natural pans. The scheme

has been so successful that there has been a huge increase in the amount of game in the park. For example, in the 1930s there were about 1000 elephant in the park; by the late 1990s there were over 30 000.

There are now 50 operational bore holes (wells) in the park, which tap the underground water and direct it to the concrete pans during the dry season.

Without these there would be large-scale mortality of wildlife, as the migration route of the wildlife to the Gwaai River has been sealed off by game fences erected to protect the interests of commercial farming. In addition, there is a 'Veterinary Fence' to prevent the spread of foot and mouth disease.

However, provision of the water has had a number of ecological impacts. Animal numbers have greatly increased and now there is an over-population of large herbivores (such as elephants) which has led to degradation of the savanna environment. Overgrazing, hoof pressure, soil compaction and the destruction of trees is most noticeable around water sources. Habitat damage is most severe in the northern part of the park due to the shallow soils and limited vegetation cover.

The problem is increasing. During the 1990s, rainfall levels have been below

Figure 4.13
Concrete watering pans

average and more erratic. The water table is sinking and some bore holes have dried up completely. But the problem is not just one of declining rainfall. There is also a severe shortage of government funding for maintenance — since the 1930s, no major bore hole maintenance has taken place. The equipment is very old and needs replacement but funds are insufficient to undertake this. In

addition, the lack of suitably trained staff and the shortage of tools and workshop facilities has resulted in many of the bore holes falling into disrepair or operating unpredictably, leaving fewer key bore holes in operation. This has led to the congregation of unsustainable concentrations of animals around the remaining bore holes and the associated degradation of the environment.

Water shortages in the park could lead to an increase in animal mortality, initially water-dependent species such as the water buck, roan and sable antelope, later herds of buffalo and elephant. Other animals may be prevented from reaching the water pans by elephants, which dominate the water reserves. This could lead to an environmental catastrophe – a huge increase in animal mortality. This would cause an economic disaster – a decrease in the tourism-potential of the park. Without the large concentration of animals in the dry season, visitors would not be attracted.

Tourism in Hwange National Park

Hwange Park is noted for its large concentrations of animals, especially in the dry season. The number of visitors to the park has risen dramatically in recent decades. In 1949 it received just 2771 visitors. This increased to over 25 000 in 1965. The numbers dropped during Zimbabwe's War of Independence (1976 to1980) but have grown rapidly since 1980 (Figure 4.14), with a peak of over 110 000 in 1992. On the north-east side of the park there are a number of hotels, lodges, and luxury bush camps, and these peripheral developments have increased pressure to improve access to the park. The most popular part of the park is Main Camp, which is the most accessible and which accounts for 78% of all visitors. Since Main Camp is more accessible, because it is nearer to centres of population and transport networks than the other camps, Sinamatella and Robins, it also attracts a disproportionate amount of day visitors and increased visitor pressure (Figure 4.15).

The popularity of Main Camp has led to overcrowding on the Ten Mile Drive, an attractive open area of savanna noted for its wildlife. Up to half of the cars in the park use Ten Mile Drive and there is a distinct concentration between 4 p.m. and 6 p.m. when the park closes at dusk. Visitors have complained that the roads are of poor quality for private cars and that the wildlife at the roadside has decreased due to traffic, dust and pollution. A survey of visitors at the game viewing platform at the Nyamandhlovu Pan found that 37% felt that the Nyamandhlovu platform was overcrowded.

In many parts of the park, notably Main Camp, overcrowding has reached a critical level. The carrying capacity – as measured in terms of accommodation and access – has been reached. However, it would be possible to develop new areas in the park if investments in water resources and tourist infrastructure were made.

Financial constraints
Zimbabwe has always offered great value for money to the tourist. The underlying philosophy of the national parks in Zimbabwe is that the natural environment should be available free or at a nominal charge. Hence, admission rates to Hwange National Park have been well below that of comparable national parks in other countries. In order to increase the revenue from national parks, a two-tier pricing system was introduced in 1993, favouring Zimbabwe residents.

Hwange National Park generates income through entrance fees and accommodation fees, as well as indirectly through lodges, camps and

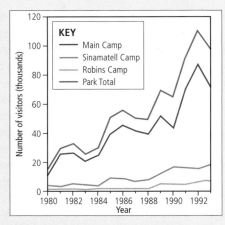

Figure 4.14 *Visitors to each camp in Hwange National Park, 1980-93*
Source: Potts, F. et al., People, wildlife and tourism in and around Hwange National Park, Zimbabwe, in Price, M., (ed.) 1996, People and tourism in fragile environments, Wiley

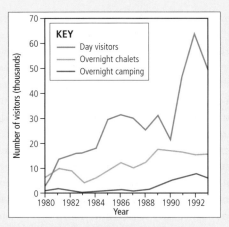

Figure 4.15 *Day and overnight visitors to Hwange National Park, 1980-93*
Source: Potts, F. et al., People, wildlife and tourism in and around Hwange National Park, Zimbabwe, in Price, M., (ed.) 1996, People and tourism in fragile environments, Wiley

operators who use the park throughout the year. HNP is one of Zimbabwe's most successful money earners. For example, in 1991-92 it earned 24% of the total revenue for the Parks and Wildlife Estate. However, the money earned goes to the government rather than to the National Parks Authority. In 1993-4 HNP earned £600 000. However, it received just £150 000 from the government to run the park: it is estimated that the park needs at least twice as much money to run effectively. This underfunding clearly underlies the problems of water supply, maintenance and overcrowding. With insufficient funding, facilities such as rest camps, picnic sites, viewing platforms and other park services have deteriorated. Many of these facilities are nearly forty years old and were designed to cope with a much smaller volume of tourists. In addition, underfunding has caused staff shortages, poor staff morale and a general decline in standards. If the park were allowed to retain the money it generated, it would be in a position to rectify some of its problems and plan for further development. But allowing the park to keep the money it generates is not something the socialist government of Zimbabwe is likely to

agree to – it may be seen as the 'thin end of the wedge' towards privatisation.

Tourism and rural communities
There is relatively little involvement of the local population in tourism. Most of the workers in Hwange National Park are drawn from a wide area and live in one of the three centres in the park. Most of the hotels, safari lodges and camps have been set up by companies and entrepreneurs from outside the area and, although they may employ some local people, it is relatively few. The financial benefit of the park for the local communities, an area of relatively sparse population, is therefore marginal.

Until the 1950s, Zimbabwe's conservation programme largely ignored local people's rights. The expropriation of land by the colonial government so that wildlife and landscapes could be preserved fuelled indigenous prejudices against wildlife. In addition, among farming communities, game animals were seen as a threat – they destroyed crops and killed livestock. Hence local people were more likely to be involved in culling and poaching and the destruction of habitat rather than involved in any wildlife conservation programme.

Zimbabwe introduced the CAMPFIRE programme (Communal Areas Management Programme for Indigenous Resources) to encourage local communities to conserve rather than exploit their wildlife resources. This is examined in detail in Chapter 8, 'Developing countries'. Hwange and the neighbouring Tsholotsho District have CAMPFIRE schemes. In Tsholtotsho, safari operators pay a concession fee to operate in the area and half of the trophy (game hunting) fees are paid to the ward (local area) in which the animal is shot. The money has been used to build schools, roads, a community hall and boreholes. Other spin-offs include the development of indigenous manufacturing. For example, Matupula Safaris encourages people from surrounding villages to bring crafts into the safari camp rather than taking visitors to Victoria Falls where there are a large number of souvenir stalls and shops. It is estimated that an average of £140 per tourist is spent in the local economy. Putting this in context, the average gross national product (GNP) per head in Zimbabwe is £1440.

By employing and training local people to work in the safari camps and sourcing supplies locally, the local economy expands. For example, old, lame or sick cows, goats and donkeys are bought as bait, thus turning something of little value into a resource for the safari industry. Safari hunting, mainly for elephant, earned the Tsholotsho district over £570 000 between 1990 and 1995. Between 1989 and 1992, 90% of total income to 12 CAMPFIRE districts in Zimbabwe came from hunting compared with 1% from other forms of tourism.

QUESTIONS

1 What are the main problems in Hwange National Park? How have they come about?

2 Comment on the way in which Hwange National Park is funded. How could the park derive more funding?

3 'Tourism should be spread throughout the park to avoid bottle-necks.' 'Tourism should be concentrated in small locations so that the rest of the park can be left free of tourist pressure and damage'. Evaluate these statements.

SUMMARY

In this chapter we have examined some of the many pressures facing wilderness areas. Much of the focus is upon the natural environment, and the examples from Antarctica, the Galapagos Islands and the Canadian Rocky Mountains illustrate the wide ranging nature of the problems. People living in wilderness areas may feel neglected by the tourist developments. This was true in the Galapagos as well as Hwange. Developing tourism may bring unwanted results – increased income inequalities in the Galapagos, increased land prices in Banff and an ecological headache trying to manage wildlife in Hwange. But for governments keen to increase their income, developing tourism is a very attractive proposition.

QUESTIONS

1 Wilderness areas should be protected at all costs. Discuss.
2 For a wilderness area you have studied, examine the impact of tourism.
3 'I should be allowed to visit any place I want.' Discuss.

WEB SITES

The virtual tourist -
  http://www.tourist.com
Friends of the Earth homepage -
  http://www.foe.co.uk
British Antarctic Survey -
  http://www.bas.nerc.ac.uk

BIBLIOGRAPHY AND RECOMMENDED READING

Jenner, P., & Smith, C., 1992, *The Tourism Industry and Environment, The Economist Special Report* 2453
Mathieson, A. and Wall, G., 1982, *Tourism economic, physical and social impacts,* Longman
Potts, F. et al., *People, wildlife and tourism in and around Hwange National Park, Zimbabwe,* in Price, M., (ed.) 1996, *People and tourism in fragile environments,* Wiley
World Trade Organisation/UNEP, 1992, *Guidelines for the Development of National Parks and Protected Areas for Tourism,* WTO/UNEP joint publication

Chapter 5
Urban and heritage tourism in developed countries

Nowhere is the distinction between tourism, recreation and leisure more blurred than in urban areas. Urban areas are important tourist destinations, but for their residents they offer recreational and leisure opportunities: tourists and residents share many of these facilities. In this chapter we examine the importance of urban tourism, the nature of urban attractions and the changing nature of urban holidays. Case studies from London, Venice and Oxford are used to show some of the range of issues in urban tourism; urban areas in developing countries are discussed in Chapter 7.

URBAN TOURISM

Urbanisation has been one of the most significant processes of the twentieth century. Urban areas are centres of population concentration and economic activity. They are also centres of a range of cultural and social activities, which offer opportunities for tourism, recreation and leisure. Large cities now constitute one of the most important types of tourist destination. Together with deindustrialisation and population dispersal, the development of tourism is one of the most important changes in large urban areas.

Urban tourism is important because urban areas are an increasingly important source of money, investment and employment in tourism. Urban areas are:

- gateways for tourist entry to the rest of the country
- centres of accommodation
- bases for excursions
- destinations in their own right.

Urban tourism is also a means of encouraging urban regeneration.

Research on tourism in urban areas is very limited and relates mostly to Europe and the United Kingdom. This research shows that it is difficult to distinguish between the tourist and non-tourist functions of a city. In addition to the tourist functions, the economic, commercial, residential and service functions of urban areas are widely used by tourists.

No two urban areas are identical. Urban areas vary in their nature, size, location, function, culture, heritage and environment. The attractions of London, Rome, Dublin and Paris – all European capital cities – are very different, as are the attractions of Oxford, Cambridge, and Heidelberg, all famous for their universities.

Cities that have a significant tourist function show some of the highest rates of urban growth. In Ireland, the tourist centre of Killarney experienced the fastest population growth in the 1990s, accompanied by a significant amount of industrial relocation and new industrial development. Similar growth was experienced in Atlanta, USA (see pages 91-2). These towns and cities do not just provide functions for the resident population, but also for visitors' recreation and leisure. As well as the growth of basic (essential) services such as education, health and housing, there is growth in the non-basic (export) services such as hotels, restaurants and clubs which cater for the tourists. These bring outside money into the area.

There are a large number of urban tourist destinations:

- capital cities, such as London, Paris, New York, and cultural capitals such as Rome (Figure 5.1)
- walled historic cities, such as Canterbury, Chester and York and small fortress cities, such as Dubrovnik in the former Yugoslavia
- university towns, such as Oxford and Cambridge
- cultural and art centres, such as Stratford-upon-Avon (Figure 5.2), Kyoto (Figure 5.3), Rome (Figure 5.4), Florence and Venice
- inner city areas, such as Castlefield and Salford Quays, Manchester and Spitalfields, London
- revitalised waterfront areas, including London Docklands and Salford Quays, Manchester
- industrial cities, such as 19th century Bradford
- seaside resorts, such as Brighton and Nice, France
- winter sports areas, such as Nagano, Japan
- tourist entertainment complexes, such as Disneyland, Paris, and Las Vegas
- specialist tourist service centres, including spas and pilgrimage destinations such as Bath and Lourdes, France.

Figure 5.1 The Coliseum, Rome

Figure 5.2 *Visitors at a cultural site, Stratford-upon-Avon*

Figure 5.3 *Urban cultural tourism, and 'wilderness', Kyoto, Japan. Kyoto was the home of the Japanese emperors from the eighth century to the nineteenth century. It is famous for its temples, shrines and 'wilderness' areas. It has over 1500 temples and 200 Shinto shrines, three palaces and nine museums*

The scale of urban tourism is thought to be immense, but unquantifiable. This is because of the difficulty of separating tourist-related activities from a host of other activities, which may or may not be carried out by tourists (see Figure 5.13 on page 71). These include:

● shopping
● sport and leisure
● relaxation
● entertainment
● visiting family and friends
● social interaction
● educational opportunities.

Any visit is likely to be the result of a combination of factors and it is often very difficult to determine a single purpose. For example, it is difficult to distinguish between religious visitors and cultural visitors to places such as Rome.

Figure 5.4 *St Peter's Square in Rome – a tourist 'honeypot', Rome is the most important tourist city in Italy, and one of Europe's finest. It contains a myriad of churches and museums. It is renowned for its architecture and its art collections.*

URBAN TOURISM AND LEISURE – A HIERARCHY

One of the most frequently-used models in human geography is that of **central place theory**. This states that there is a hierarchy of settlements, based on the number and range of services provided at each settlement. Low order settlements provide a small number of low order goods and services (such as newsagents and petrol stations) whereas settlements at the top of the hierarchy provide a wide range of high order goods and services (such as banks, solicitors, hotels, theatres and cinemas) as well as a large number of low order goods and services. Thus, low order settlements have a low range (people will not travel far to obtain these services) and a low threshold population (the number of people required to maintain these services). By contrast, large urban areas have a very high range and a large threshold population. This model has also been applied to the provision of leisure and recreational services (Figure 5.5).

International tourist cities
(e.g. London)

National and international tourist cities (e.g. Stratford-on-Avon)

Regional leisure and tourist cities (e.g. Manchester)

Local leisure towns and cities (e.g. Bedford)

Figure 5.5
The leisure-tourism urban hierarchy
Source: Carr, M., 1997, New patterns: process and change in human geography, Nelson

Hierarchy level	Rank	City	Visitor nights (million)
International	1	London	67.6
National or regional	2	Edinburgh	5.5
	3	Glasgow	3.0
	4	Oxford	2.7
	5	Birmingham	2.6
	5	Brighton/Hove	2.6
	7	Cambridge	2.5
	7	Manchester	2.5
	9	Bournemouth	1.9
	10	Bristol	1.4
	11	York	1.3
	12	Bath	1.2
	12	Liverpool	1.2

Figure 5.6 *Hierarchy of UK cities in order of visitor nights (1993)*
Source: British Tourist Authority, quoted in Carr, M., 1997, New patterns: process and change in human geography, Nelson

Figure 5.7 *The centre of Oxford from the air – a world-famous tourist attraction*

At the top of the hierarchy, the primary level, are international tourist cities such as London and Paris. These attract many millions of people annually (Figure 5.6) and serve a densely populated and large hinterland or sphere of influence. Large numbers of people commute to work in these cities and take part in many of their leisure and recreational activities there. In addition, these cities receive many international visitors.

The second level includes cities and towns of national and regional importance. Many of these, such as Stratford-upon-Avon, Oxford (Figure 5.7), Edinburgh, Bath and Cambridge in the UK, have special attractions. The third level features those with a regional hinterland, such as Birmingham. They lack the 'international appeal' of places such as York and Bath, although they are larger in size. Finally, there are a large number of large towns or small cities, such as Reading and Bradford for example, which serve a mostly local market.

The larger cities are more likely to offer specialist attractions such as national museums, galleries and zoos (Figure 5.8), whereas the local centres offer less specialised facilities,

Figure 5.8 *London Zoo – an example of a specialist attraction normally found only in large cities*

such as a recreation ground, a country park, multiplex cinema and bowling alley. These are the facilities we would expect to find in most urban centres and they cater largely for the resident population rather than attracting visitors from far away.

Figure 5.9 shows the distribution of leisure facilities around a typical small- or medium-sized town. In many small- and medium-sized cities there is a concentration of leisure facilities and tourist attractions in the central area of the city, as well as on the periphery where there are increasing numbers of sports and leisure centres and country parks. The central area (CBD) contains the main concentration of restaurants, cinemas, theatres and other facilities that do not require much space (Figure 5.10). Finally, there may be some leisure facilities dispersed into suburbs, such as parks, recreation grounds and community centres (Figure 5.11). In the 'internationally' and 'nationally' important cities, where tourist numbers are important, there is a different pattern (Figure 5.12).

Figure 5.9 *A model of tourism provision in a small city*
Source Carr, M., 1997, New patterns: process and change in human geography, Nelson

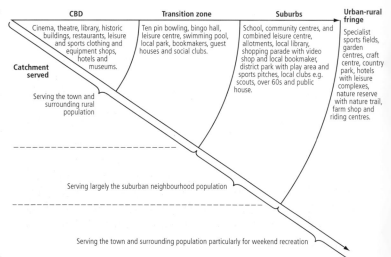

Figure 5.10 Leisure facilities in the city centre

Figure 5.11 Leisure facilities in a neighbourhood part of a city

Figure 5.12 Leisure facilities on the edge of town

THE TOURISM BUSINESS DISTRICT

In most urban areas it is possible to analyse the distribution of tourist activities and facilities and to analyse the supply of tourism services in a city. This analysis follows the ecological approach of land use patterns in a city (such as Burgess's model, see Chapter 1 in *Changing Settlements* of the city is often referred to as the RBD (recreational business district) or the TBD (tourist business district). In European cities, the tourist business district and the central business district often coincide in heritage areas. Indeed, it is often very difficult to separate the tourist business district from the CBD (Figure 5.13). It is also very difficult to differentiate the visitor-orientated services from the services that are offered to local residents (Figure 5.13).

Figure 5.13 a) The attractions, functions and services of a tourist business district *b)* Model of urban hotel location in West European cities
Source: Page, S., 1996, Urban Tourism, Routledge

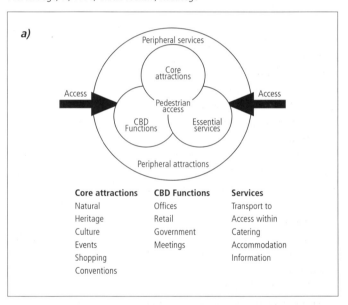

Core attractions
Natural
Heritage
Culture
Events
Shopping
Conventions

CBD Functions
Offices
Retail
Government
Meetings

Services
Transport to
Access within
Catering
Accommodation
Information

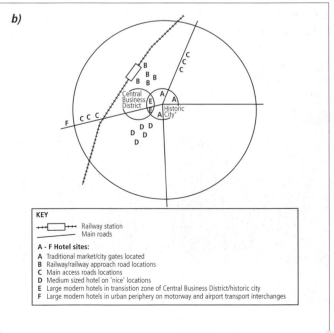

KEY
⊢⊢⊢□⊢⊢⊣ Railway station
———— Main roads

A - F Hotel sites:
A Traditional market/city gates located
B Railway/railway approach road locations
C Main access roads locations
D Medium sized hotel on 'nice' locations
E Large modern hotels in transistion zone of Central Business District/historic city
F Large modern hotels in urban periphery on motorway and airport transport interchanges

Tourist facilities provided in urban areas include accommodation, catering and shopping. Most tourist accommodation is found in urban areas, and a good urban infrastructure and accessibility is an important consideration in the location of hotels and guest houses.

Catering facilities for tourists are found in restaurants, cafes, public houses, bars, clubs, hotels and other forms of tourist accommodation. Over £2 billion each year is spent by tourists on eating and drinking in the UK.

Shopping and tourism often go hand in hand. In a survey carried out by the Historic Towns Forum, 75% of visitors combined tourism and shopping. However, not every city has the potential to be promoted for tourism as well as shopping: historic cities have a much greater attraction in terms of the built environment. City authorities have responded in a number of ways to make urban environments appealing:

- establishing pedestrian precincts
- managing parking problems and developing park and ride schemes to improve access
- marketing the destination
- investing in new and attractive indoor shopping galleries.

In the same survey, other factors which were considered to be important in attracting tourist-shoppers were:

- the cleanliness of the town
- well maintained pedestrian areas and pavements
- natural features such as rivers and parks
- architecture and shop fronts
- street furniture
- town centre activities such as live entertainment or outdoor markets.

The distinction between tourism, recreation and other activities is becoming increasingly unclear in the retail sector (see *Changing Settlements* in this series for a detailed discussion of the subject). For example, shopping for low order goods such as bread and newspapers would not normally be considered as part of the tourist infrastructure but many newsagents and small shops in tourist areas sell postcards, maps and souvenirs. At the other end of the retail scale, the growth of hypermarkets and out-of-town shopping centres is mixing food retailing with leisure facilities such as multiplex cinemas, restaurants, play areas and so on. For example, the Merry Hill shopping centre at Dudley in the West Midlands is the most popular tourist attraction in the Midlands.

One of the last out-of-town shopping centres to be built in Britain, following the government's decision to prevent further such developments, is the £1.2 billion Bluewater shopping and leisure centre at Dartford in Kent (Figure 5.14). When opened in 1999, it became the largest shopping centre in Europe. On a 110 hectare site, it contains the largest winter garden (glass-covered lounging area, with flowers) built this century and the largest new park in Kent.

Bluewater has about 10 million people living within one hour's drive: it is estimated that they spend some £5.5 billion annually. What makes Bluewater unusual, apart from its sheer scale, is the mix of retail outlets. As well as Marks and Spencer, John Lewis, House of Fraser and other high street stores, it also contains speciality up-market shops such as the Australian men's outfitters R M Williams. The centre has a range of restaurants from McDonald's to a five-star restaurant, and there are male 'creches' with beer, television and sport to attract reluctant male shoppers. The centre is open from 10 a.m. to 9 p.m. with the restaurants open until 11 p.m. so that it is possible to see a film in the evening and then dine in one of the restaurant afterwards.

Figure 5.14 *Bluewater retail and leisure centre at Dartford in Kent*

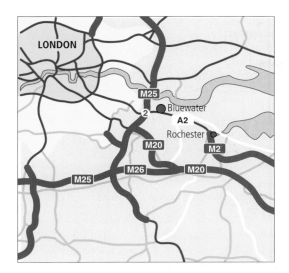
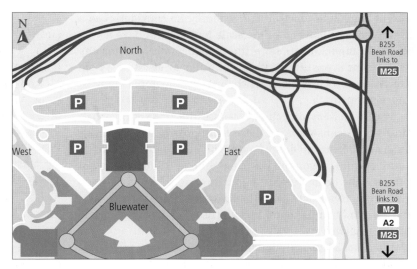

Figure 5.15 *The location of the Bluewater retail and leisure centre, Kent Source: Financial Times, 1998*

The developers predicted that people would visit the centre on account of its architecture, its lakes, the gardens and its walks as well as its shops. It is not yet known what long-term effect it will have on the Medway towns. The developers claim that Bluewater is not competing with town centres but with London's West End and other major regional shopping centres, such as Lakeside Thurrock (Figure 5.15). The projected 80 000 shoppers a day will increase the amount of traffic on the road to new heights.

Inset 3.1
The rise of professional women

In 1966, 42.2% of women of working age were in employment. By 1996 this had increased to 67%. Single professional women:

- are likely to have an active social life
- regularly go to the theatre and cinema
- actively participate in sport (67% compared with 50% of married women)
- eat out regularly
- go to the pub regularly (41% compared with 14% of women with children).

The number of single professional and managerial women aged 25 to 44 is rapidly increasing and their work patterns and lifestyles will have an increasing impact on demands for leisure, retailing and housing.

THE EFFECTS OF URBAN TOURISM

Urban tourism produces at least three types of employment:

- direct employment in tourist establishments
- indirect employment in the tourism supply sector
- 'multiplier' employment or additional employment as the locally employed population spend their money earned from tourism in the local economy.

There are social and cultural effects arising from the way in which tourism causes changes in values, behaviour, family relationships, lifestyles, and moral conduct.

Three factors can be examined:

- tourists – their demand for services, their attitudes, expectations and activities
- hosts – especially their role and attitude towards the provision of services for tourists
- the relationship between tourists and hosts and the type of contact between them (see Figure 1.29 on page 22, Doxey's index of irritation).

In a study of Queenstown, New Zealand, with a population of under 2000 and over 180 000 visitors each year, tourism was considered to have had the following effects:

- the pace of life quickened
- some people adapted to the new pace of life whereas others withdrew from the situation
- there was a limited range of low-cost entertainment, such as cinemas, of a suitable nature for local people
- the pressures associated with the number of people and vehicles in the central area of the city intensified – increased congestion and pollution
- there were more transient people (seasonal workers as well as tourists) making it difficult to establish stable social relationships
- there were high costs associated with the provision of public utilities.

The impact of tourism can generally be considered as a continuum. At one end of the scale tourism can have a very positive impact, such as in the regeneration of inner city waterfront areas. By contrast, in other areas such as old coastal resorts and historic urban areas, the impact may be more negative.

It can be very difficult to assess the impact of urban tourism because, firstly, there is often very little baseline information on the condition of the environment prior to tourism, and, secondly, it can be difficult to identify what effects have been caused by tourism and what have been caused by other activities. However, it is possible to examine certain environmental impacts of tourism (Figure 5.16). These include:

- the effect of air pollution on historic buildings
- urban sprawl in the absence of development restrictions
- insufficient transport infrastructure
- segregation of tourists from local residents
- pollution of local ecosystems from sewage, litter and too many people.

Figure 5.16 *The impact of tourism on the urban environment*
Source Page, S., 1996, Urban tourism, Routledge

Physical environment:
- land lost through development which may have been used for agriculture
- change to the hydrological system

Visual amenity
- expansion of the built area
- the effect of new architectural styles
- population growth, and therefore more houses

Infrastructure
- overloading the urban infrastructure with the utilities and developments:
  - roads
  - railways
  - car parking
  - electricity grid
  - waste disposal and water supply
- provision of new infrastructure

Urban form
- changes to the land use as tourist accommodation such as hotels and boarding houses develop
- alterations to the urban fabric (environment and infrastructure) from pedestrianisation and traffic management schemes
- changes to the built environment lead to contrasts between the quality of the urban areas used by tourists and the quality of residential areas

Restoration
- the reuse of redundant buildings
- the restoration and preservation of historic sites and buildings

---

QUESTIONS

1 What are the characteristics of the tourist business district?

2 Explain the meaning of the following terms: 'hierarchy', 'hinterland', 'tourist infrastructure'.

3 What are the benefits of urban tourism?

4 What are the environmental effects of urban tourism?

SHORT BREAKS

Short breaks are the backbone of a thriving and increasingly competitive market. Short breaks are those which involve less than 5 nights away from home. Many of these breaks are to cities – city breaks – but there are also short breaks for activities such as skiing – these are commonly Friday to Monday breaks. Other short breaks are to attractions such as Center Parcs and Oasis, which may run from Monday to Friday or Friday to Monday. Cities such as Krakow and Dresden have become 'fashionable' and have joined a growing number of cities keen to exploit this rapidly-growing sector. Nevertheless, despite an increase in the number of short-break destinations, Paris remains the most popular city for short breaks outside the UK (Figure 5.17).

The value of the UK market for short breaks abroad has grown from £611 million in 1992 to over £900 million in 1997 (Figure 5.18). While still only a small proportion of the holiday market, short breaks could account for up to 11.5% of all holidays taken abroad by the end of 1999. Increasingly, larger holiday operators, such as Thomas

City	Visitor nights (million)
London	20
Paris	16
Rome	5.6
Madrid	5.5
Athens	4.7
Vienna	4.6
Munich	2.6
Amsterdam	2.5
Brussels	2.4
Copenhagen	2.1

Figure 5.17 *International visitor nights in major European cities*
Source: Page, S., 1996, Urban tourism, Routledge/Financial Times September, 1997

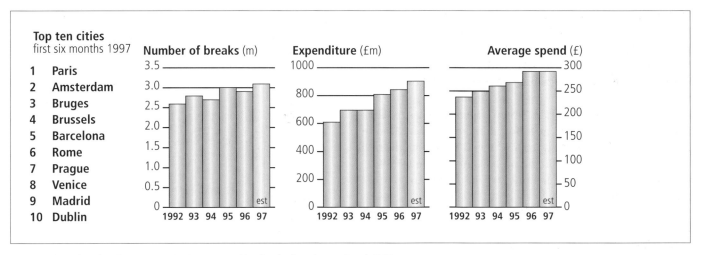

Figure 5.18 *Short breaks in Europe in the ten top cities for the first six months of 1997*
Source: Page, S., 1996, Urban tourism, Routledge/ Financial Times September 1997

Figure 5.19
Social class Source:
Economist, January 1998

Cook, are waking up to the attractions of the short breaks market, particularly to fill aircraft outside peak holiday periods.

French cities and Disneyland Paris have accounted for much of the growth in the UK market in short breaks in recent years. A number of factors have helped this increase:

- favourable economic conditions including a strong pound
- windfall gains from the conversion of building societies
- recession and high mortgage repayments mean that some people cannot afford a long holiday and so take a short break instead
- opening of the Channel Tunnel in 1994
- special promotions offered by hotels to increase off-season occupancy rates
- changes in holiday habits.

The Channel Tunnel has opened up a large new market. Initially the novelty factor was part of its attraction, but the tunnel operators now stress its convenience. Up to 20% of passengers who previously travelled from the UK to Paris by air now travel by Eurostar. The Channel Tunnel has given access to new markets such as Lille, and helped to regenerate older cities such as Bruges and Brussels.

Changes in holiday habits have also helped the short breaks market, which has traditionally appealed to well-off young couples, or couples whose children have grown up: more people have been taking two- or three-days holidays to avoid taking a week off work. In the UK, people in social categories A and B (managerial and professional occupations) (Figure 5.19) account for 40% of the market for short breaks and visits to heritage and cultural attractions. Although their leisure time may be limited, these groups generally have the highest salaries and can afford second and third holidays. Since the 1980s, urban areas in Europe have certainly benefited from the growth in short break hol-

Most social groupings include:	
A	Higher managerial, administrative or professional
B	Middle managerial, administrative or professional
C1	Supervisory, clerical or managerial
C2	Skilled manual workers
D	Semi and unskilled manual workers
E	Pensioners, the unemployed, casual or lowest grade workers

	1989	1991	1993	1995
Million breaks				
UK cities	1.8	2.1	2.9	3.3
Foreign cities	0.6	0.7	0.8	1.0
Total volume	2.4	2.8	3.7	4.3
Expenditure £ million				
UK cities	190	230	300	390
Foreign cities	170	195	250	290
Total value	360	425	550	680

Figure 5.20 *The city breaks market, 1991-95*
Source: adapted from New leisure markets, 1996, Special interest tourism, New Leisure Markets

idays from the UK of people from categories A and B.

City breaks to UK cities taken by UK tourists consist of 3.3 million visits and sales of over £390 million (Figure 5.20). This compares with sales of £290 for the foreign market. However, average spending on a domestic break is £120 compared with £300 on a foreign trip.

Short breaks in London

The Channel Tunnel has made it easier for tourists attracted by London's popular image to get there – and easier for them to get away again. It has exacerbated a growing trend for more tourists to spend less time and less money in the city. London is the dominant city-break destination in the UK, with over 40% of the market. Other important cities include Edinburgh, York, Oxford and Bournemouth. About 27 million tourists visited London in 1997, more than half from overseas. This is roughly a 50% increase over 1992; but the £8 billion spent is only 39% higher than in 1992 (Figure 5.21).

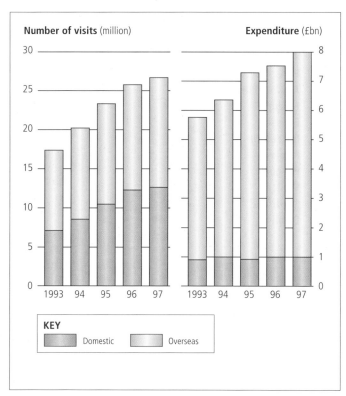

Figure 5.21 *London as a tourist attraction*
Source: Economist, January 1998

Figure 5.22 *London as a tourist attraction*

The growth of tourism spending in London – at 5 % a year – trails the world average of 8%. It mirrors a similar underperformance by the UK. London, like many large cities, relies heavily on tourist spending for much of its economic well-being (Figure 5.22). Up to 7% of London's GDP comes from tourism.

One in three of the 12 million theatre tickets sold in the West End in 1997 went to a foreign visitor; another third went to UK tourists. A third of West End shopping is done by overseas visitors, who also account for 35% of spending in the capital's restaurants.

Planners want to increase the contribution of tourism to London's economy from 7% to 20%. They want to persuade visitors to stay longer than the current average of four to five days, so that they spend more money. However, to achieve its full tourist potential, London needs better public transport and good-value hotels outside the West End tourist hot-spots. Up to half the tourists staying in hotels at the bottom end of the market complain about the quality of London hotels (Figure 5.23). American visitors, in particular, are often shocked to find that spending £80-£100 a night on a room does not necessarily guarantee them room service or en suite bathroom facilities.

In addition, if more is to be earned from tourism, London will have to target higher spending visitors. Long-distance tourists, particularly from Asia and the USA, tend to stay longer and spend more than those from mainland Europe. In 1997, Japanese tourists spent an average of £467 per visit compared with £190 by French tourists. The number of Japanese visitors, while growing rapidly, was still only 4% of overseas visitors and this proportion is likely to fall due to the collapse of the Japanese currency in 1998.

As well as persuading high spending tourists to come to London from further afield, there is also a push for them to visit less well-known parts of the city. More than 50% of tourists to London have been before, so recent tourist board campaigns have concentrated on promoting more out-of-the-way attractions, such as the Globe Theatre in Southwark and East End street markets (Figure 5.22).

Still missing from London's attractions are grand projects such as those in Paris – the Pompidou Centre, Paris's most-visited attraction, or the renovated Musee D'Orsay. Funding from the UK's National Lottery is slowly changing this, with a number of new projects, such as the Tate Gallery of Modern Art at Bankside, Southwark, and the Millennium Dome at Greenwich.

Moreover, London has described itself as the Millennium City with over £6 billion invested in attractions to mark the year 2000. The city is aiming for 31 million visitors in 2000 compared with 28 million in 1997, and expects them to generate over £10 billion. The Millennium marketing campaign is targeted mainly at high-spending visitors – those from the USA and the over 50s from Western Europe. New attractions to be marketed include the world's highest ferris wheel on the South Bank, the Vinopolis wine park in Southwark and the Tate Gallery of Modern Art at Bankside. To accommodate the extra visitors, 20 000 extra hotels beds will be required.

Figure 5.23 London – such views can prove expensive for tourists

QUESTIONS

1 What is meant by the term 'short breaks'? Why are they becoming increasingly popular for (i) tourists and (ii) tourist operators?

2 Suggest reasons why Paris is the most popular destination for short breaks for UK residents, and why London is a popular destination for UK and overseas visitors.

3 Why is tourism important to London?

4 Suggest reasons why the amount of money spent by tourists in London is declining relative to the growth in tourist numbers.

HERITAGE TOURISM IN THE UK

Heritage tourism is very important in the UK. The number of people visiting historic monuments, such as houses, churches and castles, rose to 59 million in 1997, providing a revenue of about £244 million. Overall visitor numbers increased by 2% on 1996. The highest increase (47%) was at Walmer Castle, Kent, where a new garden in honour of the Queen Mother was opened. Tourists to historic properties respond strongly to new attractions or media exposure. For example, admissions to Osborne House, Queen Victoria's family home on the Isle of Wight, increased by 30% between 1996 and 1997; the house was used in the filming of the film 'Mrs Brown'.

Historic properties are hugely popular with UK and foreign visitors alike. Up to 37% of foreign visitors cited visiting historic buildings as a reason for choosing a holiday in the UK and 32% of adults in the UK have visited a historic building in the previous 12 months (*The Guardian*, 1998). This is far more than the number who visited theme parks, galleries and museums. Visits to historic monuments are undertaken on 19% of long holiday trips, while museums and art galleries are visited on 9% of long holidays. Visitor numbers are increasing, despite admission prices rising faster than the rate of inflation.

The typical visitor to historic buildings is in their late 40s or early 50s and drawn from the top two social classes, A and B. Historic buildings are a huge money spinner. The £244 million spent on admission prices is only a tiny fraction

of the money generated in this sector. For example, the borough of Windsor and Maidenhead, with Windsor Castle as its main attraction, calculates that the tourist trade is worth over £150 million annually and generates 5000 jobs.

Many of these heritage sites are located in urban areas: there are now 58 'historic towns' each attracting more than 20 000 stays of one night or longer. In 1998, Whitby and Falmouth joined the list of historic towns which includes Woodstock (Figure 5.24), Bath and York. Whitby joined for its ruins – the ruins of Whitby Abbey (the setting for part of the novel 'Dracula'), Falmouth for Pendennis Castle, built by Henry VIII and the Church of King Charles the Martyr.

Figure 5.24 Heritage tourism – Woodstock, Oxfordshire. Blenheim Palace, and Lake, built for John Churchill, the First Duke of Marlborough

Tower of London	2.6 million
Canterbury Cathedral	1.6 million
Windsor Castle	1.1 million
St. Paul's Cathedral	964 73
Bath, Roman Bath Museum	933 489
Warwick Castle	789 000
Stonehenge	772 963
Hampton Court Palace	643 226
Leeds Castle, Kent	584 670
Chatsworth House, Derbyshire	489 672

Figure 5.25
Most visited sites in the UK, 1997 – admission charged
Source: The Guardian, July 1998

Westminster Abbey	2.5 million
York Minster	2.0 million
Chester Cathedral	1.0 million
Salisbury Cathedral	600 000
Norwich Cathedral	550 000
Durham Cathedral	495 000
Exeter Cathedral	400 000
Gloucester Cathedral	400 000
Westminster Cathedral	400 000
Lincoln Cathedral	375 000

Figure 5.27
Sites with greatest increase in visitor numbers, 1996-9
Source: The Guardian, July 1998

	Number of visitors	Percent increase
Walmer Castle, Kent	59 121	47
Kingston Lacy, Dorset	122 736	42
Eastnor Castle, Ledbury	46 778	40
Hardwick Hall, Chesterfield	102 042	38
Carlisle Castle, Cumbria	77 145	36
Osborne House, Isle of Wight	250 310	30
Hardwick Old Hall, Chesterfield	38 999	27
Aston Hall, Birmingham	43 946	26
Wimpole Hall, Cambridgeshire	78 619	24
Harewood House, Leeds	311 119	23

Figure 5.26 *Most visited sites in the UK, 1997 – free admission Source: The Guardian, July 1998*

QUESTIONS

1 Put the attractions listed in Figures 5.25, 5.26 and 5.27 into categories such as religious attractions, historic attractions, stately homes and so on. (N.B. An attraction can exist in more than one category.) What is the category with the greatest number of entries? How many of the most visited attractions listed in Figures 5.25 to 5.27 are in urban areas? What is the main characteristic of the attractions listed in Figure 5.27?

2 Why do visitor numbers at historic attractions vary so much from year to year? Give examples to support your answer.

Case study:
Tourism in Oxford

Oxford (Figure 5.28) is world famous as a historic university city. Although Oxford is not heavily promoted as a tourist destination, it attracts a large number of tourists both from within the UK and abroad. Outside London, Oxford is one of the most important visitor destinations in the UK, attracting over 5 million visitors in 1996. Tourism is an important source of employment in Oxford, providing over 7300 full-time jobs.

The most recent in-depth survey of tourists to Oxford was the 1996 Oxford Visitor Survey. Most of the people surveyed intended to visit one or more of Oxford's attractions during their visit. The most popular attractions included the Botanic Gardens (Figure 5.29), the Oxford Story and the Ashmolean Museum. A number of other attractions included Blackwell's

Figure 5.28 *Publicity material from Oxford City Council showing the location of Oxford in relation to transport links and other popular tourist places Source: Oxford City Council, 1998*

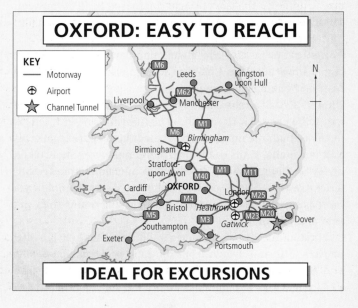

Figure 5.29 *The Botanic Gardens*

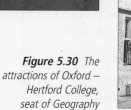

Figure 5.30 *The attractions of Oxford – Hertford College, seat of Geography*

Bookshop, the Old Bodleian Library, the Sheldonian Theatre and Carfax Tower, with its views over the Oxford rooftops. Nearly half of the visitors visited one or more of the university colleges (Figure 5.30); the three most popular choices were Christ Church, Magdalene and New College.

The results of the 1996 survey showed that in one year over 750 000 overnight trips were spent in Oxford, of which 79% were made by domestic visitors and 21% by overseas visitors. These amounted to over 3.5 million bed nights spent in the city, 50% by UK visitors and 50% by overseas visitors. In addition, a further 2.28 million day trips were made to Oxford (both domestic and overseas). Between them these trips generated £185 million spent directly in the tourist sector; with linkages and multiplier effects the value to the city's economy was about £258 million. The number of jobs sustained directly and indirectly by tourism is estimated at about 7300, or 3-4% of the economically active population in the Oxford region.

Over half of the visitors to Oxford were coming to the city for a holiday (51%). A significant number of others were using the city for business trips (7%), as language students (7%) and education (3%).

Most of the groups visiting Oxford were adult-only (85%), and a very high proportion were from the highest social groups. Eighty per cent of UK visitors were in social groups A, B and C1 compared to a national average of about 45%.

Most of the overseas visitors were from Western Europe (44%), North America (18%) and Asia and the Far East (8%). Day-visitors were drawn from a wide range of locations such as London (20%), Buckinghamshire (13%) but also Yorkshire-Humberside (4%) and the North West (4%). Most of the day visitors on holiday were staying in London.

Most of the people visiting the city arrived by car (45%) although quite a large proportion used public transport (36%). Most of those using the Park and Ride schemes considered them to be 'very good' in terms of availability of spaces, levels of charges, frequency of services and overall convenience.

The survey also investigated visitors' views and opinions on the tourist experience in Oxford. Most were very happy with the range and quality of places to visit, eat and drink and the range of shops in the city. Other comments included the attractiveness of the architecture (30%), the history of the city (17%), and the colleges (14%) as well as the nightlife and general atmosphere. However, traffic levels in the city, in particular the number of coaches and buses, the availability and cleanliness of toilets, pedestrian sign-posting and the range, standard and value for money of accommodation were not viewed as favourably. In terms of improvements, visitors said that there was too much traffic (22%), that the city was overcrowded (9%) and too expensive (5%).

The Oxford Tourism Strategy

The Oxford Tourism Strategy is to ensure visitor satisfaction, encourage an increase in tourism spending within the city and minimise the environmental problems which result from tourism. In particular, the Strategy aims to:

- provide a larger coach park and enforce on-street parking regulations (Figure 5.31)
- increase the use of public transport and Park and Ride as a means of getting into the city; as part of the publicity material that Oxford City Council send out, there are maps which show the Park and Ride locations, the major coach routes and the main bus routes (Figure 5.32)
- encourage walking tours, registered sightseeing buses and cycles

- provide comprehensive on-street information (Figure 5.33) to encourage visits to lesser known attractions and places of interest
- liaise with foreign language schools about the congestion and conflict their students cause
- increase the number of off-season visitors in order to spread the tourist load
- reinvest money generated by tourism into the fabric, infrastructure and facilities of the city, to support long-term sustainability.

There are several areas where the returns from tourism could be increased. For example, Oxford City Council is targeting high spending visitors who stay overnight. These visitors bring more money to the city and create more jobs, for example in accommodation and catering, than coach visitors stopping off en route to Woodstock or Stratford- upon-Avon, who spend little time or money in the city. The Council is trying to attract

independent day visitors not on coach trips, and business visitors. The Oxford colleges are free of university students during the University vacation and this provides an ideal opportunity to use the accommodation for conference delegates. In addition, given the number of visitors to Blenheim Palace, Woodstock, the Cotswolds and Stratford-upon-Avon, Oxford could market itself as a centre for visitors to these attractions, providing them with accommodation and varied evening entertainment.

The Oxford Tourist Strategy attempts to enhance the visitor experience. For example, the Oxford Information Centre attracts up to 500 000 people annually, making it one of the most visited places in Oxford! It is vital for visitor satisfaction that the Information Centre is able to meet demand and provide the information required. Other key locations for the provision of information are the railway station, the Gloucester Green coach and bus station

Figure 5.31 *Congestion in Oxford caused by coaches*

(Figure 5.36), Oxpen coach park and the Park and Rides. This ties in with the aim of getting people to visit the city by using public transport.

Information is also provided on the on-street information boards and there has been a improvement in the sign-posting of attractions (Figure 5.37). Signposting has a

Figure 5.32 *Promoting public transport – facilities in Oxford for coach, bus and car*
Source: Oxford City Council

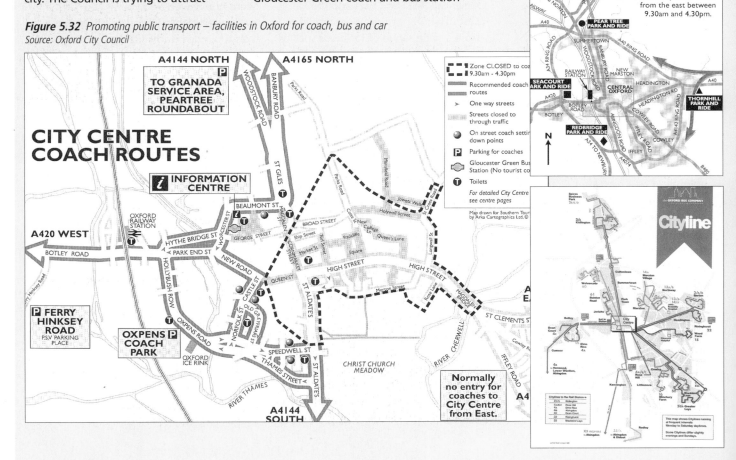

Figure 5.34 *Oxford tourist information centre*

dual role, improving the quality of the tourist experience and giving good publicity for the companies involved.

In addition, attractions need to be more varied. At present Oxford is famous for its university buildings, churches and colleges. This appeals to a particular type of visitor, but Oxford City Council are keen to provide more variety, to appeal to wider mix of people. However, there have been new tourist developments, such as the Oxford Story and Curioxity, which appeal to younger people and school groups, and new shopping developments which enhance Oxford's function as a regional shopping centre. The Riverside Walk, a walk from the Botanic Gardens around Christ Church Meadow (Figure 5.36), has a broad appeal for all age groups.

Better facilities are being provided for particular groups of people, notably the disabled. The include interpretive facilities, loop systems for the hard of hearing and ramps for people in wheel chairs.

Oxford County Council is particularly concerned to help the providers of tourist services, particularly the large number of small, independent businesses, many of which have only a few employees. Although managers in large companies can obtain advice from head office, independent businesses have very limited help. Their problems are many and range from the terms and conditions of their workforce (do Saturday staff and summer staff need a contract, for example), to practical issues such as the use of IT, recruitment and implementing sustainable practices. To help these businesses with the variety of problems they face, Oxford City Council will need to seek sponsorship for projects, such as improving IT skills, and attract additional external funding.

Figure 5.33 *On-street information board*

Figure 5.35 *Sign-posting of tourist attractions*

Figure 5.36 *Rowing during 'Eights Week' – part of the riverside walk*

QUESTIONS

1. Using examples, explain why tourism is important to Oxford.

2. What are the characteristics of (i) visitors to Oxford and (ii) the attractions they visit?

3. What main issues related to tourism need to be addressed in Oxford?

4. Evaluate the ways in which these issues are being tackled.

Case study:
Managing Blenheim Park

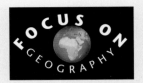

Managing Blenheim Park

Blenheim Palace and Park is an excellent example of a heritage site not located in an urban area. Away from the congested streets of Oxford, Blenheim Palace and Park are located in a semi-rural location 12 kilometres north of Oxford, next to the picturesque town of Woodstock (Figure 5.37). Blenheim Palace, home to the Duke of Marlborough, and Blenheim Park, were designated as a World Heritage Site in 1987, because of the palace, fine views and sweeping landscape. The park was designed by Capability Brown in the 1760s, and the Great Lake, formed by the damming of the River Glyme, forms the centre-piece of the parks landscape (Figure 5.38).

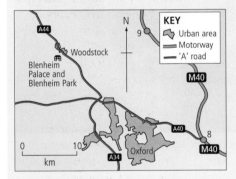

Figure 5.37 The location of Blenheim Palace and Park

Figure 5.38 The Lake, Blenheim Park

The management of the park into the twenty-first century requires considerable forward planning, especially as some of the tourist attractions are very old; yet the park is still a working farm, a nature reserve and a shooting ground.

At least three stages have been identified in the development of Blenheim Park. The first stage is the Roman-Britain stage with earthworks, crop marks, ancient boundaries and a Roman Road, Akeman Street. The second stage consists of remnants of the medieval Royal Park, used as a hunting ground by the Norman kings of England. Fifteenth- to eighteenth-century additions comprise the third stage – these make up the present park (Figure 5.39).

The present park was developed after Queen Anne made John Churchill the first Duke of Marlborough in 1705. Early designs for the park included the palace, a bridge, canals and cascades, and plantations. However, there was no overall cohesion to the design. This was to be provided by Capability Brown later in the century and it is his design that still forms the Blenheim landscape. His design includes the palace, the bridge, lakes, slopes, plantations of deciduous trees, copses, and the Column of Victory.

Problems of management

Some of the problems of managing Blenheim Palace and its lands have a very long history. For example, in the thirteenth century there was reference to the problem of maintaining the park wall. Maintaining the lake also has a long history and the dams that hold back the water in the lakes have to be continually checked and maintained.

In the 1970s, many of the plantations were affected by Dutch Elm disease, while beech bark disease affected many of the trees that had been planted in the 1700s. Given the nature of the trees, slow-maturing but long-living deciduous, it was difficult to replace them with any speed. Thus the decline of the elm and the beech had a negative impact on the visual quality of the park. At the end of the 1970s the current Duke of Marlborough and the Countryside Commission decided to introduce a Landscape Restoration Plan. The aim of the Plan was to retain and restore the historic aspects of the park, as well as promote the modern functions of tourism, farming, forestry and shooting. Later problems were unforeseen, such as the storms of 1987 and 1990, the dry summers of the 1980s and 1990s, and the introduction of grey squirrels: the dry years particularly affected beech trees since their shallow roots cannot tap deep water supplies, and the squirrels prevent natural regeneration of saplings by destroying them.

Figure 5.39 Land use on the Blenheim Estate
Source: Bond, J. and Tuler, K., 1997, Blenheim: landscape for a palace, Sutton

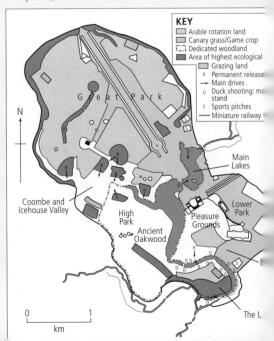

Although it would have been easy to find short-term solutions to the problems (such as planting quick-growing coniferous trees) it was decided to adopt a long-term strategy (Figure 5.40). For example, many of the trees in the park were of a similar age, being planted mostly in the 1700s, and would be felled between 2000 and 2010. More young trees were needed, which meant the selective felling of older trees and the planting of young saplings. Between 1981 and 1996, over 15 700 new trees were planted in Blenheim Park.

The current land use includes woodland, arable land, permanent pasture and the pleasure gardens. Agriculture dominates in the north and south-east of the park, while nature conservation dominates the south-west and the lakes. Part of the park contains remnants of oak woods from the mediaeval park, and this area has been designated as a Site of Special Scientific Importance (SSSI). Forestry is also important to Blenheim's economy. It has its own saw mill, which is self-financing. Most of the commercial forestry away from the main park involves coniferous trees, whereas closer to the tourist and sporting areas (pheasant shooting), deciduous trees are planted.

Tourism remains the most important function of the park. Blenheim Park attracts over 800 000 visitors each year. For this reason alone it is important to maintain the beauty of the park. Thus the management of the

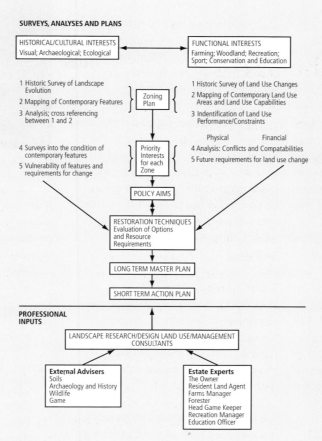

Figure 5.40 *The processes involved in implementing the Landscape Restoration Plan at Blenheim Park*
Source: Bond, J. and Tuler, K., 1997, Blenheim: landscape for a palace, Sutton

park has to reconcile the conflicting demands of users of the grounds. Decisions on the management are made by the Duke of Marlborough, the Land Agents (managers) of Blenheim Park, the Farms Manager, Forester, Head Game Keeper, Recreation Manager and Education Officer. As a result, the park has been

divided into eight land use zones (Figure 5.41):

- Great Park, where agriculture is the main function
- the main lakes and palace grounds, dominated by recreation
- the dry valleys, used for sport and recreation
- High Park, reserved for conservation, game and recreation
- Pleasure Grounds, assigned to recreation
- Lower Park, used for agriculture
- Bladon Park, mainly recreation and sport
- The Lince, used for sport and forestry.

Each of the zones is managed individually and there are different priorities for each zone. The principal objectives of the Restoration Plan are to:

- conserve the aesthetic quality of the park
- conserve historic and archaeological features
- integrate contemporary land use into the park
- maintain the character of each of the eight zones
- provide a long-term basis for landscape restoration.

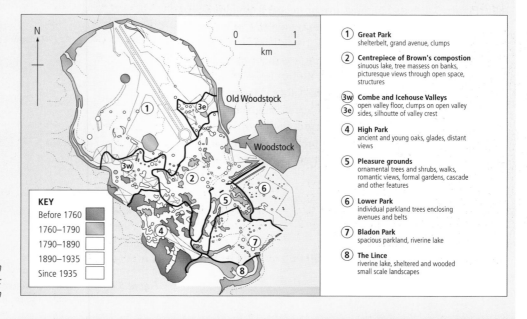

Figure 5.41 *The zoning plan at Blenheim*
Source: Bond, J. and Tuler, K., 1997, Blenheim: landscape for a palace, Sutton

The first phase of the Landscape Restoration Plan ran from 1981-1996 and the Second Phase runs from 1996 to 2011. Three main techniques are used for the restoration:

- natural regeneration – although this is difficult where there are many grazing animals. Many of the trees are very long living and regeneration proceeds slowly. For example, beech trees might be expected to live about 250 years while oak trees might live up to 500 years
- continuous replacement – whereby selective felling maintains a varied age-structure
- sequential replanting – this involves planting young, understudy tree groups approximately half-way through the life of the existing feature. Thus when the older trees die there are mature trees to replace them, rather than having to replant a whole area with new saplings.

On the western and eastern edges of the park, continuous replacement is used; in the High Park natural regeneration of oaks is encouraged; in the Great Park, clear felling of small clumps of trees on a 60-110 year rotation is to be used.

The Grand Avenue, planted with limes in the 1970s, will be replaced in the twenty-second and twenty-fourth centuries. A second avenue, on the outer edge of the Grand Avenue, is to be planted in the twenty-first century, and will require replanting in the twenty-third and twenty-fifth centuries!

Within the park there is also a 10-15 year short-term plan to maintain the environmental quality of the park. For example, intrusive vegetation is removed, so as to enhance good views, and cover is provided for game birds.

It is clear that for Blenheim Park, the detailed long-term planning that has taken place is an indication of the

Figure 5.42 Replanting is an essential part of management at Blenheim

importance of maintaining the visual quality of the park into the next century (Figure 5.42); tourism is seen as a vital part of the future prosperity of Blenheim.

QUESTIONS

1 Briefly describe the conflicting land uses in Blenheim Park.

2 Study Figure 5.42, which shows three approaches to the replanting of trees. Describe the differences between the three types. Which do you think is best, and why?

3 What main features of Blenheim Park have to be managed in order to promote tourism into the twenty-first century?

THE ENVIRONMENTAL IMPACT OF TOURISM IN VENICE

Venice is a world-famous tourist destination and an excellent example of a small historic city. It is located on a series of islands in a lagoon and is the capital of the Veneto region of Italy (Figure 5.43); its buildings are protected from alterations by government legislation. While the region has experienced massive economic growth since the 1960s, the city of Venice has experienced continued population loss during this period, falling from 175 000 in 1951 to 78 000 in 1990. Many of Venice's buildings are under constant threat from flooding, and in 1998 the Venice Flood Relief Scheme, which had been under discussion since the disastrous floods of 1966, was finally rejected because the government thought it would be ineffective. Thus, the city still has no effective flood relief scheme. Venice is suffering from:

- sinking ground level
- rising sea level
- pollution of the lagoon
- atmospheric pollution.

Tourist arrivals increased from 50 000 tourists in 1952 to

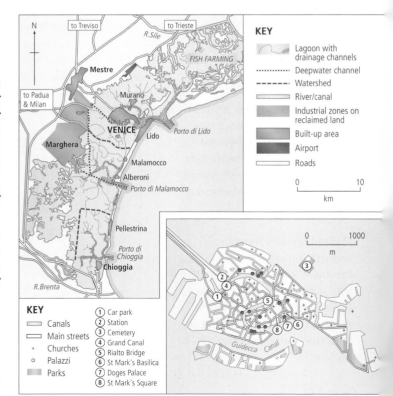

Figure 5.43 The location of Venice, 1995
Source: Page, S., 1996, Urban tourism, Routledge

1.13 million in 1987. Over the same period, the number of bed nights increased from 1.2 million to 2.49 million. These visitor numbers are swelled by day-trippers. In 1987, 4.9 million day-trippers visited Venice.

Venice's carrying capacity

As we saw in Chapter 1, the term 'carrying capacity' refers to the number of people that can supported in an environment without causing any long-term damage. Given the size of Venice (the historic centre of Venice comprises 700 hectares) and the conflict of interests between those employed in the tourist industry (and who seek to increase the number of tourists) and those not employed in the tourist industry (and who wish to keep visitor numbers down), it has been calculated (Canestrelli and Costa, 1991) that the optimum carrying capacity per day for Venice is 9780 tourists using hotel accommodation, 1460 tourists staying in non-hotel accommodation and 10 857 day trippers. This gives an annual total of over 8 million people. This is 25% greater than the number of tourists actually arriving in Venice.

However, the pattern of tourism is not even. There are clear seasonal variations, with an increase in visitor numbers in summer and at weekends. Research has estimated that an average of 37 500 day trippers a day visit Venice in August. A ceiling of 25 000 visitors (of all three categories) per day has been suggested as the maximum carrying capacity for Venice. (Optimum capacity suggests a more managed approach; maximum suggests a city bursting at the seams, with damage about to be caused.) The environmental and economic carrying capacity have different values (one concerned with preservation, the other with economic gain), but the 25 000 is a useful compromise between the economic capacity, which is higher, and the environmental, which is lower. Exceeding the carrying capacity has important implications for the environment and the long-term preservation of Venice. In 1987 the carrying capacity was exceeded on 156 days and on 22 occasions 40 000 visitors a day visited Venice. In fact there were over 60 000 visitors on six days.

The predictions for 2000 suggest an increase in the amount of tourist pressure on Venice. The carrying capacity of 25 000 visitors will be exceeded on 216 days and on 7 days the visitor numbers are predicted to exceed 100 000. When 100 000 visitors fill the city, for safety reasons the local police will be forced to close the bridge connecting the historic centre with the mainland.

The large volume of visitors who travel to Venice create a range of social and economic problems for planners (Figure 5.44). The negative externalities (negative costs such as congestion and inflated land prices that cannot be changed by one individual) of over-population stagnate the centre's economy and society through congestion and competition for scarce resources.

The proportion of visitors who are day trippers is increasing, while residential tourists are decreasing. This has resulted in a vicious circle of decline, as day-trippers, who contribute less to the local economy than resident visitors, replace the resident visitors, as it becomes less attractive to stay in the city, and cheaper to stay on the Lido. A number of measures have been made to control the influx of day trippers such as:

- denying access to the city by unauthorised tour coaches at the main coach terminal
- withdrawing Venice and Veneto region's bid for EXPO 2000.

Nevertheless, Venice continues to market itself, further alienating some of the local population

Venice is a small historic city at risk from a late twentieth century invasion by tourists and day-trippers. In this example, tourism has not been a stimulus for urban growth but has actually contributed to urban decline as the local population has continued to leave the city, leaving parts of some buildings empty. The excessive numbers of day trippers have also led to a deterioration in the quality of the tourist experience. This is significant in that it highlights problems affecting many historic cities around the world, especially those in Europe where there is a higher concentration. But it takes political will and a willingness to invest in the future to embark on a decision-making process which will address the pressures posed by tourism in Venice.

Figure 5.44 *Venice is low lying, sinking and at risk of rising sea levels.*

QUESTIONS

1 What does the term 'carrying capacity' mean?

2 What are the environmental implications of tourism in Venice?

Project Work

For an urban area near you, investigate the impact of tourism on the settlement. You could look at social, economic and environmental impacts. Social impacts include:
- the levels of irritation expressed by the host population
- the nature and scale of problems caused by tourism and tourists.

Economic questions include:
- the impact of tourism on small shopkeepers
- the importance of tourism to the local economy.

Environmental impacts include:
- overcrowding
- litter
- excess traffic (such as coaches).

A wide range of data can be collected. A questionnaire, such as that in Figure 5.45 can be used to ask residents about their views. It is important to design the questionnaire carefully (and to use a pilot study to assess its suitability). Care should also be taken to carry out the questionnaire in a variety of locations so as to get a representative cross-section of people.

Economic information is normally available from the local council. In addition, it may be possible to question specific businesses regarding the impact of tourism. Remember that getting information about money and profits is very sensitive and so you need to develop the questionnaire carefully.

Environmental impacts can be assessed by means of a questionnaire (Figure 5.46) or through an environmental quality index. This involves making a survey of the area and filling in a survey form as you proceed. The survey should be supported with annotated photographs – labelled to make very clear the point you wish the examiner to see.

Observations on the perceived quality of the environment
An environmental quality index provides a scale whereby a person rates the environmental quality from very good/attractive to very bad/unattractive. Although the scale is subjective, if the student compares two or more locations, using the same criteria, they can make value judgements about the quality of the environments and compare and contrast them.

Location: Time: Date:		
Best environment 1 2 3 4 5 6 7 8 Worst environment		
No congestion		Very congested
Plenty of parking		None available
Clean streets		Polluted streets
Many litter bins		No litter bins
Empty pavements		Congested pavements
Quiet		Noisy
No groups of people		Threatening 'gangs' of tourists

Figure 5.46 *A simple environmental survey*

Figure 5.45 *The impact of tourism – a simple questionnaire to residents*

Date and day: Time: Location of interview :			Interviewee:
Sex: Age: Place of residence:			Place of work:

Tourism brings a number of advantages to the town/city (name of settlement). How important do you think these advantages are?			
Very important	**Quite important**	**Important**	**Unimportant**
It creates many jobs			
It brings in a lot of money			
Local facilities are upgraded			
There are many spinoffs			
Any other advantages?			

Tourism brings a number of disadvantages to the town/city (name of settlement). How important do you think these disadvantages are?			
Very important	**Quite important**	**Important**	**Unimportant**
Congestion, especially coaches			
Lack of parking			
Congested streets			
Too many tourists			
Language students			
Litter			
Pollution			
Are there any other disadvantages?			

Overall, do you think that tourism is good for your town/city?

SUMMARY

We have seen in this chapter that it is very difficult to distinguish between tourism, recreation and leisure. Urban tourists use the same facilities and services when they are on holiday as local residents use during their leisure or recreational time. Moreover, it is very difficult to measure the direct and indirect impact of tourism, as it is impossible to quantify what is tourism, leisure and recreation. Nevertheless, urban tourism is big business. World cities such as London and cultural cities such as Venice and Oxford are keen to attract visitors, especially those who stay overnight or for a few days and are high spenders. What cities do not want are day visitors who add little to the economy but cause great strains on the cities' infrastructure, environment and social fabric. The concept of carrying capacity is an important one, and one which planners are using to manage the effects of urban tourism.

The examples in this chapter illustrate different approaches to the management of tourism. This reflects the nature of the attraction. Oxford is a city of 110 000 people, a regional shopping centre, an important university town and a major service centre. Many of its buildings are old and it has many narrow roads, especially in the areas frequented by tourists. By contrast, Blenheim Park, only 12 kilometres away, is a privately owned estate, where the dominant land use is agriculture and recreation. Both the Oxford City Council and the Estates Managers at Blenheim are looking towards tourism as a major source of income into the twenty-first century. Oxford is attempting to maximise economic returns and improve the tourist infrastructure and improve the visitor experience. Blenheim has adopted a land use zoning system, and is attempting to reconcile the conflicting needs of tourism, agriculture, shooting, forestry, and conservation of nature and antiquities. Both appear to be putting a great deal of attention into quite small details, for example, information boards in Oxford and the removal of individual trees at Blenheim. Without this attention to detail, the total visitor experience may well decline.

REVIEW QUESTIONS

1 To manage tourism, attention must be paid to very small details. Using examples, comment on how far you agree with this statement.
2 To what extent should Oxford and Blenheim join forces and market themselves together? Give reasons to support your answer.
3 Contact your regional tourist board and find out how they are managing tourism into the next century
4 With the use of examples (from your home town or a city know to you) describe and explain how leisure facilities vary with distance from the city centre.
5 Explain the term 'linkages' with reference to urban tourism.
6 With the use of examples, evaluate the role of tourism in urban economic development.

BIBLIOGRAPHY AND RECOMMENDED READING

Bond, J., and Tiller, K., 1997, *Blenheim; landscape for a palace*, Sutton

Canestrelli, E., and Costa, P., 1991, *Tourist carrying capacity: a fuzzy approach*, *Annals of Tourism Research*, 18(2), 295-311

Glasson. J., 1994, *Oxford: A Heritage City under Pressure, Tourism Management* 15, 2, 137-44

Law. C., 1993, *Urban tourism: attracting visitors to large cities*, Mansell

Page. S., 1995, *Urban tourism*, Routledge

Southern Tourist Board, 1997, *Oxford Visitor Survey*, 1996

WEB SITES

British Tourist Association –
http://www.visitbritain.com

Chapter 6
Tourism and sport

In this chapter we look at the impact of sport upon tourism, economic development and the environment. Previous chapters have examined the effects of beach developments, of diving, skiing and the location of tourist facilities, including sporting facilities, in urban areas. This chapter looks at other aspects of recreation, in particular the economic and environmental impact of sport. Particular attention is given to the impact of Olympic Games and contrasts are drawn between cities that have benefited from hosting the Games, those that have experienced no long-term gain, and those that have failed to host the games. We also look at some of the implications of sport from an ethical and cultural point of view.

TOURISM DEVELOPMENT AND SPORT IN DEVELOPED COUNTRIES

Sport has great potential for tourism and economic development. For example, the 1991 World Student Games held in Sheffield attracted over 5500 competitors from 110 countries. Four new sports arenas were built specially for the Games, costing almost £150 million, including the 25 000-capacity Don Valley Stadium. These facilities remain important not only for Sheffield but also for a large hinterland. On a larger scale, we can look at the impact of the Olympic Games. One of the most closely scrutinised games was held in Atlanta, USA, in 1996, where the long-term economic impact rather than the games themselves appears to have been the victor.

New developments are not necessarily linked with major sporting events, although they may have a significant impact on urban redevelopment (Figure 6.1). For example, in 1997 Wigan unveiled plans for a £150 million indoor leisure centre, one of the largest in the UK. The proposed centre aims to create 2500 jobs and attract 5 million visitors a year. The project, called Xanadu, will occupy a 30 hectare site at Leigh in Lancashire. The aim is to provide over 150 000 m^3 of leisure and retail space under a 75 metre high dome. The dome will house an indoor snow centre, complete with ski runs and an alpine village, as well as an hotel nearly 9000 m^3 in size. Xanadu will also include a £40 million swimming centre, restaurants, a multiplex cinema and virtual reality cinema. When the project is open in 2000, Wigan council hopes to attract visitors from a catchment area of 20 million people, namely those living within a 90-minute drive of the site. Many adults and children take part in sport on a regular basis (Figure 6.2) and the plan is to help

Figure 6.1 *The Don Valley Sports Stadium, Sheffield*

	% adults	
	Annually	**Monthly**
Walking	66	41
Swimming	43	16
Keep fit, aerobics	20	13
Cycling	20	11
Golf	12	5
Weight lifting	10	6
Football	9	5
Jogging, running	8	4
Tennis	7	2
Badminton	7	2
Fishing	5	2
Snooker, pool	18	10
Tenpin bowling	15	4
Darts	9	4

Figure 6.2 *Popularity of sports and physical activities with UK adults, 1995*
Source: Adapted from New leisure markets, 1996, Special interest tourism,
New Leisure Markets

regenerate the area by harnessing this market. The area is currently run down, with aging industries and high unemployment: the leisure centre will bring in significant amount of investment and revenue.

Active participation in sports has been one of the growth areas in leisure, although overall participation levels in many sports are relatively low (Figure 6.2). A large proportion of adults claim to swim regularly, but the figures include parents taking their children to fun-pools, where family leisure rather than sport is the reason for the visit. A plateau appears to have been reached, largely due to the declining numbers of 15-25 year olds (who play the most sport), resulting in lower participation rates for all adults. Men play far more sport than women do, although the gap has narrowed considerably, due to female participation in fitness-related activities such as aerobics, gym training and swimming. In addition, holiday centres in the UK have introduced facilities for taking part in keep-fit, cycling, swimming, etc.

THE BUSINESS OF SPORT

Sport is big business and more so now than ever before. It is a huge business worldwide for companies of all sizes, ranging from multinational corporations (MNCs) such as Nike, BSkyB and Coca-Cola, which invest hundreds of millions of pounds in sport every year, to small shops that sell fishing tackle and bicycle repair kits (Figure 6.3).

No one knows how much the business of sport is worth because it is impossible to measure accurately all the economic activity generated by it. However, the Georgia Institute of Technology has calculated that in the USA sport generated £94 billion of business in 1995, making it the eleventh largest industry in the country. It accounted for over £32 billion in wages and salaries and more than 2.3 million jobs. Thus the sports industry in the USA is larger in terms of the amount of employment and payments in wages/salaries than the film, radio/television, and educational services industries combined.

The Institute divided sport into three sectors:
- entertainment and recreation, which includes professional team sports and individual participation and all associated spending
- products and services
- support organisations, such as leagues and marketing groups.

Adding all the materials and functions in the three sectors gives the amount of sports business conducted. Indeed the Institute suggested that the multiplier effect from sport in the USA was worth an extra £160 billion in 1995 in related industrial activity.

The biggest sport in business terms is certainly football. The 'world game' is the most popular sport on earth, and even countries such as the USA and China, not traditionally footballing nations, are being won over. FIFA, football's governing body, estimates that football generates £123 billion of economic activity each year, and the month-long World Cup finals in 1998 drew the largest audience for a televised event in the world.

Sport has become such big business because many people (particularly unskilled and semi-skilled workers) in developed and developing economies now have more time and money to spend participating in and watching sport. Because of sport's healthy, positive and glamourous image, companies are only too happy to feed that growing demand, whether it is the clubs that compete, the television companies that broadcast it, the manufacturers that produce the equipment and clothing, or the companies that advertise their products through a sporting medium. Thus, in the business of sport, there are links with manufacturing industry, service industry and research and development.

Sport is not just about the Olympics, the top professional teams, and star players, although this is how it is presented in the media. Participation in sport – everything from fishing, cycling and golf to weekend football games in the local park – generates more business than professional sport. According to the Georgia Institute, 68% of spending on sport in the USA is related to personal participation and recreational activities.

Nevertheless, business can be bad for sport. For example, the Atlanta Olympics were estimated to have generated several billion dollars for the local economy but were also widely criticised for being over-commercialised: the influence of the corporate sponsors and the big sports goods manufacturers devalued the Olympic ideal. Consequently, the International Olympic Committee decided that future games would be less obviously commercial. Similarly, sport can be bad for business. The cost of staging the 1976 Olympic Games almost bankrupted the city of Montreal, and the Winter Olympics in 1998 at Nagano, Japan, took place at a time when the Japanese economy was in recession and skiing was becoming less popular. On a more local scale, the plans for the Oxford United football team to move from its cramped Manor Ground site to a new site on the edge of the city, Minchery Farm, have stalled (Figure 6.4) due to a lack of funds.

Figure 6.3 Small shop repairing bicycles –
part of the global sporting business

Figure 6.4 The site for the new Oxford United stadium at Minchery Farm on the outskirts of Oxford

THE OLYMPIC GAMES: THE ULTIMATE COMPETITION

The International Olympic Committee (IOC) claims that the Olympic Games are the world's greatest sporting competition, attracting the best athletes from all over the world. Held every four years, the modern Olympic Games date back to 1896. Hosting the Games brings worldwide media attention, huge investment and often the opportunity for the host city or country to benefit economically.

Barcelona, 1992

An example of a city that benefited from hosting the Olympic Games was Barcelona in south-eastern Spain. For Barcelona, the 1992 Olympics marked a watershed in the city's economic development, acting as a springboard in its drive to become one of Europe's leading cities.

The Olympics were more than just an expensive marketing campaign. They brought big investments, not just for sports facilities but in major infrastructure projects such as telecommunications and roads (Figure 6.6). These in turn attracted investment badly needed by a city that had seen its long-established and old-fashioned industrial base decline in the 1970s and 1980s.

Transport improvements were crucial for the success of the Olympics. Barcelona was attempting to become a 'Dublin' of Spain and become a fashionable area for tourists. Over £6.5 billion, raised from the public and private sector, was spent on enlarging the port for pleasure and industrial boats, building an additional runway, establishing a high-speed rail link and improving public transport. This improved infrastructure, coupled with the five existing university campuses, helped to bring high technology industries to Barcelona: Sony, Sharp, Hewlett Packard, Pioneer, Panasonic and Samsung are just some of the electronics groups with a presence in or near the city.

In the long term, tourism has also benefited, with Barcelona attracting an increasing number of visitors. More and more cruise ships either start or end their voyages at Barcelona's port. Many of their passengers choose to stay a night or two in town, either at the beginning or the end of the cruise. The city is attempting to get a bigger share of the trade fair/convention business, too.

Figure 6.5 Location of Barcelona

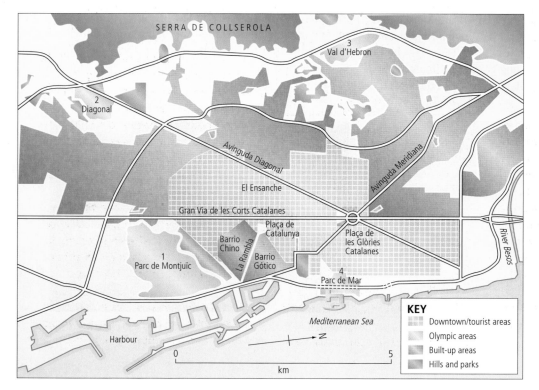

Figure 6.6 Map of Barcelona showing Olympic developments
Source: Geography Review

Case study: Atlanta, 1996

The 1996 Olympic Games held in Atlanta, USA (Figure 6.7), were a mixed blessing as far as the Games were concerned. They proved to be good from a commercial point of view, but they were criticised as a sporting event and from a spectator's point of view, because the Atlanta site was very dispersed throughout the city and transport between the many sites was difficult, and because of the lapses of security leading to the bomb blast in Centenary Park.

These were the first games to be privately sponsored, and the sponsors were more interested in long-term economic development than the sport itself. As such, they were a huge success. The Games were privately managed, and funded solely with private money, largely due to the ability of the Atlanta business community to see the economic benefits of attracting the Games and working together as a cohesive unit in cooperation with the city authorities. The goal was simple and logical – to attract business decision-makers to Atlanta, encourage them to look at the new facilities, mostly through hospitality and guided visits. They showed them the close and successful cooperation between business and government in developing housing, infrastructure and industrial units. The same strategy had been successfully used in Augusta which is home to the US Masters golf tournament. Many businesses have relocated to Augusta following inspections of the city and its facilities made by senior personnel who had initially gone there to play golf!

More so than previous Olympic Games, the Atlanta Olympic Games had a clear purpose beyond that of sport. Its organisers intended to use the games to attract new business to Atlanta, to help the economic regeneration that was already underway, and to act as a catalyst for inner city regeneration. Their target was to create 6000 new jobs and 20 new companies. By the end of the Games, 18 of the companies that took part in the programme relocated to the city, bringing with them 3100 jobs.

By the mid 1990s, Atlanta was already established as one of the fastest growing cities in the USA (Figure 6.8). Between 1986 and 1996, employment grew by 562 700 from 1.32 million to 1.82 million. During that time it also attracted the headquarters of prestigious companies such as Holiday Inn and the courier company UPS. The

Figure 6.7 *The location of Atlanta*
Source: Financial Times, December 11, 1996

Games were the final push to sell Atlanta to the outside business community, a process that had been aggressively followed since 1980.

One of the Games' great achievements was to stimulate investment in infrastructure that would have otherwise been deferred. For example, the airport was redeveloped more quickly and comprehensively than if the games not taken place. During 1996 the airport was one of the busiest in the USA. Extra facilities – accommodation space and buildings for research and sport – were gained by the Georgia State University and by the Georgia Institute of Technology, which was the home of the new Olympic Village. These facilities now form the basis for the Georgia 'research alliance' of six universities, which is intended to rival the 'research triangle' which has attracted jobs to North Carolina.

Since the Games, new housing has been built close to the former Olympic Village and old industrial buildings

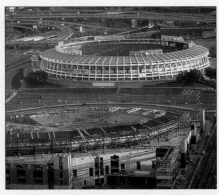

Figure 6.8 *Atlanta – the downtown area during and after the Olympic developments*

have been gentrified with conversions into 'loft' spaces resembling some of the trendiest areas of New York, but on sale at about one-third of the cost. The organisers have also reduced the amount of crime in the area by sponsoring a private force of 'ambassadors' to patrol the Atlanta streets. The downtown area has been partly redeveloped by the construction of the Olympic sports facilities. These now attract people into the area, although there are plans to develop more hotels and leisure facilities to attract people into the downtown area in the evenings.

One of the most successful attractions in the city centre is the Centenary Olympic Park, the largest urban park to be opened in the USA since 1945. The park has already become a focal point in the city, partly because of its facilities and partly because of its Olympic association. The 10 hectare park, built at a cost of £38 million, replaced a scattering of unsightly parking lots and mostly run-down buildings in the heart of downtown Atlanta.

The Games' main legacy for tourism is the various Olympic Sports stadia. The Ted Turner stadium (the main Olympic stadium) has been converted to a baseball stadium and the city planners want to use other stadia to attract important and lucrative professional and amateur sporting events. Following the success of the Games, Atlanta launched a campaign to become the nation's sports industry centre.

Economic development in Atlanta

Atlanta used its status as an Olympic city to attract new business set-ups and also to attract relocations. For example, in 1994, 223 companies moved to the Atlanta metropolitan area while in 1995 a further 260 relocated. They were attracted by the improved infrastructure, and cheaper costs compared with cities such as New York. The same pace continued during 1996 but has slowed slightly since then.

Atlanta had been a popular choice for relocation and expansion even before Atlanta was awarded the Games. Between 1985 and 1995, over 1500 businesses expanded or relocated to Atlanta. Most business investing in the south of the USA choose Atlanta because of its dominant position in the south. The city's location – within two hour's flying time of 80% of the population of the USA – and its excellent transport infrastructure remain its two main attractions. In addition, Atlanta's telecommunications capacity, especially in the wake of the Olympic-related digital and fibre-optics developments, exceeds that of any other US city. Finally, land prices in Atlanta are cheaper than in over-heated cities such as New York and Los Angeles.

An important investment in the mid-1990s was made by the South Korean Sunkyong Group, which invested £1 million in a polyester film plant. With planned expansions to 2008, it will be the largest polyester film plant in the world and it will employ 1000 people. The decision of Sunkyong to locate in Atlanta was helped by the grant of £4.5 million from the state of Georgia to purchase a 135 hectare site for the plant.

As we have seen in the model of cumulative causation (multiplier effects) in Chapter 1, where investment goes, bright young innovative workers follow. Between 1993 and 1995, over 140 000 people migrated to Atlanta, making it the top US city for domestic migration. For businesses this means a large pool of skilled and highly trained labour. This in turn is attractive to investors.

Figure 6.9 *The growth of hotel accommodation in Atlanta*
Source: Financial Times, November, 1996

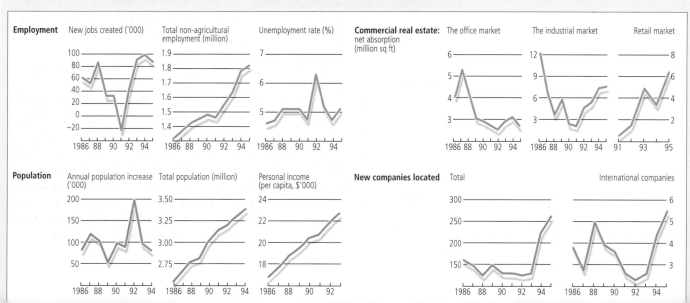

Sydney 2000: the lessons from Atlanta

The Olympic Games are a major tourist attraction. However, in the case of Atlanta, the economic motive was uppermost in the organisers' minds. The organisers of the Sydney Olympics, held in 2000, were keen not to copy the mistakes of Atlanta. For them, in terms of running the Olympic Games the main problems in Atlanta were:

- moving large numbers of people around the scattered sites
- enabling businesses to continue to operate with large numbers of sports tourists causing congestion and disrupting local businesses
- maintaining security for participants and spectators over a large number of sites.

By contrast, the 2000 Olympics at Homebush Bay are concentrated on a 2000 hectare site, about 14 kilometres west of Sydney (Figure 6.10). The athletes' village has been built next to the site (unlike at Atlanta) and the number of

Figure 6.10 *The Homebush site for the Sydney 2000 Olympics*

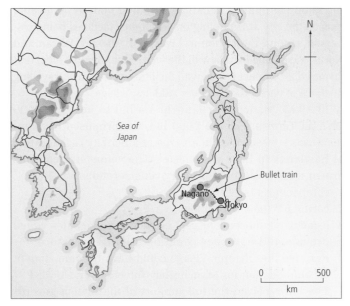

Figure 6.11 *Nagano, Japan, the host of the 1998 Winter Olympics*
Source: adapted from Philip's Modern Atlas, 90th edition, George Philip

participants has been limited to 10 000. Because the site is away from Sydney, downtown businesses as well as local ones, will not be disrupted as much.

Although the athletes will live on site, many of the spectators will travel across one of the world's largest urban areas. The Games organisers are keen to promote public transport and a rail link has been built into the centre of the Homebush site, linking it with Sydney. The trains are capable of bringing 50 000 people an hour to the site and the upgraded bus service can transport a further 28 000 people every hour to the site. Private cars will not be allowed on site, apart from transport for dignitaries, IOC officials and suppliers. Instead there is an elaborate park and ride scheme. It is estimated that up to 60% of spectators will travel by train, 30% by bus and most of the rest will walk or cycle.

Nagano – The Winter Olympics

By contrast with Atlanta, hosting the Winter Olympics in 1998 has not brought economic security for Nagano in Japan. Nagano lies on the same latitude as San Francisco, Lisbon and Athens, and is actually further south than Barcelona, but the bitter winds which blow from the Asian landmass ensure that the area experiences bitterly cold winters with plenty of snow – it is Japan's 'snow country'. Nagano is located in the middle of Japan's central island, Honshu, and is the only province without a coastline (Figure 6.11).

During the mid-1990s, Nagano experienced an economic boom partly due to the forthcoming Winter Olympics. Infrastructural developments such as the extension of the bullet train from Tokyo, boosted the region's growth rate. Its economy is based on high-technology industries, such as precision engineering and computers in the south of the province, and in the north of the province, where the winter Olympics were held, on tourism, notably walking, golf and skiing. Since 1998 there has been a slow-down in manufacturing and in tourism. Thus the economic boom, created by the construction of facilities for the winter Olympics, hid the real state of the economy. Construction created almost 300 000 jobs in the build-up to the Games; opportunities for re-employing these workers are uncertain.

Nagano officials intend to use the Olympic facilities for conferences and sporting events. Extensions to the Shinkansen (the bullet train) mean that Tokyo is now only 90 minutes away, compared with 180 minutes by conventional train. But this accessibility may reduce the benefits of tourism for Nagano, as it may encourage more day-trippers and less overnight stays. Moreover, the improved transport might lead to an increase in Nagano residents travelling to Tokyo to spend their money rather than spending it at home.

A greater concern is the decline of the skiing industry in Japan, which reflects the decline in the Japanese economy.

In the late 1980s there was a strong period of growth, and millions of new skiers headed for the slopes. By the early 1990s skiing was the most popular sport for teenagers in Japan, and the joint most popular with tennis for those in their twenties. Japanese companies responded to this growing interest. Believing that the growth would continue, companies used cheap loans from banks to build hundreds of new resorts and hotels. Ski manufacturers flooded the market with equipment, and travel agents developed package tours.

But in the early to mid-1990s, the economic bubble burst and consumers cut back. Nagano, as one of the main skiing areas, experienced this slump quite acutely. Sales of skis in Japan dropped sharply, leaving the manufacturers and retailers with large amounts of unsold stock. The number of skiers fell, although there are still some 16.5 million skiers in Japan, out of a population of 125 million. In addition, the amount of money spent per person at Japanese resorts has continued to fall since 1995. The fall in revenues and the plummeting land prices left many companies, who had borrowed heavily, in debt. Moreover, as Japan's population continues to age, there are fewer potential skiers.

Consequently, some companies are trying to attract skiers by improving accommodation and catering standards, and ski manufacturers are shifting their stocks by heavy discounting. For operators throughout the country, profit margins have slumped.

For tourism to flourish there must be economic prosperity. The demand for tourism is elastic, i.e. when people have more money they spend a higher proportion of their income on non-essential items, such as tourism and leisure. When there is a downturn in national economic fortunes less is spent on tourism and recreation. Thus it is not just developing countries that are vulnerable to changes in tourism, but developing countries too.

Manchester's bids for the Games

Manchester has made a number of bids for the Olympic Games and the Commonwealth Games. These bids have been made for a variety of reasons:

- to use sporting developments to regenerate parts of inner Manchester
- to attract tourists to major sporting events
- to upgrade transport infrastructure
- to improve housing and accommodation for students
- to place Manchester firmly on the map alongside other international cities.

Manchester put in unsuccessful bids to host the Olympic Games in 1996 and 2000, but has had a successful bid for the 2002 Commonwealth Games. The 1996 Olympic bid was an ideal opportunity to promote Manchester on the world's stage to the benefit of the city, the private sector and ultimately those working and living in the Manchester area. The plan envisaged the main stadium arena and swimming pool to be located outside the city at Dumplington with other facilities being dispersed around the region at Liverpool, Chester, Wigan and North Wales. The plan flew in the face of the Olympic ideal that favoured a compact venue with facilities within easy travelling distance of each other and the Athletes Village.

In 1993, Manchester launched a bid to host the 2000 Olympic Games. For the 2000 bid, the proposed development was concentrated in an area of inner city regeneration at Eastlands in East Manchester. The venue strategy was drawn up to meet three primary considerations:

1 compactness
2 caring for the environment
3 legacy and subsequent use, i.e. what the facilities would provide and how they could be used in the future, for example the Olympic Village could have become student accommodation for Manchester University and UMIST.

The bid received the full support of the British government but failed to win the support of the IOC. Despite losing the bid, Manchester benefited from the construction of new

Inset 6.1
Olympic scandals

The high ideals of the Olympic Movement have not been without scandal. Drug taking and the professional status of many of the amateur athletes have long haunted the IOC. However, at the end of 1998, nearly a quarter of IOC members were implicated in a 'votes for cash' scandal over the awarding of the Olympic Games to the selected host city. Twenty-four of the 115 IOC members testified in the Salt Lake City enquiry after allegations arose concerning Salt Lake's successful bid for the 2002 Winter Olympics. All 24 members were investigated. As a result: four members resigned, five where recommended for expulsion, one died and six were sacked.

Corruption also occurred at the Nagano Olympics. The Secretary of the Japanese Olympic Committee was unable to confirm or deny that the city showered IOC officials with gifts and lavish entertainment. This was because the 90 files containing records of spending during the Olympic bid were burned on the orders of the bid committee in 1998.

These scandals have led to calls for the resignation of the long-standing IOC president, Juan Antonio Samaranch.

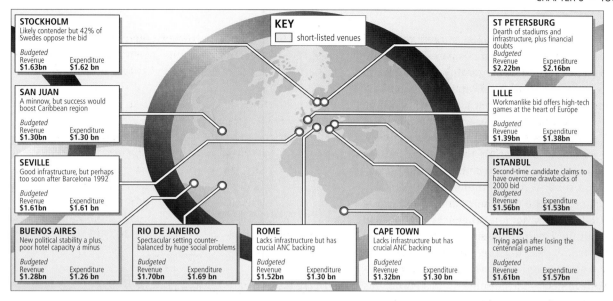

STOCKHOLM
Likely contender but 42% of Swedes oppose the bid

Budgeted
Revenue $1.63bn   Expenditure $1.62 bn

SAN JUAN
A minnow, but success would boost Caribbean region

Budgeted
Revenue $1.30bn   Expenditure $1.30 bn

SEVILLE
Good infrastructure, but perhaps too soon after Barcelona 1992

Budgeted
Revenue $1.61bn   Expenditure $1.61 bn

BUENOS AIRES
New political stability a plus, poor hotel capacity a minus

Budgeted
Revenue $1.28bn   Expenditure $1.26 bn

RIO DE JANEIRO
Spectacular setting counter-balanced by huge social problems

Budgeted
Revenue $1.70bn   Expenditure $1.69 bn

ROME
Lacks infrastructure but has crucial ANC backing

Budgeted
Revenue $1.52bn   Expenditure $1.30 bn

CAPE TOWN
Lacks infrastructure but has crucial ANC backing

Budgeted
Revenue $1.32bn   Expenditure $1.30 bn

ATHENS
Trying again after losing the centennial games

Budgeted
Revenue $1.61bn   Expenditure $1.57bn

KEY
▢ short-listed venues

ST PETERSBURG
Dearth of stadiums and infrastructure, plus financial doubts
Budgeted
Revenue $2.22bn   Expenditure $2.16bn

LILLE
Workmanlike bid offers high-tech games at the heart of Europe

Budgeted
Revenue $1.39bn   Expenditure $1.38bn

ISTANBUL
Second-time candidate claims to have overcome drawbacks of 2000 bid
Budgeted
Revenue $1.56bn   Expenditure $1.53bn

Figure 6.12
The race to host the 2004 Olympic Games
Source: Financial Times, 1998

facilities and an improved infrastructure that was started before the bid was made. For example, a new indoor arena was built near Victoria Station; it is suitable for a number of sports such as boxing, football, ice skating and ice hockey, as well as being used for concerts.

In 1995, Manchester was awarded the 2002 Commonwealth Games with the Eastlands site as the major focus for the Games. This was in spite of having no guarantee of a stadium from the government and the organising committee to stage the main event. However, over previous years (and in the course of bidding for the Olympic Games) Manchester's infrastructure had improved considerably. Greater Manchester's motorway box – the equivalent of the M25 around London, was completed in 1997. Its tram network has been extended to the Millennium Stadium site at Eastlands, and approach roads spiral into the stadium parking area, making parking relatively easy.

The central theme of Manchester's approach has been urban regeneration. The east side of Manchester has not enjoyed the same economic buoyancy of the city centre or of south Manchester, nor has it had the same developments as west Manchester, with the industrial, retail and residential redevelopment of Trafford Park and Salford Quays – the old docks for the Manchester Ship Canal.

The stadium site is within the city's inner ring road and is on derelict land once contaminated by heavy engineering waste and gasworks. Since the site has been decontaminated and cleaned up there have been a number of new developments such as the national velodrome, a world class cycling stadium, and there are plans for a national indoor tennis centre to be completed by 2002. Three universities, Manchester, UMIST and Manchester Metropolitan, are developing a village of student accommodation to link the site with the city centre. This accommodation will house athletes during the Commonwealth Games.

The race for the 2004 Olympic Games

The IOC uses a two-tier method to decide which city should host the Olympic Games. This method which short-lists favoured bids, was designed to spare the second-division bidders the unnecessary expense of continuing their bid. However, some of the 'no-hopers' prefer to continue with their bids as it enables them to develop a part of their economy, which might otherwise remain undeveloped.

Of the eleven candidates for the 2004 Olympic Games (Figure 6.12), only five were shortlisted for the second stage. These were Athens, Istanbul, Rio de Janeiro, Buenos Aires and Beijing. One of the early front runners was Rome but this failed to get onto the short-list largely due to local opposition and a poor transport infrastructure. Athens, which had lost the 1996 Centenary Games to Atlanta was ultimately awarded the 2004 Games. Most of the sporting infrastructure had been put in place during the 1970s and 1980s when it was widely expected that Athens would host the Centenary Games (the first of the modern Olympic Games took place in Athens in 1896). During the 1990s, the Greek government concentrated on upgrading the transport infrastructure to cope with the demands of hosting an Olympic games.

In neighbouring Turkey, Istanbul also bid for the 2004 Games, having lost out to Sydney for the 2000 Games. Under the logo *The meeting of continents*, the city had most of the facilities in place from its previous unsuccessful bid. Despite gridlocked traffic, water shortages, air pollution and a collapsing infrastructure, the Turkish government gave the Turkish Olympic Committee plenty of financial resources and political power to commandeer property and resources wherever necessary. However, the country continues to be rocked by political instability and there were three governments in 1997 alone. Unlike the previous bid for the 2000 Games, there was little popular appeal. With inflation reaching 80%, most Turkish people have more immediate concerns.

The Olympic Games have yet to be staged in South America, which is one reason why Buenos Aires and Rio de Janeiro made the short list. The Argentine capital made unsuccessful bids in 1936, 1944, 1956 and 1964 against a backdrop of economic decline. Its latest bid comes at a time when it has had a period of over 15 years of uninterrupted democratic rule and tentative signs of economic recovery. For the IOC the question is whether the Olympic games would help its economic recovery or whether it would strangle any recovery and send Argentina into massive debt.

Also in South America, Rio de Janeiro is a city of haves and have-nots. Undoubtedly some of the richest people in Brazil live there, but the city has massive problems ranging from high rates of crime, drug dealing, prostitution, air and water pollution, traffic congestion, as well as very widespread poverty. Rio wanted to tackle some of these problems through the investment that the Games would bring. But would it have been enough? The Atlanta model worked because Atlanta was already a successful city and the Olympic Games merely speeded up the process of development rather than attempting to start it.

Similarly, Cape Town made an unsuccessful bid to host the 2004 Games. Despite the support of President Mandela and the ruling African National Congress, Cape Town would have had to spend at least £280 million on new stadia, treble its existing hotel capacity to the Olympic requirement of 16 500 rooms, and provide infrastructure and security for at least 150 000 visitors daily. About half of the funds would have had to come from the government. In a country of massive unemployment, widespread poverty, and huge inequalities in levels of education and health, such a large investment by the government would not have been popular with voters.

	1891	1951	1971	1991
Population (000s)	27 231	41 159	46 412	48 119
Average working week (hours)	56-60	44.8	40.4	40.0
Paid annual holiday (weeks)	'rare'	1 to 2	2	>4
Licensed cars (million)	negligible	2.1	10.4	19.7
Foreign holiday-makers	negligible	3	14	30

Figure 6.13 *Growth in leisure in Britain, 1891-1991*
Source: House of Commons, 1995, p. xxi
Source: House of Commons, 1991, The environmental impact of leisure activities, HMSO, 1995

Figure 6.14 *Footpath erosion, Croagh Patrick, Ireland*

QUESTIONS

1 What are the advantages and disadvantages of hosting an Olympic Games?

2 Why might an unsuccessful bid to host the Olympic Games be useful to a city?

3 Which of the cities shown in Figure 6.14 would you have chosen to host the 2004 Olympic Games? Give reasons to support your answer. Use the web sites listed in the bibliography to access more information on the 2004 Olympic bids. What advantages do the other cities have over Athens?

Case study: **The environmental impact of leisure and tourism in the United Kingdom**

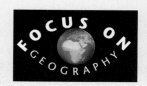

Since the early 1960s there has been a considerable increase in leisure activities of all types in the UK. The tourism and leisure industry in the UK had a turnover of over £35 billion in the mid-1990s, double that of the 1980s. It now accounts for over 5% of GDP and employs over 1.7 million people. Recreation and leisure form an important part of the tourist industry – in 1994 earnings from recreation and leisure exceeded £10 billion. Consumer spending on sports related items also accounted for over £10 billion. The sports industry employs over 500 000 people.

Leisure travel has increased by over one-third since the mid-1970s. Leisure now accounts for over 40% of all passenger mileage each year. Over 80% of all leisure journeys are made by car.

The most common negative impacts of tourism and leisure include:
- overcrowding
- traffic
- wear and tear on the natural and human environment
- disturbance and noise
- inappropriate development.

However, it is very difficult to quantify these impacts.

Rural areas have received much attention in recent years. The Government White Paper in October 1995 considered the options for managing rural areas, while recognising that they have altered considerably in recent decades. No longer are they just areas of food production but are increasingly used for industrial, residential, commercial and recreational developments. None of these is a particularly new phenomenon – in the south east the

process has been underway since the beginning of the twentieth century, but what is new is the speed and intensity with which rural areas are being developed and put under pressure. For example, the government has permitted many leisure developments and theme parks in rural areas (see Chapter 7, Theme parks and day trip attraction in the UK) and in 1992 extended the list of appropriate uses of Green Belt land to include sports.

Tourism and the demand for leisure facilities has increased dramatically over the last century. Improvements in transport, changes in work practices and the growth in disposable income have made places more accessible to a larger number of people, both in a geographic sense as well as an economic sense. Figure 6.13 shows changes in the working week and the number of paid holiday weeks, and shows how the number of cars has increased since 1891. Nevertheless, recreational pressures can create a tremendous strain on rural resources, and those pressures vary with the type of recreational use. But tourists also bring benefits. The leisure industry accounts for about 27% of consumer spending in the UK. For example, visitors to the North York Moors National Park spend about £100 million every year and 50% of jobs in the park are connected with tourism, whereas just over 40% are in farming.

Walking
One of the most popular and widespread recreational activities is walking. It is estimated that over 100 000 people are members of the Ramblers' Association and that over 5000 belong to the Long Distance Walkers' Association. The potential

impact of so many people on sensitive areas is great (Figure 6.16). For example, damage to sensitive species on popular walks may lead to soil erosion and create gullies, as along the route to Red Tarn in the Lake District. Heathlands, chalk and limestone grasslands and wetlands are particularly fragile, and breeding birds are also affected. In coastal areas destruction of sand dune vegetation and the initiation of blow out dunes are a widespread problem, as at Studland in Dorset and Ainesdale in Lancashire. Blow out dunes are formed when sand dunes which have no vegetation cover to hold the sand together are eroded by winds in gale conditions. Salt marshes are also vulnerable and trampling may lead to localised destruction of vegetation and subsequent erosion of the salt marsh. In agricultural areas there is conflict between ramblers and farmers over access to the land; walkers with dogs can be even more of a nuisance, causing disturbance to sheep, scaring people, especially children and fouling footpaths.

Angling
Angling is the most popular sport in the UK and it is estimated that over 2.5 million people fish regularly. Over 350 000 anglers belong to the three main angling organisations, the National Federation of Anglers, the Salmon and Trout Association and the National Federation of Sea Anglers. In addition, over two million fishermen do not belong to any organisation but fish on a regular basis.

Angling can have a serious effect on the environment, including visual impact, noise, damage to vegetation, trampling, litter, riverbank erosion and the dumping of rubbish. Other effects include the modification of ecosystems through the introduction of exotic species, modifications to vegetation and habitats, and disturbance to wildfowl and nesting birds. Not all of the modifications are necessarily done by anglers nor are all bad: some rivers are regularly stocked and managed. In the case of the River Cole near Swindon, the National Rivers Authority is undertaking a comprehensive restoration programme, recreating natural pool and riffle sequences and water meadows, as well as restocking fish levels.

Golf

Another very popular sport is golf. Participation increased dramatically during the late 1980s although the growth in the number of new golf courses has slowed considerably in the 1990s (Figure 6.15). New golf courses

created since 1985 have covered an area of land the size of Greater Manchester.

Controversy regarding golf courses is intense. Originally, golf courses were located on sandy, heathland areas with limited agricultural potential, such as St Andrews in Scotland. However, as the popularity of the sport has increased, the location of golf courses has changed and they have increasingly been developed in areas with good agricultural potential and close to centres of population, such as the North Oxford golf course. New golf courses, it is argued, 'rape' the environment by water abstraction, modification of natural habitats, the creation of new buildings such as clubhouses, access roads, car parks and the development of new sewage facilities. The use of fertilisers and the

regular cutting of grass inhibits natural vegetation and creates a man-made landscape. In the case of Penn, Buckinghamshire, the proposed new golf course has created fears not only about its effect on the natural environment but also its likely impact on the social character of the village. On the other hand, golf courses in some areas have created diverse semi-natural managed habitats replacing intensive arable agriculture (Inset 6.2).

A surge in course developments of 17% nationally, 40% in the south east, over the early 1990s far outstripped the rise in the number of people playing the sport. Developers were left with heavy losses, in many cases insufficient to pay interest charges. Indeed, 88 of the 388 golf courses built between 1989 and 1995 are at financial risk, and 14 of the newly built golf courses went into

Inset 6.2
Changing land use in rural areas

As a result of the Common Agricultural Policy, established between 1962 and 1968, many farmers have had to change their methods of farming. In the 1970s and 1980s, guaranteed prices and guaranteed markets led to over-production and surpluses in many commodities. However, from the mid-1980s farmers were affected by restrictive policies which reduced the amount they could produce. A number of strategies were introduced by The Common Agricultural Policy and the Ministry of Agriculture Fisheries and Food to reduce the impact of farming on the environment: **set-aside land, Environmentally Sensitive Areas (ESAs), Nitrate Sensitive Areas,** to protect groundwater areas, Habitat Schemes to improve or create wildlife habitats, **Organic Aid Schemes** to encourage farmers to convert to organic production methods, and **Countryside Access Schemes** to grant new opportunities for public access to set-aside land and suitable farmland in ESAs.

In addition, many farmers diversified. Diversification is a recent trend but is increasingly important and it developed

as the costs of farm inputs increased more than the price received for farm products. There are a number of forms of diversification

- **direct marketing**, such as pick-your-owns (PYOs), farm gate sales and farm shops
- **accommodation**, such as bed and breakfast, camping and caravanning
- **recreation**, such as golf courses, 'horsiculture', and nature trails
- **commercial**, such as new crops or livestock.

Successful diversification requires a number of conditions:
- availability of capital
- good marketing and advertising
- planning permission to develop if the farm is on Green Belt land
- absence of conflicts with farming activities at key times of the year, e.g. during lambing season.

The changing fortunes of golf

A surge in course developments of 17% nationally, 40% in the south east, over the early 1990s far outstripped the rise in the number of people playing the sport.

Developers were left with heavy losses, in many cases insufficient to pay interest charges. Indeed, 88 of the 388 golf courses built between 1989 and 1995 are at financial risk, and 14 of the newly built golf courses went into receivership within five years of opening. Over-development in the 1980s and early 1990s led to a proliferation of ill-conceived golf courses which the developers had borrowed heavily to finance. Many of them were in the wrong place – either too close to competitors or too far from the

market. Land prices were at their peak in the late 1980s and this has left many of the new developments with huge debts.

American Golf UK, a sister company of American Golf Corporation, the world's largest course operator, paid £10 million to acquire seven courses in the UK that had been built at a cost of over £20 million. One of the most spectacular sales involved the Quietwaters golf and hotel development in Essex which cost more than £30 million to develop and was sold in 1994 for £5 million.

Despite the failure of so many companies, there are still a large number of proposals for golf courses waiting to go through the planning process.

Figure 6.15 The changing fortunes of golf

receivership within five years of opening. Over-development in the 1980s and early 1990s led to a proliferation of ill-conceived golf courses which the developers had borrowed heavily to finance. Many of them were in the wrong place – either too close to competitors or too far from the market. Land prices were at their peak in the late 1980s and this has left many of the new developments with huge debts.

American Golf UK, a sister company of American Golf Corporation, the world's largest course operator, paid £10 million to acquire seven courses in the UK that had been built at a cost of over £20 million. One of the most spectacular sales involved the Quietwaters golf and hotel development in Essex which cost more than £30 million to develop and was sold in 1994 for £5 million.

Despite the failure of so many companies, there are still a large number of proposals for golf courses waiting to go through the planning process.

Off-road cycling

Off-road cycling, like trampling, can damage vegetation and lead to soil erosion in particularly popular locations. Chalk downlands, bridleways, peat in wet conditions and the New Forest have been identified as especially vulnerable due to a mixture of environmental sensitivity and population pressure. Some bikers are considered to be over-enthusiastic and this leads to conflicts with other users, especially walkers including those with young children. The impacts of four-wheel vehicles and trail bikes are more severe. Soil and vegetation losses are increased; there has been extreme damage in parts of the North York Moors, the Peak District and the Yorkshire Dales. Noise disturbances are also a problem.

Water sports

People in Britain are becoming increasingly involved in water sports. Like other forms of recreation, the popularity of water sports has increased as disposable income and leisure time have increased. Sailing has become increasingly popular, and there

are even 'honeypot' waterways such as the Norfolk Broads, Poole Harbour and Lake Windermere, where traffic congestion and heated tempers are common.

With the number of people involved in sailing and powerboat racing forecast to grow by 50% in the 1990s, there was a rapid increase in new marina developments. Many of these were in fragile environments such as the Thames Estuary, an important salt marsh and a habitat for migrating birds. During the 1980s, 2000 boat berths were created in the Essex Marshes on the north side of the Thames Estuary and there are now nearly twenty marinas on the Blackwater estuary and eight on the Crouch. In 1992 permission was granted to build a new marina and boating lake on mudflats in Cardiff Bay which was already designated as a Site of Special Scientific Interest.

Other water sports such as scuba-diving, water-skiing, jet-skiing and boardsailing (windsurfing) are quite recent, expanding since the late 1970s. Boardsailing was only introduced into the UK in 1974 and within a decade over 100 000 boards were being used. Both scuba diving and water-skiing have experienced rapid increases in growth, the latter as a family sport, for families with teenage children. Most of the growth in water sports occurred during the economically prosperous years of the 1980s; with the recession of the late 1980s and early 1990s, growth faltered and in the late 1990s has not recovered.

There are a number of recreational activities which generate strong emotions and fierce debate. Water skiing is one of the higher profile activities. It causes problems because of its high noise levels, pollution due to the emission of fuel, increased swash on shores, and conflict with other users.

Water skiing has taken place on part of the Norfolk and Suffolk Broads since the early 1950s. The Broads are a man-made environment, formed by the flooding of areas of medieval peat cuttings. This has created a series of attractive lakes in the valleys of the Bure, Yare and Waveney rivers. It is an excellent example of a conflict in a National Park – the conflict between water skiers, with their power boats, and other users, desiring peace and quiet, is an obvious one.

In the 1950s, water skiers had access to some of the Broads as well as to the rivers. Bylaws were introduced to control water skiing in 1978, and this limited skiing to five areas on the River Yare and five areas on the River Waveney. In addition, time restrictions were introduced, concentrating the activity into shorter periods. Although the areas have largely been successful, the time zoning has not. This is partly due to the lack of flexibility within the bylaws, preventing any change or expansion of these times: queuing at the start of popular times is common.

There are those who wish to ban water skiing from the area altogether. The BWSF has expressed disappointment with the lack of attempts to manage water-skiing on the Norfolk Broads: they feel that the BA is not interested in water-skiing. In 1993, the BA produced its draft plan, 'No Easy Answers', which proposed a policy for the removal of water skiing from the rivers. Concerns were raised over wash, noise and environmental impact etc., and safety on the rivers, but the results were largely inconclusive. In response the Water Ski Working Group (comprising members of the BWSF and other waterskiers) suggested a number of alternatives in the management of water skiing.

The BWSF does have some support: the Sports Council has identified the Broads as a centre of regional importance and believes that water skiing should not be removed from the rivers until an equivalent opportunity is made available elsewhere. In addition, the House of Commons Environment Committee Report 'The Environmental Impact of Leisure Activities' stated: 'We are concerned that certain activities ... water skiing for example, are denied facilities and hounded from area to area ... Recently, planning decisions excluded water skiers from sites previously used, in most cases without offering them alternatives ... We would like to see much more emphasis on positive planning ... codes of practice and a framework of voluntary co-operation are part of the way forward.'

QUESTIONS

1 How will the diversification options for farmers vary between (i) south-east England and northern Scotland, and (ii) a farm on the urban fringe and one in a remote rural area? Give reasons for your answers.

2 Explain why the environmental impacts of recreation and leisure are increasing.

3 What impacts do (i) golf and (ii) water skiing have on the environment?

4 What are the environmental impacts of recreation in urban areas? Give reasons, and local examples, to support your answer.

SPORT AND ETHICS

So far we have looked at a the impact of a major sporting event, the Olympic Games, and at economic and environmental effects of sport. But there are also ethical and cultural issues connected with the growth of sport. Here we look at two examples, the development of golf courses in Vietnam and hunting in Western Europe.

The impact of golf in Vietnam

The demand for golf courses in the Far East has led to many controversial developments. One plan was for the South Korean car manufacturer, Daewoo, to build an 18-hole golf course in Kim No commune near the Vietnamese capital, Hanoi (Figure 6.17). In 1997, Vietnamese peasants clashed with police after the government decided to convert the peasants' maize fields into the Daewoo golf course (Figure 6.18). What made this all the more remarkable is that public protest in Vietnam is almost unheard of – nor is it generally reported to the West.

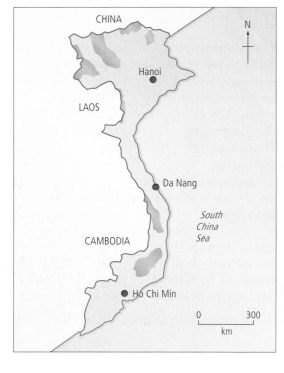

Figure 6.16
Map of Vietnam
Source: adapted from World Reference Atlas, 1994, Dorling Kindersley

This relatively small incident points to one of the fundamental conflicts that is developing in Vietnamese society, a decade after economic reforms began to change people's livelihoods. Since 1986, the state has followed a liberal economic policy known as *doi moi* (renovation) and there has been large-scale foreign investment. However, economic change has not coincided with any major political change – Vietnamese people are now more inclined to protect and defend their increased wealth, but the political system has yet to provide channels for redressing public grievances. These sort of problems of increasing materialism with limited freedom of speech, are likely to increase as large foreign investment projects increase in number and scale.

The land issue is a particularly contentious one. Vietnam allows its citizens *usufructure* rights, i.e. the right to use the land but not to own it. The government refuses to allow private ownership of the land. Since unification at the end of the Vietnamese war in 1975, all land has been owned by the state, but many villages, such as those in Kim No, recall the days before the Communist government, when the land was held in common not by the state. Although the peasants did not own the land individually, the land was held for their benefit and could not be sold to outside organisations. To make matters worse, the land that the government intends to develop will become a 'playground for foreigners'.

Foreigners are part of the problem. Although land is in short supply, the Vietnamese government has been willing to clear large tracts of land for major projects, often at the expense of local residents. For example, a group of Taiwanese investors in 'Saigon South', a £1 billion satellite city on the edge of Ho Chi Minh City, faced months of delay after protests by coconut farmers who refused to be relocated from the site without any compensation.

Figure 6.17 *New golf course development in Vietnam*

Hunting in Europe

One of the most controversial sports is hunting. In the mid-1980s over six million people in Europe were involved in hunting, creating an industry which employed about 100 000 people including equipment manufacturers, retailers, gamekeepers, specialist magazine publishers, generating revenues of about £4 billion. France, Italy, Spain and the UK accounted for 80% of the European hunters. France had over 1.8 million hunters who paid £180 million for land access rights, i.e. the cost of gamekeepers, game rearing and the use of land.

Much hunting is done in forests as these provide the breeding, roosting and feeding grounds for much of the traditional game, such as deer, foxes, rabbits and wild birds. Hunting pressure on some wildlife populations is increasing significantly as residential, commercial and industrial development, and transport infrastructure cause habitat fragmentation and landscape and vegetation damage. Hunting also affects non-target species. For example, water fowl are poisoned by lead through the ingestion of lead shot; this is leading to increased bird mortality and unsuccessful nesting and hatching of chicks. There is also evidence in the UK that lead weights used in recreational fishing have been ingested by water fowl, especially swans.

Nevertheless, the main controversy in the UK is whether blood sports, such as fox hunting, inflict too much pain and distress on the hunted animals (Figure 6.18) or whether such sports support an important rural industry, thereby maintaining people on the land, and are an important agent for landscape and vegetation conservation and management (Figure 6.19).

Figure 6.18 *Blood sports in Britain – hare coursing*

Figure 6.19
Landscape conservation as a result of hunting/shooting – a grouse moor

SUMMARY

This chapter has shown that sport – taking part and being a spectator – is a significant economic activity, and that it has been used by city planners to regenerate cities, improve the economy, and create employment. As we saw with the examples of Atlanta, Barcelona and Manchester, sport can transform a city and give it renewed growth. However, it cannot be a solution to all economic problems; the example of Nagano shows that the wider economy and demographic characteristics have a part to play. But it can also have important environmental effects, both good and bad, as well as ethical and cultural ones.

QUESTIONS

1 Using examples explain why sport is important for tourism, recreation and leisure.
2 For an area that you have studied, such as your home area or nearby town, describe and explain the importance of sport in the local economy. You may find it useful to get in touch with the Recreation Department of your local City or County Council. For example, what facilities are there? How many people are employed? How many people use the facilities? What is the sphere of influence of the facilities that you have investigated?

BIBLIOGRAPHY AND RECOMMENDED READING

House of Commons, 1995, *The Environmental Impact of Leisure Activities*, HMSO
New leisure markets, 1996, *Special interest tourism, New Leisure Markets*
Odell, B., 1998, *Water skiing on the Norfolk Broads*, UK CEED Bulletin, 54
Wall, G. and Wright, C., 1971, *The environmental impact of outdoor recreation*, University of Waterloo, Ontario

WEB SITES

Bids for the 2004 Olympic Games -
Http//www.athens2004.net/
Http//www.Olympic_games/host_city_bids/2004/
Http//www.istanbul2004.org/

Chapter 7
Theme parks and day-trip attractions in the UK

Figure 7.1 *Visitors to Box Hill, Surrey*

Although the main topic of this chapter is theme parks, we look also at leisure parks and other day-trip attractions which all compete for tourist or leisure spending. We have seen already that it is very difficult to distinguish between tourism, recreation and leisure, to classify types of tourism and to measure their impact. This is certainly true again in this chapter where we look at attractions such as leisure parks, theme parks and multiplex cinemas. At first it may seem that these are clear-cut categories, but as we will see, theme parks may be classified as a short-break, leisure parks could be defined as coastal attractions, and multiplex cinemas and virtual reality theme parks are largely aspects of urban tourism. This chapter focuses on day-trip attractions, theme parks and short stay attractions such as Centre Parcs. The chapter examines the reasons for their growth, and their economic and environmental impact.

DAY-TRIP ATTRACTIONS

The most common form of leisure park is seaside sites offering fairground attractions, with others offering sport, such as crazy golf and boating, or arcade amusements. Total admissions to leisure parks have increased from 33.6 million in 1991 to 40.5 million in 1994, although the growth was somewhat erratic over that period.

The market for day-trip attractions is not restricted to leisure parks, as the attractions for day-trippers are very diverse, ranging from country parks (Figure 7.1) to urban-industrial heritage (Figure 7.2). The highest number of visitors is achieved by country parks (Figure 7.3), but these are characterised by stays of less than a full day and little

Figure 7.2 *Cadbury world in Bourneville, an industrial theme park; outdoor attractions can see a drop in visitor numbers if the weather is poor.*

	Number of attractions		Million visits	
	Total	Over 100 000 admissions	1992	1994
Country parks	200	150	48.0	57.1
Leisure parks	60	46	33.3	40.5
Wildlife attractions	150	124	21.5	22.8
Workplaces	335	122	9.5	11.1
Farms	165	n/a	5.5	8.3
Steam railways	98	54	4.8	4.9
Visitor centres	215	n/a	11.0	17.1
Total	**1223**	**750**	**133.6**	**161.8**

Figure 7.3 *Visits to main types of day-trip attraction, 1992 and 1994*
Source: adapted from New leisure markets, 1996, Theme parks, New Leisure Market

expenditure. Many country parks are operated by local authorities as public services and have free entry to visitors.

Figure 7.4 shows the number of people visiting leisure parks. The data needs to be treated with caution. For example, 1992 was a poor year owing to the economic recession, whereas 1994 was an above-average year, with good summer weather and a return of customer confidence.

There is an underlying trend amongst certain sectors of the population for more people to take more day-trips and short-breaks away from home and to take fewer longer long-haul holidays. In response, there has been a growth in the number of day-trip or short-break attractions. For example, the Sea Life Centres (Figure 7.5) were developed in the early

1990s, and there are now about a dozen centres around Britain. The Blackpool Sea Life Centre is the most popular, attracting over 550 000 people each year. The group as a whole attracts some 2.5 million visitors annually. Along with Cadbury World in Birmingham, the Sea Life Centres dominate the English Tourist Board's list of most popular recently opened attractions. Cadbury World opened in 1990 as a tourist attraction. Previously, tours around the factory were common but had to be discontinued because of health and hygiene considerations. Cadbury World now attracts over 500 000 visitors a year. Much of the exhibition there relates to the National Curriculum and school parties are an important source of visitors.

Figure 7.5 *Visitors at Birmingham Sea Life Centre*

LEISURE AND THE COUNTRYSIDE

More than 45% of all car journeys are for leisure and a third of them are trips to the countryside. The leisure industry is transforming the face of the countryside, with theme parks, golf courses, health farms, hang gliding and war games, for example, all competing for rural land. After agriculture, recreation is the biggest source of damage to Britain's sites of special scientific interest (SSSI) and theme parks and other attractions, such as war games, mountain biking, are among the main culprits in causing environmental destruction.

An important recent trend has been for farms to diversify away from food production and into leisure; the distinction between farming and recreation is becoming increasingly blurred. For example, some farms offer camping and caravanning, war games, nature trails, pick-your-own farm, family visits (Figure 7.6) and educational visits. Some farms may adopt a certain theme – such as working Victorian farm or may farm unusual animals, such as ostriches and deer (Figure 7.7). War games are among one of the most popular new developments with over 400 sites in Britain. Although it can benefit farmers, financially it can damage the environment. For example, at Bonny Wood near Stowmarket in Suffolk, the ancient 20 hectare oak and ash woodland was badly damaged by a war games development.

One of the main reasons for this change in rural areas is

	1991	1994
Number of leisure parks	57	76
– free admission	9	21
– paid entry	48	55
Admissions	33.6	40.5
Parks with over 2 million admissions in 1994		
Blackpool Pleasure Beach	6.5	7.3
Palace Pier, Brighton	3.5	3.8
Alton Towers	1.9	2.7
Rotunda, Folkestone	1.0	2.5
Eastbourne	–	2.3
Pleasure Beach, Great Yarmouth	2.5	2.0
Pleasureland, Southport	1.7	2.0

Figure 7.4 *Visits to leisure parks, 1991 and 1994*
Source: adapted from New leisure markets, 1996, Theme parks, New Leisure Markets

Figure 7.6 *Family visits to a farm*

Figure 7.7 *A 'theme' farm. The Museum of Welsh Life at St. Fagans*

the Common Agricultural Policy (CAP) of the European Union. This policy has placed limits on the amount of crops that can be grown and the amount of milk that can be produced. (See Chapter 4 in *Development and under- development* in this series for a full discussion of the CAP and its implications.) This means that farmers have had to look to ways other than farming to make a profit from their land.

By the end of the 1990s, farmers had taken out over 600 000 hectares of land from agricultural use and much of this has gone into leisure activities. The notion that the main purpose of rural land is to produce food is no longer true in some areas, especially those close to large centres of population.

The conversion of farmland to leisure land is not without problems. There are conflicts concerning the tranquillity of the land, its use (whether for farming, recreation, housing developments, etc), environmental issues, the economic needs of rural people and the conflict between personal property and common rights. There are conflicts between those who wish to use it for peace and quiet and those who use it to fly model aeroplanes, clay-pigeon shooting, rock concerts and so on. Some of these problems, such as footpath erosion and damage done by sailing and water sports are localised and heavily publicised. But other developments in the countryside cause more widespread damage but attract less attention, the most obvious pressure being from the construction industry. For example, the Conservative government of the early 1990s welcomed the development of the new Center Parcs at Longleat. Even though the development was within an Area of Outstanding Natural Beauty (AONB), the Planning Minister claimed that it would create 750 jobs and would not undermine the beauty of the area. The village can accommodate up to 3500 visitors at a time, and has not destroyed the local environment, whilst providing short-term construction employment and long-term service employment. There are similar plans for a holiday village at Alton Towers on land adjacent to the theme park. Already Alton Towers covers 200 hectares and can accommodate 30 000 people, 7000 cars and 400 coaches.

However, many leisure developments are on rural land, which is derelict or redundant. The Cotswolds Water Park (Figure 7.8) is on a series of former gravel works and the Sherwood Forest Center Parcs led to improving land use and habitats. At Longleat, Center Parcs created a new lake, and increased the variety of landscapes present.

Figure 7.8 *The Cotswold Water Park – rehabilitating a derelict gravel works*

THEME PARKS

A theme park has a number of characteristics:

- attractions which use a special theme, such historical, fantastic, animal or geographical, for example, Disneyland in California, Parc Asterix in Paris
- mechanical rides ranging from the 'white knuckle rides' to gentler rides such as carousels for younger children
- the ability to entertain a family for a whole day
- an inclusive entry price.

Permanent fairgrounds at major resorts, such as Blackpool and Great Yarmouth, sited on the seafront or on piers, are officially referred to as 'leisure parks'.

Theme park development is unusual in that it is both capital intensive and labour intensive – most industries are either one or the other. Large capital sums are required to be invested initially in the rides and indoor attractions, for landscaping and creating a safe, pleasant infrastructure, including water and sewage facilities, roads and paths. The parks are labour intensive for a number of reasons: safety is of paramount importance and requires proper supervision of all parts of the park. Cleanliness is also very important – the UK theme parks resemble the Disney format with teams of cleaners and wandering entertainers.

Important European theme parks include Futuroscope and Parc Asterix (France), Efteling (Netherlands), Europa Park (Germany) and Liseburg (Sweden). In the late 1990s, Warner Brothers, the American entertainment group, opened a huge theme park and studio complex in Bottrop, once the hub of the Ruhr industrial region. The potential market consists of some 27 million people from northern Germany and Belgium.

Theme parks in the UK

The major theme parks in the UK include Alton Towers, Chessington World of Adventure, Legoland, Thorpe Park and Drayton Manor (Figure 7.9). Legoland, Berkshire, opened in 1996 and therefore does not appear on Figure 7.9.

Although the Disney parks in the USA date back to the 1970s, most British people gained their first experience of theme parks on day-trips to much smaller, more modest operations, such as Alton Towers, Thorpe Park and Chessington World of Adventure.

Some parks have a central theme, such as Camelot (Arthurian legends) or American adventure (the Wild West), while others have a range of themes, such as Alton Towers

---

QUESTIONS

1 Choose an appropriate technique to illustrate the data in Figure 7.3. What are the most important forms of day-trips, in terms of volume, as shown in Figure 7.3? Explain why these forms of trip are important.

2 Briefly explain why rural areas are increasingly turning towards recreation and leisure as a means of generating income.

3 How does the potential for rural tourism vary with distance from large centres of population? Give reasons to support your answer.

and Chessington World of Adventure. Legoland and Disneyland exploit the company's other markets such as toys, films and videos.

In 1995, 22% of adults and 36% of children visited a theme park. The higher proportion of children indicates family attendance and school parties. UK residents are increasingly likely to visit a theme park abroad. Over one million people from the UK visited Disneyland Paris in 1995, while over 500 000 have visited Disneyworld in Florida each year since the mid-1990s.

Catchment areas for the parks

Catchment areas are mainly regional for many of the UK theme parks, although catchment areas for the larger theme parks can be international. Typically, the regional catchment area is about two-hours drive time. This means that a family with young children can leave home at 9 a.m., arrive by 11 a.m., stay for six hours and be home by 7 p.m.

Regional visitors account for 80% of admissions to the smaller theme parks but only 60% for the larger ones. Alton Towers is a special case and is almost a 'national' theme park. Over half of its visitors come from outside the region: special train services from London and coach services from other cities and resorts are available.

Value of the market in the UK

Expenditure at the twelve main theme parks in 1995 was worth about £138 million (Figure 7.10). Primary expenditure is that spent on admission charges, and those charges account for between 60% and 65% of consumer spending in the theme park. Catering is the second most important source of revenue, accounting for 20-25% of spending, while gifts and souvenirs make up the rest. During economic recession the amount of secondary expenditure is reduced, even if primary expenditure holds its own.

Figure 7.10 shows the economic attraction of operating a theme park. During the early 1990s, admissions were fairly static, with an increase of only 5.5% between 1992 and 1995. But during this time, total revenues increased by 57% and the amount spent per customer increased by almost 50% – few industries can match this level of growth.

Alton Towers	Staffordshire	2.7 million
Chessington World of Adventure	Surrey	1.8 million
Frontierland	Lancashire	1.3 million
Thorpe Park	Surrey	1.2 million
Drayton Manor Park	Staffordshire	1.0 million
Flamingo Land	N Yorkshire	1.0 million
American Adventure	Derbyshire	0.6 million
Camelot	Lancashire	0.5 million
Lightwater Valley	N Yorkshire	0.5 million
Flambards	Cornwall	0.5 million
Pleasurewood Hills	Suffolk	0.4 million
Paulton's Park	Hampshire	0.4 million
Blackgang Chine Lands of Fantasy	Isle of Wight	0.3 million

Figure 7.9 *Visitors to the 12 major theme parks in the UK, 1995*
Source: adapted from New leisure markets, 1996, Theme parks, New Leisure Markets

	1992	1995	% change
1992-5			
Admissions (12 major parks) (millions)	11.0	11.6	5.5
Revenue (£ million)	88.0	138.0	57
Spending per visitor (£)	8.00	11.90	49

Figure 7.10 *Estimated value of theme park markets, 1992 and 1995*
Source: adapted from New leisure markets, 1996, Theme parks, New Leisure Markets

Since 1995, admissions and receipts have risen. Annual promotions and the regular addition of new rides and attractions appears to influence admissions to individual parks more than general economic trends, although these trends do have some influence on theme parks.

Ownership of the main theme parks is dominated by just three companies – Pearson, Granada and Ready Mixed Concrete (RMC). Pearson, for example, is a publishing and media conglomerate, which publishes the Financial Times. It owns the Tussauds Group which controls Alton Towers, Chessington World of Adventure, the London Planetarium, Warwick Castle, Rock Circus and Madame Tussaud's Waxworks in London.

The industry is moving from a domestic to an international base. This applies not only to UK visitors travelling to the USA and to mainland Europe but also to Europeans and North Americans visiting UK theme parks as part of their holiday.

(000s)	1990	1991	1992	1993	1994	1995
Alton Towers	2070	1968	2501	2618	3011	2707
Chessington World of Adventure	1515	1410	1170	1495	1614	1770
Frontierland	1300	1300	1300	1300	1300	1300
Thorpe Park	974	921	1026	1327	1235	1166
Drayton Manor Park	989	990	950	1060	1104	1000
Flamingo Land	1138	1087	991	1000	1100	1000
American Adventure	750	1000	860	800	723	600
Camelot	600	700	600	550	528	500
Lightwater Valley	400	409	479	500	480	480
Total	**9736**	**9785**	**9877**	**10 650**	**11 095**	**10 523**

Figure 7.11 *Admissions to the nine largest theme parks, 1990-95*
Source: New leisure markets, 1996, Theme parks, New Leisure Markets

Figure 7.12 *Attracting the younger visitor – Legoland's fairy-tale ride works*

Admissions to theme parks

Figure 7.11 shows that the volume of admissions to theme parks was reasonably static during the recession years of 1989 to 1992 at about 10 million people. The prospect of paying £50 or more for a family day out limited the number of people visiting theme parks. From 1993, due to recovery from the recession, an increase in domestic tourism and leisure and investment in new attractions, theme parks increased the number of visitors they attracted and passed 11 million for the first time in 1994. Parks discovered that 'white knuckle rides' were a secure way of attracting high admissions, although it was important to offer attractions to those with infants (Figure 7.12) as well as older children, teenagers and adults. The market was diversifying in order to widen its appeal.

At the same time, 1994, EuroDisney opened and struggled. Renamed Disneyland Paris in 1996 with lower prices, it began to recover; surprisingly it also provided other theme parks with an uplift – attendances at other theme parks increased rather than fell. This is because those who visited theme parks as part of a holiday abroad had an experience which was positive enough to stimulate further exploration of theme parks at home.

Experts within the tourism industry believe that the creation of more quality parks and other attractions will encourage new customers into the market. Theme parks are aimed at satisfying basic needs in the leisure industry – entertainment, familiar food, safety, cleanliness and value for money. As long as customer satisfaction is maintained, there is potential for the market to grow. Evidence to support this is the increasing number of people travelling greater distances to visit theme parks, including overseas parks.

Figure 7.13 *Miniland, Legoland*

Legoland, Windsor

Legoland Windsor opened in 1996 advertising itself as 'a safe, happy land-within-a-land where the imagination knows no bounds'. The park was built at a cost of £85 million on the site of the former Windsor Safari Park, which closed in 1992. Legoland was able to develop a market base from a population who already knew its products, Lego and Duplo. Legoland is located about 40 kilometres from central London, within sight of Windsor Castle, which itself attracts about 600 000 people every year. The park is extremely consumer-friendly. There are cash machines, a camera shop, lockers and pushchair hire. There are workshops, stunt shows, puppet shows, theme restaurants, food carts (such as hot dog stands), play areas as well as rides. Miniland (Figure 7.13) consists of Lego models of famous cities and landscapes. Legoland aims to attract 1.4 million visitors every year.

Figure 7.14 *The driving school, Legoland*

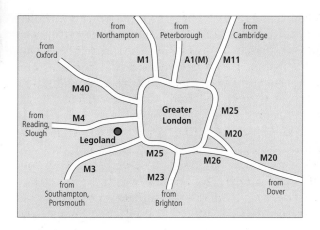

Figure 7.15 *The location of Legoland showing motorway links*
Source: adapted from Geofile, January 1996

Legoland's strategy was to win the hearts and minds of younger visitors and the minds of their parents. Instead of white-knuckle rides there are children's driving schools (Figure 7.14) complete with electric buggies and traffic lights. Instead of arcade games, it has a room full of computers linked up to robotic models. For parents and children, the day is an educational and entertaining day out.

Within an hour's drive of Legoland there is a potential market of 9 million families with children aged between 2 and 13, its target market (Figure 7.15). Legoland boasts an important advantage over other theme parks, for example Alton Towers and Chessington, in that its central theme, Lego and Duplo bricks, are familiar to its customers long before they even enter the theme park.

The owners of Legoland, the Danish company Lego Group, hope that visits to Legoland will boost sales of Lego and Duplo as well as some of their more innovative computer software packages.

Figure 7.16 *The location of Alton Towers, showing nearby conurbations and motorway links*

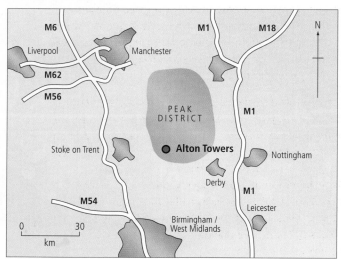

ALTON TOWERS

Alton Towers is situated near Alton in Staffordshire (Figure 7.16) and was opened in 1974. It attracted over 3 million visitors in 1994 and over 2.7 million visitors in 1995. The site covers about 350 hectares, including a stately home and gardens, nature trails, show farm, 'adventureland', eight restaurants and cafeterias and a hotel. There are over 120 rides including Nemesis (Figure 7.17), Black Hole and Skyride. These 'white knuckle rides' are the heart of the park's attraction, although there are attractions for all ages, especially young children.

Alton Towers is unusual in that it is located in the Peak District. As Figure 7.16 shows, it is accessible to a number of conurbations such as Birmingham, Stoke, Derby and Sheffield. By contrast, most of its main rivals are found very close to large urban centres. As visitors walk by the lakes and parks of the derelict stately home, peace and quiet give way to screams from the gravity-defying Nemesis ride.

At Alton Towers, the Alton Towers Hotel and Storybook Land were opened in 1996. Storybook Land centres on an ice rink with shows based on stories by Beatrice Potter. This is mainly to attract families with young children. In another move, the owners are attempting to introduce a Disney-style dimension to the park: Alton Towers was the first park to open a hotel in its bid to attract overnight visitors. For those who stay overnight, the second day in the park is available at a much reduced price. A large restaurant was also built in an attempt to entice non-staying park visitors to see the hotel and decide to stay overnight.

When the hotel at Alton Towers was opened, the then National Heritage Secretary, Virginia Bottomley, said that theme parks had a part to play in bringing together family and community groups. But theme parks are facing a growing challenge from computer-based indoor entertainment centres and multi-leisure centres offering indoor attractions, such as cinemas, ten-pin bowling and restaurants. Theme parks are facing this challenge through large-scale capital investment and in new attractions. Consequently, what started out as a family business running fairground rides at the seaside, is now a corporate concern.

Figure 7.17
The Nemesis ride at Alton Towers

Figure 7.18
Segaworld at the Trocadero Centre, Piccadilly

Virtual theme park

Europe's first interactive theme park, Segaworld, opened in 1996 in London after a £50 million investment from between Sega Enterprises, one of Japan's leading games groups, and Trocadero, a UK-based leisure company. Segaworld occupies seven floors and over 12 000 m^3 of the Trocadero Centre, the retail and entertainment centre in Piccadilly, London (Figure 7.18).

Unlike the other theme parks, Segaworld combines virtual reality and advanced computer graphics to create interactive entertainment rather than physical movement on which the traditional theme parks rely. For example, Aqua Planet, one of six adventure rides at Segaworld, uses new technology by combining motion simulation with virtual reality. Visitors wear 3-D glasses and sit in chairs, which spin through 360° for an underwater interactive adventure that involves fighting off attacks by a giant octopus.

Video games lie at the heart of Segaworld, divided into six theme zones including flight deck, which features the take-off roar of a Harrier jump jet suspended from the ceiling. The smell of rubber periodically pervades Race Track, the racing car zone, where eight drivers compete against each other.

Segaworld expects to attract 1.75 million visitors a year with an average spend of £15 per head. Being an indoor theme park, it has the advantage of not being at the mercy of the weather.

Inset 7.1
Disneyland Paris

Disneyland Paris attracted 1.6 million British visitors in its first full year, 1991, but this fell back to 1.2 million in 1995. Total admissions increased from 8.4 million in 1991 to 10.7 million in 1995, with the French accounting for 40% of visitors and the British about 12%. Visitor numbers from Britain are affected by fluctuations in the currency exchange. During 1995-96 there was a very unfavourable exchange rate, although a number of short-breaks 'deals' maintained numbers. In addition, the opening of the Channel Tunnel and widespread advertising by the Disney company, 'The magic is closer than you think' has led to an increase in visitor numbers. Disneyland Paris hopes to attract 2 million UK visitors each year by 2000.

The experience of Europe's Disney park show that theme parks can get it wrong. The cost of building the park was double the budget (reaching £3.4 billion) and the recession in Europe in the early 1990s kept many visitors away, especially given the prices originally charged. The park did not make a profit in its first four years. Moreover, many Europeans wanted the park to be based around American culture as seen by Disney (Figure 7.19), rather than having a Disney version of European culture.

Disneyland Paris plans to develop a new town including a shopping mall, houses and leisure facilities on the outskirts of its site. This is the first time that the initiative for a new town in France has come largely from a private developer. By 2000, a 90 000 square metre shopping mall, with 150 shops, will attract some of the 400 000 local shoppers. The new town, to be called Val d'Europe, will have a

Figure 7.19 *Disneyland Paris – Europe's premier theme park*

population of 1500 and will contain 370 000 square metres of space for business, public facilities, hotels and restaurants. A second campus for the local Marne La Vallee university may also be located at the site. The aim is to create more than 2000 new jobs.

The development of Disneyland Paris had side-effects which were not anticipated by the Disney company. Although it dominates European theme parks, with three times as many visitors as any other park, it has stimulated the theme park sector generally. Other theme parks in France to open included Futuroscope, Parc Asterix and Nausicaa, while Legoland opened in the UK.

One of the greatest ironies is that since Disneyland Paris opened, the long-haul holiday market has grown, carrying more visitors to attractions in the USA, in particular Florida, the world's centre for theme parks. Admissions to the main attractions in Florida, in 1995, were:

- Magic Kingdom at Walt Disney World – 12.9 million
- Epcot Centre, Walt Disney World – 10.7 million
- MGM Studios at Walt Disney World – 9.5 million
- Universal Studios – 8 million
- Sea World – 5 million.

MULTIPLEX CINEMAS

Since the early 1980s, North America has developed hundreds of new multiplex cinemas (cinemas with more than five screens) and megaplexes (more than 12 screens). By contrast, in Europe the number of cinema screens fell from over 26 000 in 1980 to under 19 000 in 1995. However, since 1995 there have been scores of new developments across Europe, yet Europe is still relatively underdeveloped compared with North America.

The North American market is now considered to be saturated or 'mature' in that there is at least one multiplex in every large city and many US cinema companies have turned their attention to Europe. For example, Warner Brothers diversified into the UK at the end of the 1980s and now has eight cinemas here. Admissions to UK cinemas have doubled since 1985 when the first multiplex in Britain opened in Milton Keynes. There are now 900 multiplexes throughout the UK and attendances reached 130 million in 1997. Warner Brothers plans to open another 23 cinemas in the UK by 2000 when audiences are expected to reach 180 million. They also plan to open another 275 multiplexes across Europe by 2000.

The stimulus for these developments was not the shortage of cinemas, but the shortage of clean, modern cinemas that offered a wide choice of films and a selection of eating and drinking places.

Britain's largest multiplex cinema, a 'megalopolex' with 30 screens, is to be built at Birmingham, although this is 'small' compared with the 40-screen cinema being built in Helsinki, Finland.

CENTER PARCS

Center Parcs is a relatively new company in the UK and is one of the most successful leisure concepts, as compared with UK seaside resorts. It combines the concept of a theme park (based largely around water and sport) with holidays with outdoor activities such as swimming, and evening entertainment, such as comedians and bands. One of the main attractions in each complex is a large indoor pool with 'rapids', 'beaches' and 'waves' in a controlled climate which enables visitors to enjoy a family holiday at any time of the year. There are three Center Parcs in the UK: the first was opened in Sherwood Forest in 1987, followed by Elveden in Norfolk and Longleat Forest in Wiltshire in 1994 (Figure 7.20).

The Center Parcs concept creates a relaxed atmosphere in a woodland setting (Figure 7.21). The sites are car-free zones and people travel around the site by bicycle or on foot. Most of the activities are centred on a dome, which contains a number of swimming pools (catering for all ages and abilities), restaurants, play areas and shops. Other activities, such as tennis, horse riding, football, badminton, take place outside the dome.

Center Parcs has a reputation for attracting middle-class people (A, B and C1): they have been described as a 'suburbanised forest'. This is partly on account of the high cost of a holiday there. In addition to the cost of accommodation, most activities have to be paid for, with the exception of the swimming and activities for young children.

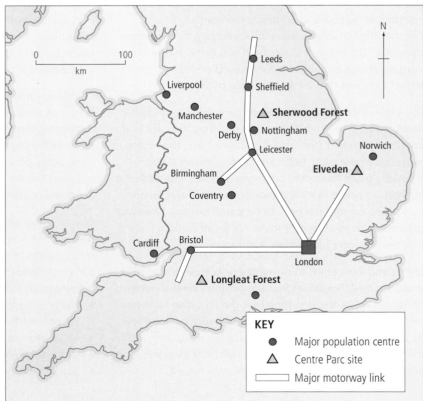

Figure 7.20 *The location of Center Parcs showing nearby population centres and motorway links*
Source: Geofile, January 1996, 278

The Center Parcs developments have been very successful. The keys to their success include:

- successful marketing and targeting of middle-class families
- an indoor environment which makes Britain's unreliable weather irrelevant
- a tranquil and natural environment.

Profits and turnover are high; occupancy rates are 95% throughout the year. However, one of the main constrains on expanding the Center Parcs chain is the availability of suitable sites close to large centres of population.

Figure 7.21 *The forest and dome at Centre Parcs, Longleat*

SUMMARY

Most people in Britain regard the countryside as common property, and they wish to enjoy it. This begs the question: what is the countryside for? It is for people to earn a living and it is for people to enjoy, but sometimes these two aims are irreconcilable.

QUESTIONS

1 Conduct a survey of your home area. What attractions, such as cinemas, theme parks, special interest activities (such as an ice-rink or a bowling alley) are there? What are the characteristics of the locations of these facilities? What geographic factors help to explain their location?
2 Account for the rise in popularity of theme parks.

BIBLIOGRAPHY AND RECOMMENDED READING

New leisure markets, 1996, *Special interest tourism*, New Leisure Markets

New leisure markets, 1996, *Theme parks*, New Leisure Markets

WEB SITES

Cadbury World -
http://www.cadbury.co.uk

Chapter 8
Developing countries

This chapter focuses on tourism in developing countries and looks at several countries, which illustrate some of the key issues that arise with the promotion of tourism. We examine the way in which rural communities have been integrated into tourism in Zimbabwe, the problems of integrating rural communities in Kenya into tourism, the health and safety problems caused by tourism in the Dominican Republic, the effects of terrorism on Egypt's tourist industry, attempts by Burma's military dictatorship and Cuba's communist government to attract tourism, sex tourism in Thailand and the growth of fast food chains in India. The effects of tourism vary widely from country to country and it would be wrong to think of all developing countries as having the same characteristics.

THE ATTRACTIONS OF DEVELOPING COUNTRIES

Inset

Developing countries, as far as it is possible to generalise, are characterised by lower standards of living, less GNP/head, a poorer urban infrastructure, and a higher percentage of people engaged in agriculture or manufacturing compared with more developed countries. They are economically less developed rather than being socially, culturally or politically less developed.

Worldwide, mostly from developed countries, tourists are attracted to developing countries, such as Zimbabwe, Kenya and the Dominican Republic, for a number of reasons. These include:

- their rich and varied wildlife and world famous game reserves (Figure 8.1)
- tropical climates, attractive to European visitors especially in December and January
- glorious beaches, often deserted (Figure 8.2)
- rich cultural heritage and traditions (Figure 8.3)
- relatively low cost of living compared with developed countries
- European languages being widely spoken, with many links with Europe.

Tourism can bring a number of benefits to a developing economy, including foreign currency, employment, investment and improved infrastructure. For example, thousands of people are employed in formal (registered) and informal (unregistered) occupations ranging from hotel staff and tour operators to cleaners, gardeners and souvenir hawkers. In addition, tourism is a more profitable way to use land than for farming. Estimates of the annual returns per hectare of land range from £10 for pastoralism to £35 for dry-land farming and £140 for game parks and tourism.

However, there are a number of problems that have arisen as a result of the tourist industry:

- undue pressure on natural ecosystems, leading to soil erosion, litter pollution, decline of animal numbers
- much tourist-related employment is unskilled, seasonal, part-time, poorly paid and lacking any rights for the workers
- resources are spent on providing for tourists while local people may have to manage without
- a large proportion of profits go overseas, for example to holiday companies, tour operators, hotel chains
- crime is increasingly directed at tourists; much is petty crime but there have been very serious incidents
- tourism is very unpredictable, varying in volume with the strength of the economy, cost, safety, alternative opportunities, stage in the family life-cycle.

Figure 8.1 *Wildlife is an important attraction in many developing countries*

Figure 8.2 *'Almost' deserted sandy beach, South Africa*

Figure 8.3 *'Cultural heritage' provided in a music and dance session*

TOURISM IN ZIMBABWE

Zimbabwe has experienced a rapid increase in the number of tourists during the 1990s: during the first quarter of 1998 the number of visitors increased by 71% compared with the same period in 1997, although income from tourism was up by only 23%.

The main sources of tourists include South Africa, Zambia, the USA, Canada and Western Europe. As a tourist destination, Zimbabwe has a broad range of attractions. Victoria Falls (Figure 8.5), National Parks such as Gonarezhou in the south-east, the Zambezi Valley and Hwange (Figure 8.6), historic and cultural monuments such as the Great Zimbabwe Monument, and rock paintings in the hills close to Bulawayo dating as far back as 30 000 years (Figure 8.7). Zimbabwe has a number of different environments including rainforest, savanna woodlands, semi-desert, lowlands and highlands. These produce a variety of different ecosystems (Figure 8.8) with many different species of game animals.

There are also sporting attractions. These include golf courses, trout fishing, game fishing, hunting, white-water rafting, sailing, canoeing, riding, horse racing and polo. Zimbabwe is rapidly becoming a popular haunt for rich golfers, offering spectacular settings. Year-round good weather, uncrowded fairways and reasonable green fees make the sport attractive. There are forty 18-hole courses located throughout the country and Zimbabwe offers the sport as a golfing 'safari'. Adventure tourism, including wildlife safaris, luxurious lodges and of course visits to the spectacular Victoria Falls, is gaining in popularity, and there has also been a golf renaissance. For example, the Elephant Hills Hotel complex, with an excellent golf course, has magnificent views across the Zambezi River and is within sight of the Fall's spray.

Zimbabwe's tourism industry is based on an environment both natural and man-made which is highly susceptible to degradation. Limited revenues from tourism are used for the protection of the environment. With increased awareness of conservation, there is new enthusiasm from the tourists to

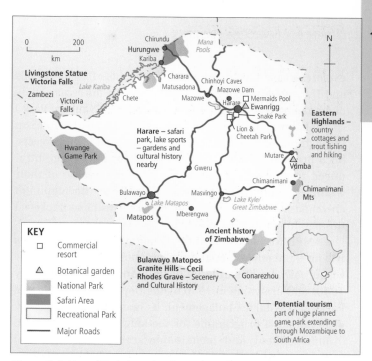

Figure 8.4 *Map of Zimbabwe showing parks and main tourist attractions*
Source: Carr, M., 1997, New patterns processes and change, Nelson

Figure 8.5 *Victoria Falls, Zimbabwe*

Figure 8.6 *Hwange National Park, Zimbabwe*

QUESTIONS

1 Why are more people from the developed world taking holidays in the developing world?

2 What are the advantages and disadvantages of tourism in developing countries?

explore areas other than the famous sights of Victoria Falls and Hwange National Park. (See Chapter 4 for a case study of managing wildlife and tourism in Hwange National Park.)

Zimbabwe has pioneered ecologically sustainable tourism through innovative schemes known as CAMPFIRE projects. Such projects, which are growing rapidly, have been introduced to show local people the economic value of their wildlife. Zimbabwe's controlled tourism development encompasses rural areas, and people's lives have improved through integrated projects.

CAMPFIRE is based on the rationale that communities will invest in environmental conservation if they can use the resources on a sustainable basis. Conceived in the early 1980s and drawn up in 1986 by the Department of National Parks and Wildlife Management, its main objectives were:

- to initiate a programme for the long term development, management and sustainable utilisation of natural resources in the communal areas (land held for the use of a community, but not owned by any one person)
- to achieve management of resources by placing their custody and responsibility with the resident communities
- to allow communities to benefit directly from the exploitation of natural resources within the communal areas
- to establish the administrative and institutional structures necessary to make the programme work.

Under CAMPFIRE, participating communities have:

- full legal rights to manage and benefit directly from their own wildlife
- territorial rights over wildlife in their area
- the right to establish wildlife management institutions at lower levels, at ward and village levels. (Small-scale electoral/communal wards – often comprising a village plus surrounding rural area.)

Figure 8.7 Rock art and a lizard charmer at the Matopas, Zimbabwe

Figure 8.8 Rain forest by the Zambezi River, Zimbabwe

A percentage of the revenue goes to the local village/ward committee, which decides what the money should be spent on – whether it should be used to fund infrastructure developments for the benefit of both people and wildlife, or whether it should be invested in income-generating projects. Infrastructure developments include:

- installation of boreholes with engines for clean water
- pre-school, school and health clinic developments
- fencing of arable land to protect it from crop pests
- small dam/pan construction to supply water for people and wildlife
- road development
- maintenance funds for electric fences.

Revenues are also used to pay community members for removal of snares, which used to be set by the local Zimbabwe people to kill the larger animals, particularly carnivores, which threatened their herds, or antelopes, which ate the grass. The money is also used to buy food during periods of drought.

Country	1997 arrivals (000s)	% change 1996-97	1997 receipts (£ million)	% change 1996-97
1 South Africa	5530	11.9	1417	15.1
2 Tunisia	4263	9.7	950	6.1
3 Morocco	3115	15.7	740	-13.1
4 Zimbabwe	1894	8.7	154	14.2
5 Kenya	750	4.6	309	5.9
6 Botswana	728	3.0	112	1.7
7 Algeria	635	5.0	–	–
8 Nigeria	611	-25.7	53	1.2
9 Mauritius	536	10.1	311	0.0
10 Eritrea	492	18.0	46	8.7
11 Namibia	410	1.2	130	1.0
12 Reunion	368	6.1	168	5.8
13 Tanzania	350	12.9	222	11.8
14 Ghana	325	6.6	164	6.8
15 Swaziland	322	2.2	–	–

Figure 8.9 Changes in the number of tourists to Africa
Source: World Tourism Organisation, 1998

QUESTIONS

1 Study Figure 8.9 which shows the number of tourists to the main tourist destinations in Africa. Choose an appropriate method to show this data on an outline map of Africa. Describe, and comment on, the geographical pattern you have drawn.

2 What are the attractions of Zimbabwe as a tourist destination?

3 Briefly explain what happens in the CAMPFIRE scheme. How useful is this for rural communities in Zimbabwe?

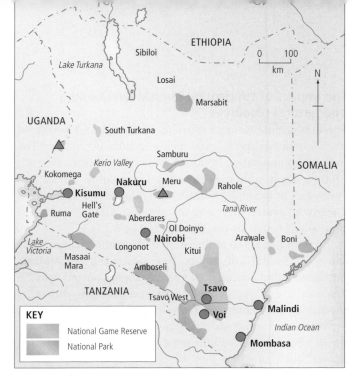

Figure 8.10 *Map of Kenya showing parks and main tourist attractions*
Source: Carr, M., 1997, New patterns, Nelson

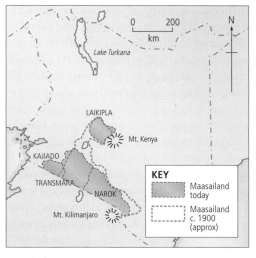

Figure 8.11
Maasailand – past and present. Berger, D., The challenge of integrating Maasai tradition with tourism, in Price, M., (ed.), 1996, People and tourism in fragile environments, Wiley

INTEGRATING THE MAASAI WITH TOURISM IN KENYA

Tourism in Kenya is mainly safari and beach orientated. It is vital to the economy and is a major source of foreign exchange. However, despite moving into the package holiday market in the 1980s, the number of tourists visiting Kenya decreased in the 1990s. The main reasons were the well-publicised murder of several tourists, political upheaval within Kenya and economic recession worldwide.

Wildlife-related tourism is Kenya's most valuable industry, creating jobs and bringing in foreign exchange. Between 1955 and 1991, visitor numbers rose from 36 000 to 805 000 and over the same period, the revenues from tourism rose from £1.6 million to £24 million. Wildlife-related tourism accounts for about 40% of all tourism in Kenya and much of this is concentrated in parks such as Nairobi, Maasai Mara, Amboseli and Tsavo West (Figure 8.10) in Maasailand (Figure 8.11). However, the participation of the Maasai people in tourism – either as managers or beneficiaries – has been minimal, but is increasing.

Kenya's protected lands can be divided into two main types: National Parks and National Game Reserves. National Parks are protected for the national interest and funded and managed by the Kenya Wildlife Service (KWS); National Game Reserves are owned by local authorities on behalf of indigenous people.

The indigenous Maasai people have coexisted with wildlife and the natural ecosystem for hundreds of years, manipulating the environment to sustain their livestock. Their use of the savanna has followed the seasonal movement of animals. Their knowledge of the environment and skill in working with the environment has the potential to be used in the management of Kenya's environment to create sustainable tourism.

The Maasai are the most famous of Kenya's ten or so pastoralist groups. They are the best known of Kenya's pastoralists because they are located in protected areas, which are famous for their diversity of wildlife and are a popular destination for safari tourists. The Maasai occupied the Great Rift Valley of Kenya from about the fifteenth century, but in the nineteenth and twentieth centuries lost most of their territory. Now the 400 000-strong Maasai occupy four districts in the southwest of Kenya and their traditional way of life is breaking down. Many of the younger Maasai are intermarrying with people from other tribes, adopting the languages and customs of neighbouring groups and contributing to the national economy.

To fully understand the challenges of integrating Maasai tradition with modern tourism, it is important to distinguish between the popular traditional image of the Maasai and their current way of life. The image is of a pastoral group dependent on meat, milk and blood, with women plastering mud huts, elders sitting discussing matters of the Maasai world and warriors dancing their war songs. These images of the Maasai, which are formed when tourists visit a 'traditional' Maasai village are far from the truth. Maasai culture is changing. Values, aspirations and beliefs are changing as the Maasai become steadily influenced by a modern cash economy (Figure 8.12).

Figure 8.12 *The modern Maasai are mostly integrated into Kenya's everyday lifestyle*

The Maasai are increasingly part of an economy in which they have to earn money in order to buy goods and services that they would have previously produced themselves. These include food, consumer goods, school fees, medical bills and so on. Some Maasai are involved in the tourist trade and own bars, shops, and trading stalls while others are involved in accommodation and transport. Some Maasai lease their land to companies to build on. Thus there are some Maasai who are making a considerable profit out of tourism.

These changes are possible because there has been a change in land tenure. During the colonial era of the nineteenth and early twentieth centuries, communal areas were administered by local authorities on behalf of the indigenous people. After Kenya's Independence in 1963, the government encouraged privatisation of land by converting communal land into private ranches for groups and individuals. The government viewed pastoralism as inefficient, unproductive and environmentally damaging. Privatisation has led to changes in land use. For example, many of the smaller plots have been sold to farmers, some from outside the area who farm them intensively; the larger holdings have been sold to developers keen to exploit Kenya's rangeland (the savanna or grazing land), forest, water and wildlife resources. The pastoralists no longer have sufficient land to support themselves using traditional methods and have to supplement their income by other means.

The cooperation and cohesion which characterises the traditional Maasai community are increasingly being replaced by modern 'values' of individualism, where competition and entrepreneurial activity predominate. The government view is that the Maasai are modernising and contributing to the national economy. The alternative view, held by many geographers, is that the Maasai are losing their land, their rights, their culture and livelihood.

The impact of tourism on Maasai livelihood and natural resources

For a long time Kenyan tourism promoted and marketed wildlife-tourism and ignored the indigenous population. The indigenous population became more disadvantaged as much of their land was expropriated for wildlife parks and reserves. For example, Nairobi and Amboseli Parks had previously provided dry season grazing and a source of permanent water for the Maasai (Figure 8.13).

Tourism has led to an increase in consumer prices, while the construction of roads has destroyed vegetation, increased pollution and endangered human life and wildlife. The increase in population in the tourist areas – drawn by the prospects of increased wealth through tourism – has adverse social and environmental effects, such as the breakdown of communities and the destruction of parts of the natural environment.

However, in the 1990s an increasing number of Maasai are benefiting from tourism, although at a cost. For example, there are external business links and political links, which have enabled the tourist infrastructure to be developed, and which will mean the area will be increasingly marketed, but these developments have weakened local cohesion. The Maasai are able to sell some of their crafts to visitors and there is no doubt that a small minority of the Maasai have become very rich and powerful through their ownership of tourist-related resources.

Attempts to reduce environmental destruction inside the national parks have often increased pressures just outside the parks. Near entrance gates, unplanned trading centres have emerged, such as Talek township on the edge of the Maasai Mara Reserve (Figure 8.13). Partly as a result of Kenya's reputation for poor environmental management of tourism, it is now facing increased competition from other developing countries, such as Zimbabwe, which have a better reputation.

The Maasai culture is increasingly being used as a bait to attract tourists to Kenya. It is now an integral part of many tourist itineraries. Some Maasai pastoralists have managed to combine livestock-rearing with ecotourism, while others have engaged in a variety of wildlife projects and enterprises (Figure 8.14). Oldonyo Waus Camp is an example of a development for a small number of visitors who are prepared to pay a high price for an exclusive experience. Many Maasai were involved in planning the development, and many now work there. The lodge owner has diversified so that there is a wildlife management plan, an ostrich rearing section, beadwork by local women and regulated culling of elephants and other large herbivores. Some of the profit is ploughed back into local projects such as dam construction and reforestation. Other examples include Kimana, owned by an

Figure 8.13 A township on the edge of the Maasai Mara Reserve

organisation called Kuku Group Ranch, which has set land aside as a wildlife sanctuary to conserve vegetation, to provide vital water source around a swamp and to earn money from tourism. Over fifty projects were developed on ranches between 1993 and 1994 surrounding Amboseli National Park. Revenues earned in the parks are increasingly shared with neighbouring communities to support community development; local communities are more likely to protect wildlife and land surrounding national parks if they benefit from tourism.

The Olanana Cultural Centre (Figure 8.15) is an attempt by a private company to market Maasai culture in a culturally sensitive way. The Maasai were involved in the construction of the centre and are employed there; a percentage of the revenue goes towards local development. There have also been a number of educational programmes. One of the most successful is a programme that enables North American students to visit Maasai communities and learn about rangeland ecosystems, Maasai traditions, development and cultural issues.

The ways in which pastoralists and wildlife-based tourism attempt to preserve their resource base are often in conflict. Pastoralists follow a seasonal pattern of movement, thereby preventing long-term damage to vegetation and water resources. By contrast, wildlife-based tourism has depended on areas being used exclusively by wildlife and tourists. Nevertheless, pastoralists continue to graze their herds ille-

gally in parks and reserves, and grazing competition between wildlife and the Maasai herds has increased. The amount of grazing land has decreased but, as livestock continues to be owned individually, some pastoralists increase their herd size in order to command a larger part of the common resource. Those with the largest herds cause most environmental destruction.

The Maasai social structure is also breaking down. A new group of elite landowners has been formed, many of whom are Maasai, who want to be part of capitalist Kenya, rather than traditional Maasai life. They feel little reason to cling to their traditions, but desire a greater share of Kenya's riches. They control most of the resources in Maasailand, including those related to tourism. A lack of formal education for the pastoralists means that they find it difficult to unite and claim legally what is rightfully theirs. Maasai communities rarely have the entrepreneurial skill or contacts to start up and manage tourism ventures. Thus many go into partnerships with agents who have overseas contacts, marketing skills and managerial skills whose historical role has been one of exploitation.

Thus there is a change in the way in which tourism is organised. In the past, the government and the tourist industry have 'mined' the parks and reserves and used the Maasai culture to attract tourists, although there was very little benefit to the Maasai themselves. Increasingly, however, traditional land use systems are being integrated into tourism: some tour operators are investing in the Maasai as a long term tourist attraction/resource with the Maasai being encouraged to take part in sustainable management of wildlife. There are clear parallels with the CAMPFIRE schemes in Zimbabwe.

For tourism to continue in Kenya, the land must retain its attractions, such as its natural landscapes and its spectacular biodiversity. Pastoral communities that have the skills and knowledge to work in a sustainable way with natural processes should be encouraged to use this knowledge for the sustainable development of tourism in Maasailand. However, they must be rewarded for their work. Without reward they will return to unsustainable activities such as intensive commercial farming. The more the Maasai community are involved in developments in their own land, the greater the chance that the developments will be successful.

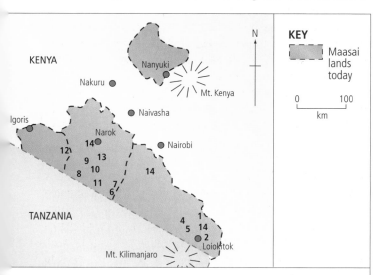

Multiple land use – Imbirkani
Wildlife sanctuary – Kimana
Camel treks – Ilingwezi
KWS revenue sharing projects – Ambrose/Tsavo
Group ranch wildlife scouts – training wildlife scouts
Naimina Enkiyio Conservation Trust
Ethnobotany project – vegetation survey & conservation

8 Waste management – Mara lodges
9 Community conservation project – Mara
10 Wood fuel survey/energy conservation – Talek
11 Rhino scouts – Naikara/Loleta
12 Olanana cultural centre
13 Explore Mara training
14 KWS Community Wildlife Service

Figure 8.14 *Wildlife projects and enterprises in Maasailand*
Berger, D., The challenge of integrating Maasai tradition with tourism, in Price, M., (ed.) 1996, People and tourism in fragile environments, Wiley

---

QUESTIONS

1 Compare and contrast the popular image of the Maasai with their real characteristics.

2 Why is there a conflict between Maasai pastoralists and tourism?

3 Briefly describe some of the ways in which the Maasai have been integrated into tourism.

4 What problems are the in attempting to integrate the Maasai into tourist developments?

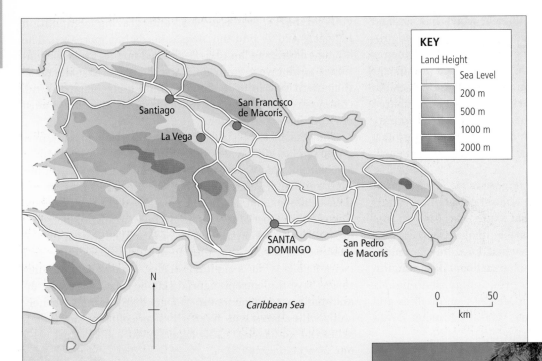

Figure 8.15
The Dominican Republic
Source: adapted from Dorling Kindersley, World Reference Atlas, 1994

Figure 8.16 *Stunning white, sandy beaches in the Dominican Republic*

VISITOR VULNERABILITY – TOURISM IN THE DOMINICAN REPUBLIC

In the late 1990s the Dominican Republic offered the seemingly impossible – the Caribbean for the budget traveller (Figure 8.16). With its white, sandy beaches, dramatic mountains and the promise of £500 all-inclusive tropical holidays, the Dominican Republic rapidly became one of the most popular tourist destinations (Figure 8.16). Overtaking Florida as the top long-haul destination for UK tourists, the island was swamped by 250 000 UK tourists in 1997 – double that of 1996. However, the explosion of visitor numbers was not met with a similar increase in infrastructure developments and the industry quickly became unsustainable; in 1997, 35% of UK visitors fell ill, mostly with food poisoning.

The Dominican Republic shares the island of Hispaniola with Haiti, occupying the eastern end.

In 1998, Airtours, the second largest UK tour operator to the island, announced it was cutting 10 000 holidays, one quarter of its total, amid concerns about hygiene standards in parts of the tourist sector. In 1997, Thomson Holidays evacuated 350 guests from one hotel after at least three people contracted typhoid.

One of the main problems was hygiene (or the lack of it) and the risk this posed through disease. One in three visitors to the problem hotels had suffered diarrhoea or sickness. Indeed, the figures might be even higher, because many people with diarrhoea often do not go to their doctor.

Airtours blames the island for failing to improve the water and sewage systems to keep pace with the growth of tourism, and, despite assurances that health and hygiene standards would be improved generally, this did not happen. Although a hygiene improvement programme had been established in 1996, some hotels had failed to comply with it.

Indeed, the pressure group Holiday Travelwatch received 10 000 letters of complaint regarding serious illness on the island between July and August 1997 – including twelve notifiable diseases, such as typhoid, cholera, salmonella, *E Coli* bacteria, hepatitis and legionnaire's disease (Figure 8.17) – up to 2000 UK visitors to the island sued their tour operators.

For the first time, a developing country has become a number one travel destination and officials admit that the island, which relies on tourism for almost half its economy, has a major hygiene problem. The Dominican Republic attracts people who are not familiar with travelling to the tropics and do not take sufficient care – for example, by drinking bottled water. According to the Dominican Republic

Figure 8.17 Poor environmental standards in the Dominican Republic

Tourist Board, less than 1% of UK tourists visited their doctors on their return from holiday, showing that the alleged health problems were not as bad as the tourists claimed.

Aggressive steps have now been taken to identify and eradicate the hygiene problems. In 1998, forty-six of the 84 hotels used by UK tour operators on the island signed up to a programme backed by the Federation of Tour Operators specifying European Union levels of hygiene. Hotels failing to implement such standards, checked fortnightly, will be dropped from the UK market. New health regulations imposed in 1998 include strict guidelines on the storage and separation of food, and further investment in water and sewage systems.

Health problems have not been the only difficulty on the island. Figure 8.18 lists some of the less attractive aspects of the island.

Paradise Lost:
the negative side of the Dominican Republic

Armed crime has soared after 1500 criminals from the island were deported back there by the US in 1996.
- Two locally-recruited tour guides raped a British holidaymaker in 1997. The 44-year-old woman has had a nervous breakdown while awaiting the outcome of an HIV test.

- There are high levels of Aids, HIV, hepatitis, polio and typhoid.
- Banks and supermarkets are guarded by security men with guns while gangs roam the streets. Once they arrive at their holiday destination, tourists are warned not to stray from the beaten track.

Figure 8.18 Paradise Lost – the negative side of the Dominican Republic

TERRORISM AND RECENT CHANGES IN TOURISM IN EGYPT

Egypt's wealth of antiquities has made it a popular tourist destination since the 1880s. Together with the pyramids and ancient temples, it offers cruises on the Nile and top class scuba diving, especially at the coral reefs near Hurghada on the Red Sea.

In the 1970s, the Egyptian president Anwar Sadat challenged his people to conquer the desert. Model New Towns were built, but few Egyptians moved out to the 'tenements in the sand'. Now, however, Egypt is in the midst of a land rush. Egyptians are deserting the Nile valley but bypassing Sadat's ghost towns and flocking to resorts with names such as Santa Monica, Virginia Beach and Dreamland. From the white beaches west of Alexandria to the coral-studded shores of the Red Sea, the country's 3000 kilometre coastline is being developed into tourist 'villages' (Figure 8.19). In the mid-1980s, the government built condominiums next to a number of beaches. The condominiums were very popular with Egypt's middle class, encouraging a series of similar projects that have cost £7 billion and destroyed up to a quarter of Egypt's Mediterranean coastline, by removing sand, increasing the pollution in the area, and ruining the landscape. Egyptians themselves account for the building booms near Cairo and on the Mediterranean coast, but rapid construction on the Red Sea coast is largely to accommodate tourists.

Figure 8.19 Map of Egypt showing main resorts Source: The Economist, August 17, 1996

Egypt has long been a popular tourist attraction. Throughout the 1970s and 1980s, tourism in Egypt prospered, and indeed it became Egypt's main source of foreign currency (other than aid currency). However, a spate of terrorist attacks between 1993 and 1995 and isolated incidents in 1996 and 1997 led to a sharp decline in tourism. Islamic fundamentalists began attacking western tourists in order to put pressure on the Egyptian government to make Egypt an Islamic state. As a result, tourist numbers fell from

3.2 million in 1992 to 2.6 million in 1993 and there was a major drop in foreign earnings. In the late 1990s there has been renewed investment in tourism and tourists are back, but not all, as they once were, in pursuit of Egypt's antiquities. Instead a small, but increasing number head for the relative safety of the beaches, which are a less obvious attraction, and so far remain untargeted by Islamic anti-tourist groups (Figure 8.20).

Tourism is important for Egypt. Even in 1995-96, a period when the number of tourists was low, tourism earned £1.9 billion in foreign exchange and reached £2.33 billion in 1997-98.

In the late 1990s the Red Sea coast attracted only one-tenth of Egypt's tourists. Given current growth rates, the Egyptian government sees that share rising to about half the 10 million visitors expected each year by 2020. At least 90 000 hotel rooms must be built to accommodate them (which is 25% more than the capacity for the whole country in 1998). To service these, the local population will have to increase fivefold from its current level of 200 000 and water will somehow have to be piped in from the already over-exploited Nile.

All this leads some to predict a planning disaster. Critics point to a 60 kilometre stretch between Hurghada and Safaga (Figure 8.19), where the government has allocated land for building 65 000 rooms, and where delicate coral reefs run parallel to the shoreline. Environmental laws forbid alteration of the coast. But at Hurghada, where chain hotels already stand elbow to elbow, developers have excavated lagoons and levelled reefs, completely ignoring the rules.

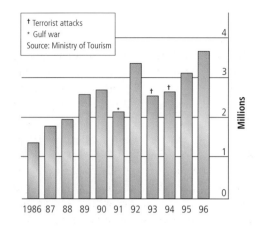

Figure 8.20
Foreign visitors to Egypt, 986-96
Source: The Economist, August 17, 1996

TOURISM AND INTERNAL POLITICS – THE CASE OF ZANZIBAR

In 1964 the island of Zanzibar united with the African country, Tanganyika, to form Tanzania (Figure 8.21) but a large number of residents in Zanzibar have never recognised the 1964 union and separatists are a growing force.

INSET

The HDI, Human Development Index, is an index varying between 1 at the higher end of the scale and 0.0 at the lower end, and is calculated by using data for Purchasing Power (GNP/head at local costs), educational attainment, and life expectancy. Tanzania has a low HDI, just 0.306.

Tanzania is a very poor country. It has a low Gross Domestic Product per head, a high infant mortality rate, low daily calorie intake and a low HDI. In the early 1990s it received just 186 000 tourists a year. However, it possesses landscapes of considerable beauty and important biodiversity. One-third of Tanzania is game reserve or national park. The Serengeti and the Ngorongoro Crater are among the top attractions. Increasingly, the Tanzanian government is looking towards tourism as a way of developing the country.

Zanzibar's traditional cash crop economy, based on cloves, faces a bleak future. The economic collapse in Indonesia will almost certainly curtail demand for the scented hreteh cigarettes that absorb the bulk of the world's clove crop, most of which is grown in Tanzania. The Zanzibar Opposition Party (CUE) wants to restructure the islands along the lines of Singapore or Hong Kong, with finance and trans-shipment of goods from East Africa placed at the core of a service-oriented economy. But, while the Tanzanian government based on the mainland controls banking licences and customs regulations, such a change is impossible.

If the links with mainland Tanzania are to remain as they

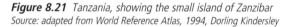

Figure 8.21 Tanzania, showing the small island of Zanzibar
Source: adapted from World Reference Atlas, 1994, Dorling Kindersley

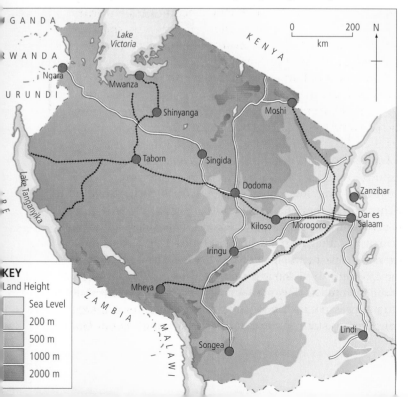

are, the only plausible source of economic growth is tourism. This, indeed, is beginning to take off. Some 86 500 tourists visited Zanzibar in 1997, a fivefold increase on 1987. The Zanzibar Investment Promotion Agency has approved £175 million worth of projects in tourism, ten times the total for other industries. Tourist revenue in 1997 was twice that of 1996.

But tourism is causing anger among many Zanzibaris. A quarter of all visitors in 1997 were package tourists from Italy, accustomed to wandering hand-in-hand and baring flesh to the sun (Figure 8.22). This does not suit the conservative norms of Zanzibar, which is racially mixed, Arabs and Africans, but overwhelmingly Muslim. Underdressed tourists are reported to have been attacked outside mosques.

Like many other issues in Zanzibar, the 'moral irresponsibility' of tourists threatens to become a political issue. According to the Zanzibar Opposition Party, if their hands were not tied by the mainland they would not have to depend on 'half-naked visitors for a living'. In response, the Tanzanian ruling party accuses the CUE of depriving Zanzibaris of a golden future by opposing the development of tourism. However, as many of the top jobs in the tourist industry are held by people from the mainland, the Zanzibaris have less of a vested interest in tourism than the mainland.

TOURISM UNDER DICTATORSHIPS

We now turn from countries afflicted by terrorism and internal political conflict to two countries which have markedly contrasting political systems, Burma and Cuba, both of whom have experienced pressure from developed countries as they attempt to develop their tourism industries.

BURMA (MYANMAR)

In 1988, the military in Burma (officially known as the Union of Myanmar) seized political power from the Socialist Programme Party (the sole legal party), supposedly to maintain order until multiparty elections could be held. These elections were held in 1990 and won by the National League for Democracy, taking 81% of the seats. However, the League was prevented from taking power by the State Law and Order Restoration Council (the military) who failed to relinquish power. Against this background of political tension and Burma's abuse of human rights, tourism has nevertheless developed, because of the attraction of mountains, rain forests, tropical beaches and historic buildings and temples.

Between 1962 and 1988 tourists to Burma were limited to a one-week stay. However, Burma has recently adopted an open door policy designed to attract foreign income. Old hotels are being renovated and new ones built in joint ventures with private capital. Much of the investment comes

Figure 8.22
Tourism – an exchange of culture and dress code

QUESTIONS

1 Describe why the Dominican Republic is such a popular location for UK tourists.

2 Describe and explain the problems that tourists may experience on a holiday to the Dominican Republic.

3 Study Figure 8.20 which shows changes in the numbers of tourists to Egypt. What impacts did the Gulf War and the terrorist attacks in Cairo have on the number of people visiting the country?

4 Using Tanzania as an example, show how political conflict within a country can influence tourism.

---

from Japan, Singapore and Korea. Since 1990, the military junta has begun face-lifting historic monuments and relocating 'unsightly' villages away from temples at Pagan, Mandalay, Sagaing, and Amarpura (Figure 8.23).

Mainly due to Burma's bloated defence budget, the country is in desperate need of foreign currency, and has made an all-out effort to attract foreign visitors. Tourism revenue increased tenfold between 1992 and 1996, earning the country over £120 million annually. As such, it is the country's second largest legal source of foreign exchange (agricultural exports are the top earner). Other, illegal, sources of foreign exchange include heroin. Most of the visitors are drawn from the Far East, in particular Japan and Singapore. The number of French and German visitors is increasing too.

In 1996 the government undertook a massive publicity campaign. Visit Myanmar Year was an attempt to increase foreign tourism to Burma. However, most of the publicity was inside the country rather than outside and the number of foreign tourists did not change significantly. In addition, the campaign led to a rash of overbuilding and renovation, destroying some of the colonial splendour of inner city areas. The government has also been criticised for its use of forced labour and for forcibly relocating entire villages in preparation for Visit Myanmar Year (Figure 8.25).

There is disagreement on whether tourism is having a beneficial effect on the actions of the government. Tourist chiefs and the government's tourism spokesperson claim that the presence of tourists is helping to change the way of the regime and is providing local people with an income. By contrast, critics argue that the revenue derived from tourism is used to prop up the authoritarian government. For the government's part, foreign exchange rather than social change is the main reason for opening up Burma to tourism. After nearly three decades of isolation the government is still wary of outside influences and change. Ironically, the ease with which tourists can now obtain visas means that it is easier for journalists and human rights groups to visit Burma and publicise its human rights abuses, such as the house arrest of Aung San Suu Kyi, leader of the pro-democracy movement.

CUBA

Cuba (Figure 8.24), once the playground for wealthy Americans, limited tourism in 1959 following the overthrow of the military dictator Batista and the ascent to power of communist Fidel Castro. Cuba's economy was subsequently modelled on the Soviet Union and tourism was regarded as undesirable for a socialist country. Cuba is the only communist country in the Caribbean and was viewed by the USA as a major threat to peace in the region. However, since the collapse of communism in the Soviet Union, the USA feels the threat has diminished, although Cuba is still subject to US sanctions.

Tourism to Cuba is increasing, with about 750 000 people visiting the island each year. The industry is worth about £0.8 billion to the economy. Most tourist arrivals are from Canada, Germany, Mexico and Spain, and some Americans visit Cuba via Mexico. In addition, Cuba attracts a number of wealthy Latin American 'health tourists' who use the island's

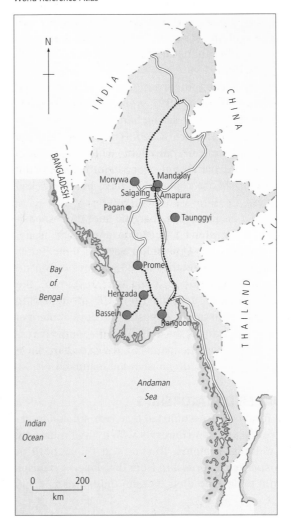

Figure 8.23 *The location of Burma*
Source: adapted from Dorling Kindersley, 1994, World Reference Atlas

low-cost advanced health care, or to stay at one of the many sanatoria, both of which Castro invested fairly heavily in.

Since the mid-1990s there has been a rapid increase in the number of new hotels built as Cuba attempts to increase

Figure 8.24 *The location of Cuba*
Source: Dorling Kindersley, 1994, World Reference Atlas

the number of tourists and increase its foreign exchange. The government's decision to transform Cuba into a big tourist destination has produced a large number of joint ventures and management contracts, mostly with European and Canadian hoteliers. This is in spite of US legislation aimed at reducing foreign investment to the island.

For Cuba, these foreign investors provide:
- fast economic growth
- know-how about the tourist demand/trends/infrastructure
- marketing to foreign tourists
- the use of internationally known and dependable hotel names, for example Spain's Sol-Melia, Canada's Delta Hotels, Germany's LTI International, and France's Club Mediterranee.

Cuba hopes to attract over a million tourists a year by the year 2000 and plans to increase the number of hotel rooms from 25 000 in 1996 to 50 000 in 2000, at a cost of over £1.75 billion. The government needs to raise tourism receipts not only to finance economic recovery but also to offset adverse balance of payments caused by a fall in prices of its exports, sugar and nickel, and a rise in the costs of essential imports.

Cuba has had to improve its environment in some places, particularly its infrastructure in tourist resorts. For example,

in the resort of Varadero, a special tourist zone (a concentrated development for tourism, police launched a crackdown against hundreds of prostitutes who worked the resort, and they shut down dozens of unregulated private home restaurants and unregulated taxis with unreliable drivers and prohibited Cubans from privately renting out accommodation. It is also a location vulnerable to hurricanes, which destroy beaches and destroy the infrastructure – for example, in 1996 it was struck by Hurricane Lili.

QUESTIONS

1 Using examples, explain how political developments influence the provision of tourism.

2 How far do you agree with the statement that politics should be kept out of tourism? Use examples to support your answer.

TOURISM IN THAILAND

By contrast to Cuba and Burma, Thailand (Figure 8.25) has not experienced extreme political conflict, although it has experienced a financial crisis (1997-98). As far as tourism goes, Thailand had an up-market appeal, but it also has a reputation for being a source of sex tourism.

Thailand is an excellent example of a developing country that has developed tourism in that it has attracted large amounts of foreign currency: tourism is Thailand's main foreign exchange earner. Almost 7 million tourists visited Thailand in 1995, representing an increase of over 12% on 1994; annual growth in 1997 was about 5% . Nevertheless, this represented a slow-down compared to the rate of growth in the 1980s, when the growth rate was 14%.

Thailand has a range of attractions for tourists:
- Bangkok, the capital, offers cultural diversity and historic attractions, such as excursions to the famous bridge over the River Kwai, an important landmark from World War II
- attractive water markets (Figure 8.26)
- large, sandy coastal beaches such as those at Pattaya and Phuket, set in a tropical climate
- temples and religious attractions, especially in the north around Chiang Mai
- attractive countryside, with irrigated rice fields and orchid cultivation
- hill tribes in the north of the country
- tropical vegetation and wildlife, such as elephants.

In addition, Thailand is only a few hours flight from Tokyo, and is a favoured stopover on the long-haul flights between Europe and Australia. Over half of Thailand's

Figure 8.25 *The location of Thailand*
Source: Dorling Kindersley, 1994, World Reference Atlas

Figure 8.26 *Attractions in Thailand – a water market in Bangkok*

tourists come from south-east Asia, but a significant number come from Europe and North America. Increasing number of tourists come from eastern Europe and Russia.

Tourism in Thailand caters for all sections of the tourist market. The cream of the industry is epitomised by the Chiang Mai Regent Hotel catering for the high-spending tourist, who is happy to spend a few days in the north of the country. The majority of tourists are package holiday-makers whose holidays include travel and accommodation; they want to visit the attractions of Thailand but to travel in conditions of comfort. Tourists from Eastern Europe and Russia typically stay in budget hotels, although they spend their money shopping and eating, which increases their total holiday spending. Thailand also attracts many backpackers with little money to spend.

In the mid-1980s the Thai tourist trade had exploded into life, as western holidaymakers discovered a fashionably exotic land at the end of a newly-affordable long-haul flight. In 1987, a promotion to increase tourism, 'Visit Thailand Year 1987', increased arrivals by nearly one quarter. In the late 1990s, East European and Asian tourists have descended on Pattaya and transformed it into a holiday resort comparable with a Spanish resort of the 1970s. Places such as Bangkok and Chiang Mai, the primary tourist destinations in the 1980s, have become secondary to Pattaya.

Many countries have since tried to copy Thailand's promotion. One problem facing Thailand is that the competition for ever more discerning tourists is becoming greater. The Tourist Association of Thailand (TAT) believes that Thailand cannot cater for every tourist need. It wants to attract high-spending wealthy tourists.

The TAT's aim is to try to:
- spread tourists around the country more, away from overcrowding in Pattaya and other coastal resorts

- encourage tourists to take participate in more of the diverse activities on offer, trekking, cultural discoveries, ecotourism
- take more care of the environment, by dealing with water pollution along the coast, by designing better new buildings which do not ruin the city skylines of places such as Chiang Mai.

Thailand's tourist market is going through a structural change. The industry has been losing steam for a number of years. The industry is likely to adjust itself and cater for niche customers. These are not just the traditionally wealthy (European, American and Japanese), but also the Korean honeymoon market, Chinese and Vietnamese nouveau riche.

Thailand also expects to benefit from its proximity to Indo-China and Burma, the frontier of south-east Asia. In addition, it hopes to attract some of the visitors en route to the Olympic Games in Sydney in 2000.

Inset 8.1
Sex tourism

Small boys and girls are sold into prostitution as soon as they have left primary school. They hang out on the pavements, among the skinny, diseased dogs lying curled in front of shops that sell very little. Up to 90% of girls from the poorest villages end up in prostitution or some kind of sex work. They are often sold by families who are offered a lump sum of money. They do this to pay off debts that have amassed.

Mae Sai is a village in northern Thailand. It is part of an area of subsistence farming. However, the nature of farming has been disrupted by Thailand's rapid urbanisation. Many families are also dependent upon the heroin trade. Mae Sai lies within the notorious heroin-trading Golden Triangle.

Agents or 'middle men' arrange children for big operators in the large cities. The market for 'sex tourists' has grown dramatically. South East Asia is desperate for foreign currency and is a place where young lives can be bought cheap. Many children find themselves tied into bonded labour, working in brothels, bars, and massage parlours. They live in appalling conditions. Many children, boys as well as girls, may have to 'service' up to ten clients a night.

Source: adapted from *You* magazine, 1 December 1996

Sex tourism

In Thailand there are over 700 000 prostitutes, mostly aged between 17 and 24, many of them serving tourists (generally Western). These are mostly poorly educated young women who migrate to Bangkok from rural areas. As well as involving women, sex tourism also involves many young children, sometimes as young as eight years old. The historic reason was the large presence of US military personnel during the Vietnam War. Many prostitutes also go to the coastal resorts, mainly Pattaya, but there are other centres around Thailand. The male to female ratio in some resorts, such as Pattaya, is two to one (both resident and tourist population). Up to 250 000 sex tourists travel to Thailand every year from developed countries such as the USA, the UK, Germany and Japan. It is thought that about half a million of Thailand's fifty-nine million people are HIV positive, largely due to prostitution.

The first international conference to examine the issue of commercial sexual exploitation of children took place in Stockholm, Sweden in 1996. The conference focused on establishing methods to combat child pornography and the sale and trafficking of children for sexual purposes. One of its tasks was to agree a consensus on how to tackle 'sex tourism' in developing countries whereby paedophiles, mostly from developed countries, sexually abuse children while abroad. Methods discussed included the extradition of convicted offenders, tougher legal sanctions, including seizure of paedophiles' assets, improved trans-national police coordination and greater victim support.

In 1997, an agreement was reached between the UK and the Philippines in an attempt to crack down on the trade. But is it enough? The sale of children for sex in countries such as Sri Lanka, Thailand and the Philippines is a growing trade (Figure 8.27). Some accounts suggest that Asia's financial crisis has driven more people into prostitution and led to more parents selling their children to pimps. There are reports of a growing traffic through Thailand of young women kidnapped from Burma, Laos, southern China and Cambodia. Some of these people are destined for the 'tourist trade'.

QUESTIONS

1 Using an atlas, travel brochures and any other information, describe the attractions that Thailand offers for tourists.

2 Why is Thailand reluctant to stop sex tourism?

Trading Partners

THAILAND there may be as many as 400 000 children under the age of 16 working in brothels, bars and clubs. Many are reportedly trafficked from northern rural areas, where incomes are much lower than the national average, or from nearby countries including Burma and Laos.

PHILIPPINES up to 40 000 children involved in prostitution in Manila, and some 25 000 children in tourist areas and towns near Olongapo, the site of a recently closed United States military base. Research shows that poverty forces girls into prostitution in a country where about half of the urban population lives below the poverty line.

INDIA 300 000 to 400 000 children involved in prostitution. Criminal gangs lure or abduct children, and thousands of girls enter prostitution as part of customary practices now banned by law. Girls from Bangladesh and Nepal are also sold for prostitution in India.

SRI LANKA More than 10 000 boys may be involved in sex tourism. Large numbers of girls may also be involved in prostitution in the country's free trade zone.

LATIN AMERICA child prostitution, linked to poverty, the plight of street children, drugs and sex tourism, exists in virtually all countries. Many of Brazil's 500 000 street children turn to prostitution for survival. There are also reports of thousands of girls forced into prostitution in mining camps in the Amazon region.

In **INDUSTRIALISED COUNTRIES** poverty, disintegration of families, drug abuse and greater mobility of population have contributed to greater levels of child prostitution. The use of new technologies such as computer networks and video recorders makes it easier for criminals to involve children in pornography with less risk of detection. In the United States alone, up to 300 000 under 18s are estimated to be involved in prostitution.

Figure 8.27 Trading partners *Source: The Guardian, April 1, 1998*

CULTURAL AND AGRICULTURAL CHANGE IN INDIA

Many tourist destinations have to import foodstuffs to cater for their visitors. Another effect of tourism is that through the introduction of restaurants and fast-food chains, eating habits and agricultural practices may change. Restaurants and eating houses, initially catering for a tourist population, are frequented increasingly by local middle-class people. Nowhere is this more true than with the growth of fast-food chains. But the implications are not just for eating patterns, it also affects agriculture and land use. A good example is the impact of fast-food chains in India.

In 1996, Indian farmers ransacked a Kentucky Fried Chicken (KFC) restaurant in Bangalore as a political protest against the increasing presence of fast-food chains in India. The protesters were members of the Karnataka Rajya Raitha Sangha (KRRS), an association representing several million farmers in Karnataka State. They demanded that KFC leave India, claiming that it and other foreign food operations were threatening traditional agriculture by expanding the meat industry and forcing Western farming methods and seed varieties on farmers.

At the same time PepsiCo Restaurants International, the fast-food arm of the American group Pepsi and the owner of KFC, opened a Pizza Hut in Bangalore and McDonald's opened its first two Indian outlets in New Delhi and Bombay. Environmental and political groups opposed the openings.

For example, the director of the Research Foundation for Science, Technology and Natural Resource Policy in New Delhi, described the arrival of foreign fast-food chains in India as an attack on sustainable agriculture, claiming that the fast-food chains would move people into a meat-based diet that the country could not afford. He also thought that the intensive breeding of poultry and other livestock which fast-food restaurants encourage would have serious implications for India's ability to feed itself. The director also stated that using food crops such as maize to feed chickens was a poor use of resources; grain can feed five times as many people if consumed directly rather than being given to animals to be transformed into meat, milk and eggs. In addition, the 375 gallons of water needed to produce a pound of chicken is twenty times the amount an average Indian family is supposed to use in one day – if it gets water at all. He predicted that the price of grain would increase because supply could not meet demand since the land was growing meat for the rich of the country and for export. Indeed, the director added that some of India's middle-class were increasingly replacing home-cooked meals of vegetables and lentils with non-vegetarian pre-prepared food.

While it is open to question whether multinational food companies are affecting Indian eating habits, their impact on local agriculture is undeniable. Contract farming, where a company governs and buys the entire crop of a large group of farmers, is common. For instance, PepsiCo Restaurants International, the group's beverage and snack foods arm, has controlled the output of about 1000 farmers in the state of Punjab for the past 5 years, telling them what to grow and how to grow it.

SUMMARY

In this chapter we have looked at the advantages and disadvantages of tourism in developing countries. The first two case studies, Zimbabwe and the Maasai in Kenya, showed how rural communities were marginalised by tourism. We then saw the way in which rural communities are being integrated into tourism in Zimbabwe, but problems remain in integrating rural communities in Kenya into tourism. In other places, tourism has developed so fast as to endanger the health and safety of visitors. A variety of examples showed the political and cultural issues associated with tourist development, such as terrorism in Egypt, attempts by Cuba's communist government and Burma's military dictatorship to attract tourism, sex tourism in Thailand and the impact of fast-food chains in India. As we have seen, developing countries see tourism as an important economic asset, but it would be wrong to think that all developing countries have to deal with the same issues. Environmental degradation, alienation of the local communities and clashes with cultural values are common to many of the countries, but the way in which these issues affect each country depends very much on the historical, political and cultural climate of each nation.

QUESTIONS

1 What are the advantages and disadvantages of tourism to developing countries? Use examples to support your answer.
2 Using examples, describe and explain the environmental, social and economic impact of tourism in developing countries.

BIBLIOGRAPHY AND RECOMMENDED READING

Berger, D., *The challenge of integrating Maasai tradition with tourism*, in Price, M., (ed.) 1996, People and tourism in fragile environments, Wiley
Economist Intelligence Unit, 1995, 'Thailand', *International Tourism Report*, 3:67-81
Harrison, D., (ed.) 1994, *Tourism and the less-developed countries*, Routledge
Lea, J., 1988, *Tourism and the developing world*, Routledge

Chapter 9
Sustainable tourism and ecotourism

The terms 'sustainable tourism' and 'ecotourism' are used frequently. In some cases they are even used interchangeably. But they are not the same. Sustainable tourism is that which can continue without damaging the environment, as well as integrating the local community and involving them in the planning and implementation of tourist development. Ecotourism is a type of low density, low impact tourism, thus it can be considered as a form of sustainable tourism. However, some have described ecotourism as 'snob tourism' with wealthy/intellectual people enjoying the pleasures of a remote environment or culture; often what passes for ecotourism is far from sustainable. In this chapter we look at tourism in three developing countries, Monteverde Cloud Forest in Costa Rica, ecotourism in Belize and trekking in Nepal, where attempts have been made to conserve the environment.

PRINCIPLES OF SUSTAINABLE TOURISM

Sustainable tourism is tourism which:

- operates within natural capacities for the regeneration and future productivity of natural resources (Figure 9.1)
- recognises the contribution of people in the local communities, with customs and lifestyles linked to the tourism experience
- accepts that local people must have an equitable share in the economic benefits of tourism (Figure 9.2).

This entails:

- **using resources sustainably** – the sustainable use of natural, social and cultural resources is crucial and makes long term business sense
- **reducing over-consumption and waste** – this avoids the cost of restoring long-term environmental damage and contributes to the quality of tourism
- **maintaining biodiversity** – maintaining and promoting natural, social and cultural diversities is essential for long-term sustainable tourism and creates a resilient base for industry
- **supporting local economies** – tourism that supports a wide range of local economic activities and which takes environmental costs and values into account both protects these economies and avoids environmental damage (Figure 9.3)
- **involving local communities** – the full involvement of local communities in the tourism sector not only benefits

---

Benefits to the environment
- Safeguarding the resource for the benefit of future generations
- The protection and enhancement of the special landscapes and features which appeal to visitors.

Benefits to the community
- Real opportunities for community involvement in tourism and the creation of a better climate for development
- Supporting the local economy and local services – for instance helping to support local transport systems in rural areas
- Creating new business opportunities.

Benefits to the tourism industry
- Economic benefits for operators – for example, reducing energy bills by as much as 20% by installing efficient insulation, and spending less on consumables, such as paper and plastic goods, by choosing reusable containers, washable table linen etc.
- Better working relationship with the local community
- Enhanced appeal for visitors from those market areas which have a high proportion of discerning and ecologically aware consumers
- Opportunities for the development and promotion of environment-friendly activity tourism such as cycling, walking, birdwatching, many water-based activities and newer interests including conservation holidays.

Benefits for the visitor
- The development of a quality tourism service
- Better relationships with the local community
- Closer involvement with and better understanding of both the people and the holiday destination

---

Figure 9.1 *Sustainable tourism – a tourist on a board walk in an Australian rainforest*

Figure 9.2 *Sustainable tourism: the benefits* Source: Northern Ireland Tourist Board, 1993, Tourism in Northern Ireland – a sustainable approach

Figure 9.3 Practical steps towards sustainable tourism *Source: Northern Ireland Tourist Board, 1993, Tourism in Northern Ireland – a sustainable approach*

them and the environment in general but also improves the quality of the tourism experience

- **consulting stake holders and the public** – consultation between the tourism industry and local communities, organisations and institutions is essential if they are to work alongside each other and resolve potential conflicts of interest

- **training staff** – staff training which integrates sustainable tourism into work practices, together with the recruitment of local personnel at all levels improves the quality of the tourism product

- **marketing tourism responsibly** – encouraging tourists to visit sites during off-peak periods to reduce visitor numbers or to visit when ecosystems are most robust helps preserve the environment; it provides tourists with complete and responsible information, increases respect for the natural social and cultural environments of destination areas and enhances customer satisfaction

- **undertaking research** – on-going monitoring by the industry using effective data collection analysis is essential to help solve problems and to bring benefits to destinations, the industry, tourists and the local community

- **integrating tourism into planning** – integrating tourism development into national and local planning policies, and producing management plans which undertake environmental impact assessments projects, plans and policies increases the long term viability of tourism (Figures 9.4 and 9.5)

- **better information provision** – providing tourists with information in advance and in situ, for example, through visitor centres about tourist destinations.

Figure 9.4 Methods of sustainable tourism – cable car in Costa Rica

If it is a proposed development, ask yourself:

Is it in the right place, or would it be visually more acceptable elsewhere?

Might it damage or destroy valuable habitats or archaeological sites?

Is the design appropriate to the location?
- consider the importance of reflecting the local style both inside and outside

Is the scale of the proposals in keeping with its surroundings?
- could it be better landscaped? Is the development the right size and shape?

Are the specified materials the most appropriate for the project?
- use local stone, slate and wood if possible. How can you enhance insulating materials?

Has full consideration been given to all ancillary services?
- what additional features, e.g. access roads, sewerage and waste disposal, will be needed?

If it is an existing operation, ask yourself:

Is the business being run in a sustainable manner?
- consider an environmental audit of the operation. Is there scope for new environment-friendly technology, e.g. electric vehicles and solar heating?

Is it damaging the local or wider environment in any way?
- is it inadvertently polluting a water course or burning harmful plastics? Are the waste and sewage disposal methods the most effective?

Are the suppliers environmentally friendly?
- do they recycle, save energy, avoid unnecessary waste or use materials from sustainable sources?

What is the relationship between the business and the local community?
- employ local people where possible. Use local shops and services and encourage your visitors to do the same. Look at the potential for group purchasing of goods. Link your business to local community and environmental projects and organisations.

Is the operation efficient?
- how much energy could you save? Regular maintenance of energy-consuming appliances and equipment can reduce energy consumption and fuel bills. Install energy and temperature controls in all rooms.

Is it generating unnecessary waste?
- economise on the amount of waste water by installing more efficient washing machines. Use phosphate-free detergents. Organic waste could be composted.

Can the use of disposable goods be reduced?
- use goods that can be used more than once.

Can more be done to recycle material?
- install recycling procedures.

Can more be done to promote the business's environmental credentials?
- consider cooperative marketing with other environment-friendly operators. Tell visitors what you are doing.

Are visitors being informed about the area and the community?
- provide visitors with advance information and advice about the area, local customs, traditions and other areas.

Does the development have new opportunities for tourism?
- explore the potential for introducing creative, cultural, nature study and environmental holiday activities.

1. **Controls on land use** – Cyprus uses land-use zoning. In Denmark, a new 3 kilometre coastal planning zone imposes strong restrictions on tourist development on open coastlines. EU legislation on environmental impact assessment has influenced large-scale tourist projects in Europe.

2. **Planning controls on new buildings**, as for example, in the Ria Formosa National Park, Portugal, where planning permission for tourist facilities in the park is now dependent on operators adopting one of several National Park approved designs.

3. **Controls on bed capacity or infrastructure**, such as in Malta where downmarket bed capacity has been gradually limited and accommodation has been developed in collaboration with tour operators in four or five star hotels. In 1993, Majorca removed 25 000 bed spaces to ease tourism pressure.

4. **Controls on the illegal building of second homes** in Sweden and Denmark have been in place for several decades. In Norway, a more restrictive approach to building second homes has now been adopted

5. **Environmental standards** for drinking water, bathing water, waste water and air emissions. Such standards were first enforced in Majorca in 1984. Guidelines have also been developed for open space and densities of new development. Similar regulations have been introduced into Cyprus.

6. **Establishment of protected areas** around sensitive areas such as wetlands and sand dunes, for example, the Green Lungs example in Central and Eastern Europe (a set of environments in Europe which are being protected to promote conservation, and provide access to open space).

7. **Traffic management** schemes and restrictions on the use of private cars such as at Glossglockner, Hochalpenstrasses in Austria, where stringent road pricing measures and conversion of car parks have been introduced to discourage car users. The target is to shift 90% of the 1.3 million visitors arriving by car to 70% by coach and bus by the year 2000. Many towns and cities throughout Europe have introduced pedestrianised zones in their centres.

8. **Limits to tourist numbers** have been introduced in popular areas, such as in Denmark, where government planners and tourist organisations have developed procedures for jointly controlling the impacts of tourism.

9. **Economic measures** can indirectly help relieve environmental pressure; measures such as the 10% land levy on new development in Cyprus can help reduce some unfavourable developments.

10. **Environmental awareness** for tourists, host communities and tour operators is vital. Numerous good practice guides have been developed by hotel chains, theme parks and automobile clubs. Blue flags are awarded to beaches meeting certain standards such as EU regulations, provision of certain facilities and good beach area management. These blue flags have been promoted by the Foundation for Environmental Education in Europe and they have influenced tourists' choice of beaches.

11. **Training** of those involved in the management of tourist areas. For instance, partnerships have been developed between Central and Eastern Europe and Western European National Parks, such as Sumava in Bohemia and Bayerischer Wald in Germany, and between Ojcow in Poland and the Peak District in the UK. A manual has been written on how to encourage ecological practices in hotels; initiatives such as the Walled Towns Friendship Circle – an alliance of 109 towns in fifteen countries – have produced a handbook of good practice for sustainable tourism in walled towns.

12. **Monitoring** the affects of tourism. A policy action is to refine and improve strategy, such as the use of indicators to monitor effectiveness of tourism policies.

Figure 9.5 *Examples of legislation and policy being used to manage the impact of tourism and recreation in Europe*
Source: *European Environment Agency, 1995, Europe's environment: The Dobris assessment, European Environment Agency*

ECOTOURISM

Ecotourism has been described as a 'green' or 'alternative' (unconventional) form of sustainable tourism. Ecotourism generally takes place in remote areas, with a low density of tourists – the facilities were originally at a fairly basic level, but are gradually becoming more comfortable. Ecotourism often involves tourism that explores ecology and ecosystems such as game parks, nature reserves, coral reefs and forest parks. It aims to give people a first-hand experience of natural environments and to show them the importance of conservation. The characteristics of ecotourism include:

- planning and control of tourist developments so that they fit in with local conditions
- increasing involvement and control by local or regional communities
- activities appropriate to the local area
- a balance between conservation and development and between environment and economics.

The key objectives for sustainable tourism are:

- maintaining the quality of the environment whilst
- maximising the economic benefit.

However, in areas where ecotourism occurs there is often a conflict between:

- allowing total access to visitors and providing them with all the facilities they desire and
- conserving the landscape, plants and animals of the area.

Another conflict arises when local people wish to use the resource for their own benefit rather than for the benefit of wildlife or conservation.

Ecotourism has also been described as 'egotourism'. Critics argue that ecotourists are trying to get closer to the environment and are perhaps causing much more damage than mass tourism. Backpackers are thought to be the greatest threat: they put little into the local economy but want to visit beautiful, undiscovered places, destroying the natural environment as they go off the beaten track. By contrast, mass tourists are concentrated onto set routes, such as those used by coach tours.

Figure 9.7
Spectacular scenery and biodiversity, Monteverde Cloud Forest, Costa Rica

Figure 9.6 *The location of the Monteverde cloud forest*
Source: Baez, A., Learning from experience in the Monteverde Cloud Forest, Costa Rica in Price, M. (ed.), 1996, People and tourism in fragile environments, Wiley

species of birds, 120 species of reptiles and amphibians and several thousand species of insect.

Like ecosystems throughout the world, Monteverde has been subject from the 1970s to increasing population pressure and expansion of agricultural activities. However, by chance, in the 1950s a number of North American Quaker families emigrated to Monteverde in search of a peaceful life in the isolated region of Monteverde.

Today, there are three main Quaker communities in the Monteverde area with a total population of about 5000. Access to the area is difficult and as a result the area is largely self-sufficient in agriculture. One of the reasons why the Quaker community appears to have successfully colonised the area is that their interests are similar to that of the indigenous population – they work for the well-being of the community and have group decision-making. Thus, when tourism developed in Monteverde in the 1960s and 1970s, its characteristics were very different from mainstream tourism because of the way in which locals and Quakers controlled the way they developed their resources in a conservational, sustainable way, rather than in a commercial, exploitative fashion.

The early tourists were mostly scientists and conservationists from the USA visiting Monteverde to study the area's rich biodiversity. Many of these published papers in learned journals.

The Tropical Science Center, a Costa Rican non-government organisation, bought 324 hectares of forest in 1972

THE MONTEVERDE CLOUD FOREST, COSTA RICA

Monteverde, in Costa Rica, is one of the best examples of ecotourism. It attracts about 1 million visitors each year. Well-organised government promotions and a reputation as the safest country in Central America attract a large number of North American and European visitors. Costa Rica's tourism is unusual in that a large part of it relates to special interest groups, such as bird-watchers, and its dispersed small-scale nature is a form of sustainable ecotourism.

Monteverde is located in the Tilaran Mountains of Costa Rica (Figure 9.6) and the cloud forest is situated at a height of around 1700 metres, where it is often enveloped by clouds. Due to its location, Monteverde is influenced by weather systems from both the Atlantic and Pacific Oceans, as well as by temperature changes with altitude. Due to this climatic range there is a great variety of ecosystems in the cloud forest: there are over 100 species of mammals, 400

for a reserve in Monteverde and reached an agreement with the Quakers to manage the land. This became the original Monteverde Private Cloud Forest Reserve. From the mid-1980s, all conservation work on Monteverde was carried out under the auspices of the Monteverde Conservation League, whose aim was the long-term preservation and conservation of Monteverde's natural resources.

From the 1970s, the Monteverde Cloud Forest attracted the attention of the popular media, while the Costa Rican government were keen to develop tourism. Monteverde was correctly portrayed as an area rich in biodiversity and with spectacular scenery (Figure 9.7). This attracted naturalists, bird watchers and other special interest groups.

To cater for these small groups, local people became involved in the small-scale provision of services, such as accommodation and catering for tourists. This small-scale unobtrusive form of tourism, today called ecotourism, became the established pattern for the Monteverde area. Tourism has increased rapidly: in 1974 there were just 471 visitors; this had grown to 49 552 by 1992, and continues to grow. The major period of growth was between 1987 and 1991 and led to a large expansion in the accommodation, food and transport provided. Since the early 1990s, the numbers of tourists have stabilised at about 50 000.

However, the nature of the tourist has changed. Initially, the visitors were mainly researchers. Now most of the tourists have a more general interest in the forest and seek a balance between entertainment, adventure and knowledge. They require a higher standard of accommodation than the earlier tourists and are drawn from a broader age range. Monteverde now accounts for about 18% of Costa Rica's total tourist revenue.

The growth and development of tourism in Costa Rica, especially Monteverde, came at a time when there was a long-term decline in the price received for many of the agricultural products for which Costa Rica was renowned, notably coffee and bananas. The type of tourism that developed was able to absorb some of the displaced agricultural workers in their own villages. Much of this development was small-scale. For example, 70% of the hotels in Costa Rica have less than 20 rooms. This small-scale tourism, which developed in protected reserves provided by the government and other organisations, provided jobs in tourism together with opportunities to start small businesses linked to the tourist industry.

As agriculture in the Monteverde region declined as people switched to tourism, it became necessary to import food from San Jose, Costa Rica's capital, or neighbouring cities, increasing the cost of food locally.

Although employment in tourism is often criticised as low paid, unskilled and insecure, the same can be said of agriculture. Consequently, most of the young people in the

Figure 9.8 *Local business*

area are turning to employment connected with tourism instead of agriculture because it is higher paid, has a higher social status and better working conditions.

Over 80 new businesses have been created in Monteverde since the mid-1970s, including hotels, bed and breakfast accommodation, restaurants, craft stalls, supermarkets, bars, riding stables and a butterfly and botanical garden (Figure 9.8). Many of these are locally owned. Over 400 full-time and 140 part-time jobs have been created. There are also indirect employment and multiplier effects, such as food suppliers, transport providers and storage and warehousing staff. Private reserves have also generated employment and attracted foreign income. The Monteverde Cloud Forest Reserve employs over 50 people. Part of the reserve's budget is used for support and extension services, such as training and education programmes, and road maintenance and refuse collection.

Unlike many rural areas in developing countries, Monteverde is not experiencing out-migration. Indeed, quite the opposite. Because of the developments in tourism there have been increased employment opportunities and this has attracted many young people. The growth in the resident and tourist population has placed a great strain on the existing infrastructure, such as water supplies, refuse collection, electricity and telecommunications. The price of land has soared and is now as expensive in Monteverde as in San Jose. Also, the atmosphere of the region has changed. The Quakers sought a peaceful life, free from the stresses and pressures of modern materialism in a capitalist country; traditionally, villagers in Central America work between 6 a.m. and 3 p.m., Monday to Friday. But tourism is a 24-hour,

365-day industry. Thus cultural changes and adjustments need to be made to a new way of life.

There have been benefits other than employment and income generation. Controlled access to the cloud forest, by limiting numbers and always using local people as guides means that not only are jobs created, but visitor impact is kept to a minimum. Local arts and crafts have been rejuvenated. The success of small businesses means that income should be more evenly distributed. Formal and informal education programmes have been strengthened and the local community are even more aware of the value of their natural resources than they were when they were farmers.

Another benefit is that the private sector is now keen to conserve and restore the natural environment. A number of former cattle ranches, farms and timber companies have realised that using the forest in situ, for tourism, is more profitable than removing the forest for other uses. This demonstrates that for developing countries to preserve their natural resources, local people must have access to and benefit from the resource, such as through common ownership or use; we have seen how this was not the case in Zimbabwe and it was not until the establishment of CAMPFIRE projects that this issue was addressed.

Monteverde is among one of the most prosperous and successful rural communities in Costa Rica. Much of this has been attributed to the capacity of the Quakers and the indigenous people for organisation, an ability to work in groups and their shared interest in a common good, namely the cloud forest. Another reason for success is the active participation of women in the tourist developments, in providing bed and breakfast accommodation: this gives the women economic power. As tourism has developed there have been increased opportunities for women in areas such as employment, education and training and as entrepreneurs.

Tourism in Monteverde continues to change. In recent years local people have tried to diversify the attractions of the area and have opened and developed a butterfly farm and gardens, arts and crafts, and traditional forms of farming. Access remains controlled and restricted, and prices have been increased to a high but affordable level for overseas tourists. The high level of local ownership of the tourist infrastructure is a reason to expect tourism to remain important in the Monteverde region.

QUESTIONS

1 Why has Costa Rica such a large and unique biodiversity?

2 To what extent can the type of tourism that has developed in the Monteverde Cloud Forest be described as ecotourism? Support your answer with examples.

3 What pressures on the Monteverde environment are threatening its tourism? How are these pressures likely to change in the future? Give reasons to support your answer

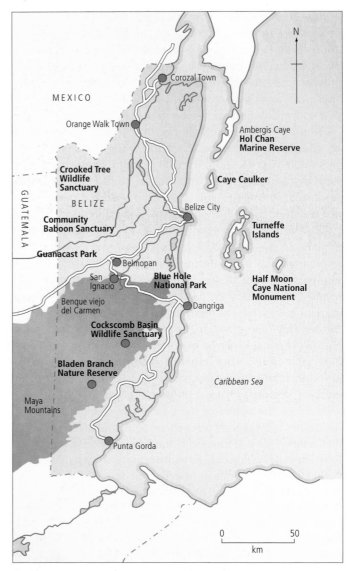

Figure 9.9 Map of Belize showing nature reserves and wildlife sanctuaries
Source: Carr, M., 1997, New patterns, process and change, Nelson

ECOTOURISM IN BELIZE

Another example of a country, which has encouraged ecotourism, is Belize. It has been less successful in meeting its aims, and is thus a useful contrast with Costa Rica.

Until 1983, the Belize government limited tourism partly to reduce the foreign impact, but also because it did not have the infrastructure to deal with an influx of tourists. However, the government now encourages ecotourism since it meets the needs of the local people, it attempt to safeguard the natural environment and it brings in foreign currency. Belize is located in Central America (Figure 9.9) and has many attractions including:

● a coral barrier reef

● over 450 cayes (low-lying islands) which are especially favoured by scuba divers

Figure 9.11 *An attempt to halt environmental damage in Belize*

Figure 9.10 *Belize's Mayan pyramids*

- antiquities from the Mayan civilisation (Figure 9.10)
- political stability
- a sub-tropical climate
- close proximity to the cities of the southern USA
- an alternative to the over-developed resorts of Mexico.

After agricultural exports, tourism is Belize's second most important source of foreign currency. In 1980, it earned approximately £4 million from tourism but this had increased to over £40 million by 1990. Belize has concentrated on the elite market, attracting fewer visitors but those who spend more money. There have been notable successes in the attempt to develop ecotourism. For example, at Hopkins Village the Sandy Beach Lodge hotel and cultural centre was developed by the Sandy Beach Women's Cooperative. In this instance, the local community was involved in the planning and management of the new facilities.

Up to one-quarter of the country has been designated as a nature reserve in some form, and there have been a number of private initiatives, which have been successful in preserving wildlife. Threatened species include the jaguar and the Black Howler monkey.

However, there are many signs that ecotourism is not working. For example, up to 90% of recent developments are foreign-owned and there has been a shift away from small, locally-owned hotels to large, overseas chains. There is also environmental degradation. Coral at the Hol Chan Marine Reserve (located on the Ambergis Caye) has been damaged, and there is evidence of overfishing as stocks of conch and lobster decline. Mangrove swamps are being drained and part of the Caye Caulker was levelled to make a landing strip, destroying important nesting grounds in the process. In addition, unsupervised groups of tourists are visiting nature reserves and failing to take sufficient care of the environment.

However, the biggest threats come from pressures outside tourism. The expansion of logging in the rainforest and the arrival of refugees from Guatemala and El Salvador, who clear the rain forest and use the land for shifting cultivation is threatening the environment (Figure 9.11).

QUESTIONS

1 Briefly explain why tourism is increasing rapidly in Belize.

2 What pressures external to Belize and not related to tourism are threatening its tourism?

3 To what extent can ecotourism in Belize be classified as ecotourism? Use examples to support your answer.

EXAMINATION QUESTION

The Annapurna Conservation Project

The Annapurna Conservation Area Project (Figure 9.12) is a good example of community involvement in tourism. In the 1960s, deforestation on the steep slopes of the Himalayas in Nepal led to severe erosion, removal of topsoil and flooding. Since the 1970s, the Nepalese government has encouraged community reforestation with local people involved in the decision-making and running of the conservation projects. From a number of small schemes, a large project, the Annapurna Conservation Project, has developed. It has four distinctive characteristics:

- the scheme covers a large area, over 2200 square kilometres, and involves over 40 000 people
- it is managed by local people, since the government believes that it will only work if it involves and benefits the local community
- it is based on land-use zoning, as shown in Figure 9.19
- part of the funding comes from the tourist revenue.

Tourism has grown rapidly in Nepal (Figures 9.13 and 9.14), in particular trekking (Figure 9.15). However, there has been a considerable impact on the natural environment (Figure 9.16), especially on rates of soil erosion (Figure 9.17), as well as other impacts on the human environment, both good and bad (Figure 9.18). In response to the growth of tourism, and in an effort to give greater local control over the development of tourism, the Annapurna Conservation Area Project was established and developed (Figure 9.19).

Figure 9.12 *Trekkers in the spectacular scenery of the Annapurna Conservation Area Project*

Year	Tourists	Trekkers (permits issued)
1960	4 000	100
1970	4 500	1 000
1980	163 000	40 000
1990	255 000	60 000
1995	350 000	70 000
2000 (est.)	500 000	(no data)

Figure 9.13 *The growth of tourists and trekkers Source: Edexcel Foundation, June 1998*

Figure 9.14 *Growth in tourist receipts Source: adapted from Edexcel Foundation, June 1998*

Year	Receipts (£ million)
1960	0.03
1970	4
1980	20
1990	45
1995	87

Figure 9.15 *Trekking tourism Source: Edexcel Foundation, June 1998*

There are few roads in the Nepalese Himalayas, so tourists must walk to enjoy the mountains. The word 'trekking' has today come to mean exotic back-packing holidays. Trekkers in Nepal either walk independently or in groups, and often hire Nepalese guides and porters. Trekking means travel by foot for many days. During this time travellers can spend nights either in the homes of local people or in simple hotels, or they can camp by themselves.

Most of Nepal is not wilderness as it is understood in the West. Trekking routes pass through rural, sparsely settled areas in the homeland of the Nepali people. Except in the more popular routes, trails are in poor condition; acute deforestation has led to frequent landslides; boarding and lodging facilities are poor and clean drinking water is not always available. Yet, because tourism is the country's second highest foreign exchange earner (after carpet exports), contributing nearly 4% of gross domestic product, the government is keen to attract more tourists.

Figure 9.17 *Soil loss and rainfall intensity* Source: Edexcel Foundation, June 1998

Rainfall intensity (mm/hr)	Average soil losses (kg/ha) by percentage of area forested			
	20-30%	40-50%	60-70%	80-90%
0 - 10	6.1	4.0	2.9	2.6
10 - 20	19.1	19.2	9.8	10.6
> 20	43.6	25.2	28.1	16.9

Figure 9.16 *The impact of trekking on the physical environment* Source: Edexcel Foundation, June 1998

Hordes of trekkers have eroded the most common routes and left huge volumes of non-biodegradable litter in their path. The increase in trekkers has lead to an increased demand for firewood to allow them to take hot showers and have camp fires. A two month trek can use as much firewood as a Nepalese family uses in a year (over 8000 kilograms). Once cleared of the natural protective rhododendron forest and left exposed to monsoon rains, the rates of soil erosion increase dramatically. The wealth generated locally by tourism is often spent on larger herds of livestock or building more hotels. The overcutting of the trees to provide fodder and fuelwood has further reduced the capacity of the forest to regenerate itself. The pressure is especially great in the high valleys of the Annapurna region, an area visited by 60% of trekkers.

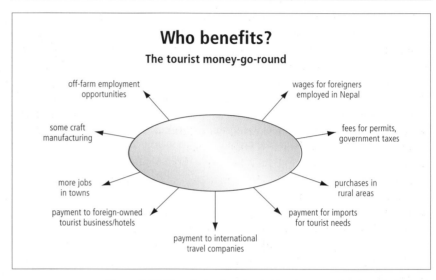

Who benefits?
The tourist money-go-round

off-farm employment opportunities

wages for foreigners employed in Nepal

some craft manufacturing

fees for permits, government taxes

more jobs in towns

purchases in rural areas

payment to foreign-owned tourist business/hotels

payment for imports for tourist needs

payment to international travel companies

Figure 9.18 *The effects of tourism in Nepal* Source: Edexcel Foundation, 1998

Figure 9.19 *Land use zoning in the Annapurna Range, Nepal* Source: Edexcel Foundation, 1998

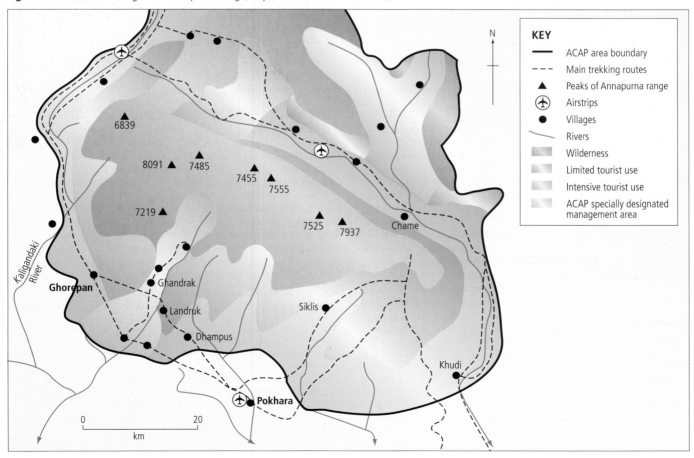

KEY

———	ACAP area boundary
- - -	Main trekking routes
▲	Peaks of Annapurna range
✈	Airstrips
●	Villages
～	Rivers
	Wilderness
	Limited tourist use
	Intensive tourist use
	ACAP specially designated management area

Village control of forests

Annapurna Conservation Area Project (ACAP) was established in 1986. Unlike many other national parks worldwide, the conservation area does not exclude human habitation. The needs of the local people are integral to the project. Although there was some initial scepticism, local people have come to realise that they have much to gain from the project. The traditional method of managing Nepal's forests (known as ritithi) is balanced cutting and growth. However, the traditional practices died out and decades of deforestation ensued as the population grew. Since the formation of ACAP however, the responsibility of managing forests and wildlife has been handed back to villagers.

New ideas

ACAP is funded by the fees paid by trekkers passing through the Annapurnas. It has devised a multitude of simple fuel-saving devices, including solar-heated showers, and it runs health-related workshops. These workshops include hygiene (the necessity of boiling water or digging latrines) and using flues to prevent buildings filling up with smoke and contributing to one of the biggest health problems, tuberculosis.

Consequences?

The Annapurna Conservation Area is visited by over 80 000 people a year. Over 700 tea shops (simple huts, which provide refreshments,) and lodges have been built. Today, the local people are learning to maintain a high level of control over their resources and their future by building an endowment fund from entry fees to the area, and working together on education, community development, biodiversity and energy conservation projects. The concern of mountain people is that they will lose control over their culture, their economy and their environment as tourism develops. Merely restricting tourism cannot be the solution to this imbalance, because people's desire to see new places will not disappear. Instead, mountain communities must achieve greater control over the rate at which tourism grows and the ways in which it develops.

Plans for a new road

Plans to build a new road up the Ghandrak Valley make a mockery of all the environmentally and culturally sensitive issues raised. Funded by the Chinese, it will cost far more in environmental terms than any possible economic benefit, but ACAP cannot prevent the road being built. 'If you live in a remote area, you are entitled to certain government benefits. Many people actually live in Pokhara and commute to their remote villages as the need arises. The people would clearly like to see the road built,' commented the ACAP director.

Figure 9.20 The Annapurna Conservation Area Project – a success story?
Source: Edexcel Foundation, 1998

QUESTIONS

1 Study Figures 9.13 and 9.14. Describe the pattern of growth in tourists, trekkers and tourist revenue to Nepal since 1960.

2 Using examples, describe and explain the positive and negative impacts of tourism in Nepal.

3 To what extent is the Annapurna Conservation Area Project working? Give reasons to support your answer.

SUMMARY

We have seen the principles of sustainable development and it is clear that they can be applied to most communities, most hotels and forms of tourist accommodation, as well as to the resorts themselves. The case studies have illustrated a variety of issues. For example, ecotourism in Belize is influenced by external forces (refugees from Latin America) as well as the development of outside interest in Belize as a tourist destination. The experience of trekking in Nepal has provided good economic returns, but at a social cost (through loss of cultural identity) and environmental cost. Despite the presence of a sustainable scheme, local people seem to have little control over what takes place. The Monteverde Cloud Forest is a remarkable and unique example of how ecotourism can work and how it can be sustainable. And yet the conditions that have allowed it to develop are so unusual as to suggest that to be sustainable, ecotourism has to be managed strictly from the start; paradoxically, this approach is almost the opposite of the philosophy of ecotourism which is to experience something completely natural and unmanaged.

QUESTIONS

1 What is ecotourism?
2 Is ecotourism sustainable?
3 Refer to Figures 9.2, 9.3 and 9.5 for the characteristics of sustainable tourism. Using examples, describe and explain the characteristics of (i) tourism that is sustainable and (ii) tourism that is not sustainable.

BIBLIOGRAPHY AND RECOMMENDED READING

Baez, A., 1996, *Learning from experience in the Monteverde cloud forest, Costa Rica in Price,* M. (ed.), People and tourism in fragile environments, Wiley

European Environment Agency, 1995, *Europe's Environment: The Dobris Assessment,* European Environment Agency

Nagle, G, 1995, 'Killarney National Park', *Geogrphical Magazine,* May, 61-3.

Nagle, G. and Spencer K., 1997, *Sustainable Development,* Hodder

World Wildlife Fund/UK, 1992, *Beyond the Green Horizon Principles for Sustainable Tourism,* Worldwide Fund for Nature/UK

Northern Ireland Tourist Board, 1994, *Tourism in Northern Ireland – a sustainable approach,* Northern Ireland Tourist Board

WEB SITES

Environment Agency homepage – http://www.environment.agency.gov.uk

Greenpeace International homepage – http://www.greenpeach.org/greenpeace.html

Glossary

Access   The ease with a place can be reached; it implies cost and time, not just distance

Accommodation   In the tourist industry accommodation is sometimes divided into the serviced such as hotels and registered bed and breakfast accommodation, and unserviced such as house exchanges or making rooms available unregistered

Agenda 21   Plans drawn up by local authorities to achieve sustainable forms of development

Alienation   The process whereby a group of people become economically and socially excluded from the main community

All-inclusive resorts   A form of tourism in which tourists stay in a resort or enclave that provides all their needs and entertainment; contact with the surrounding population is minimal

Avalanches   A form of mass movement in which snow and ice travel downhill rapidly

Bank Holidays   Set days when a large proportion of the working population is given a day's paid holiday

Biodiversity   Biological diversity or the gene pool; the sum total of genetic diversity within an ecosystem

Blood sports   'Sports' which involve the killing of animals such as fox hunting and deer hunting; in these cases the animals experience considerable fear and pain as well as being killed in a slow, painful way

CAMPFIRE   A scheme in Zimbabwe whereby local communities derive some benefit from the spoils of tourism

Carrying capacity   The maximum number of people that an environment can support without inflicting any long-term damage on that environment

Catchment   The area from which people are drawn to an attraction

Charter holidays   A form of organised holidays in which flight, accommodation and meals are booked and paid for in advance

Climate   The sum total of extremes and averages of weather over a period of not less than 30 years

Climate change   The long-term change in climate, largely as a result of human activity

coastal resorts   Tourist centres which have developed around a coastal location, usually a sandy beach

Colonies   Countries which were at one time part of an Empire and ruled by another country

Commonwealth Games   A sporting event in which members of the former British Empire (the Commonwealth) take part

Communism   A form of politics in which government control is very powerful

Comparative advantage   The advantages that one region possesses over another; the theory states that a region should exploit its comparative as it is better able to exploit that resource than other regions

Conservation   The attempt to preserve landscapes, environments, species and cultures

Coral reefs   Large accumulations of coral (animals called polyps) usually on the edge of land masses such as the Great Barrier Reef of the coast of Australia

Core-periphery   The economic centre of an area is often referred to as the core whereas the less developed areas are referred to as the periphery

Country parks   Large parks, often with a rural theme, found on the edge of town acting as a honeypot for urban residents

Cruising   A form of tourism in which the tourists sleep on board a ship and enjoy excursions to islands and coastal areas by day

Culture   The language, beliefs, arts, folklore, history, customs and legends of a people

Cumulative causation   A process whereby prosperous areas become more prosperous whereas less endowed areas become worse off

Destination factsheet   An information sheet providing background information about an area as well as useful tips for sustainability

Disposable income   The amount of money left after all the essentials have been paid for the amount of disposable income in developed countries has risen steadily over the century

Drought   A period of long-term water shortage

Ecological impacts   The effects on the biosphere including vegetation, soil, flora and fauna

Economies of scale   The savings made by increasing the scale of the operations

Ecotourism   A specialised form of tourism in which people visit relatively isolated, untouched natural environments, such as coral reefs, rainforests and mountain forests

Enclaves   Small areas which are reserved for tourists and are physically and socially isolated from the community in which they are found

Environment tax   A tax raised to provide funds to manage the environment

Environmental management   Any form of plan or policy designed to protect and enhance the environment

Exchange rates   The relative strength of one currency set against another

Extinctions   The irreversible removal of a species from the gene pool

Farm visits   A new form of recreation in which people pay to watch farming processes or buy farm products direct from the farmer; it is an example of farm diversification

Foot path erosion   The compaction of soil following trampling and break down of vegetation

Funicular railway   A chain operated railway (based on the pulley system) to help get people up steep slopes and to high ground

Game animals   Usually refers to exotic species found in savanna areas such as lions, elephants and rhinos

Game reserve   Areas set aside for the protection of wild animals, reserves can be national parks or owned by individuals

Global warming   The increase in global temperatures largely as a result of the build up of carbon dioxide

Hazards   Extreme physical events which endanger people's lives and their livelihoods

Heritage tourism   Tourism based around a historic theme ranging from industrial sites to rural life, castles and cathedrals

Historic buildings   All forms of castles, palaces, cathedrals etc.

Holiday homes   Homes which are either rented out to visitors for the holiday period or those which are owned as second home and are used only during the holiday period

Honeypot   A tourist location which attracts large numbers (swarms) of tourists

Hygiene   The level of cleanliness (or otherwise) with respect to water, food and sanitation

Immigration   The inward movement of people for a relatively long period of time

Information technology   The use of high technology, computers, and the Internet to store, process and transfer information around the world extremely rapidly

Infrastructure   The combination of transport facilities such as roads and railways, utilities such as electricity, water and gas, and sewage systems

International Olympic Committee   The committee responsible for the Olympic Games

Language students   Visitors to an area whose primary aim is to learn another language while on their visit

Leakage   The amount of money that escapes from a tourist destination and makes its way to other countries via airline companies, multinational corporations, food exporters

Leisure   The time that an individual has to relax, get involved in an activity etc.

Management   Any form of plan or policy designed to protect and enhance the environment

Mass tourism   An organised form of tourism in which travel, accommodation and meals are booked and paid for in advance

Multiplier effects   The way in which expanding industries create more demand for workers, who in turn create demand for more housing and services, which in turn attracts more industry, and so on

National parks   Areas of outstanding natural beauty in which human activity is carefully controlled

National Park Authorities   The bodies (in the UK) responsible for the management of the national parks, and having two main aims to protect and enhance the character of the landscape and to provide access and facilities for enjoying the area

Negative externalities   Results or effects of an activity which canot be costed but which damage the area, such as air and water pollution

Olympic Games   The world's premier sporting event, involving athletes from most of the world's nations, held every four years

Pollution   A concentration of a substance that is too great for the environment to deal with

Protected areas   Areas where human activity is carefully managed and regulated such as national parks, Areas of Outstanding Natural Beauty, and Sites of Special Scientific Importance

Recession   A downturn in the economy leading to lower levels of disposable income and poor exchange rates

Recreation   The use of leisure time for enjoyment

Refugees   People who have fled an area on account of persecution

Restoration   The return of a natural environment to its previous state

Seasonal unemployment   Unemployment which occurs for only part of the year, in the case of tourism this is mostly in winter

Sex tourism   A form of tourism in which the motive for travel is sexual encounters with prostitutes or children

Short breaks   Breaks in which the visit lasts for less than five nights away from home

Sites of Special Scientific Importance   Areas with important ecological or other value which are given some form of protection, however limited

Social class   A system for categorising people by the occupational status of the head of household

Sustainable tourism   A form of tourism which does not cause any long-term damage to the environment but allows the environment to be used and managed

Theme parks   A relatively new form of tourism often based around a concept (Disneyland or Legoland) and usually found close to urban areas

Thomas Cook   Founder of the travel firm bearing his name, and widely accredited as the founder of modern tourism

Tourist business district   The concentration of tourist related facilities usually in the centre of a town or city

Tourist life cycle   The process whereby a tourist destination initially grows and then declines

Trampling   The destruction of vegetation and soil structure as a result of concentrated trampling along selected paths

Trekking   Walking holidays usually taken in mountainous areas such as Nepal

Urban tourism   A form of tourism in urban areas but very difficult to differentiate from the recreational activities of residents of that city

War games   Enactment of military scenarios by civilians for leisure or training purposes

Waste   Unwanted materials or by-products resulting from the over-consumption of resources

Water sports   Sports such as scuba diving, windsurfing, water skiing

White knuckle rides   Rides at a theme park where the object of the ride is to scare the passenger

Wilderness areas   Remote, isolated areas which are ecologically vulnerable and are beginning to attract significant numbers of tourists

Winter sports   Sports such as skiing, skating

World Heritage Site   A site designated as having international significance and recognition, such as Blenheim Palace, Woodstock

World Tourism Organisation   One of the main organisations involved in the business of travel

Zoning   The process by which different activities are placed in contrasting areas such as concentrating the largest number of tourists in 'honeypots' with car parks, tea shops, souvenir shops, and toilets, while at the same time limiting or even preventing tourists from entering other parts

Index